The New York Times

LITTLE BLACK & WHITE
BOOK OF HOLIDAY CROSSWORDS

The New York Times

LITTLE BLACK & WHITE
BOOK OF HOLIDAY CROSSWORDS

Edited by Will Shortz

ST. MARTIN'S GRIFFIN ✦ NEW YORK

DIFFICULTY KEY

Easy:

Moderate:

Hard:

The New York Times

1

ACROSS

1 Fastener that may have a Phillips head
6 "One more thing . . ."
10 Eject, as 16-Across
14 Tara's Scarlett
15 Factory whistle time
16 Material from a volcano
17 Roger Bannister was the first
20 "You've got mail" co.
21 Trudge (along)
22 Sheeplike
23 In the proper manner
24 Agents' customers
26 Women's quarters, in sultans' homes
29 Fan sound
30 Emergency removal of people, for short
31 "Rise and ___!"
32 "Paper or plastic?" item
35 How something may be done, nostalgically
39 Old competitor of Pan Am
40 Heeded the alarm
41 ___ and proper
42 Mensa-eligible
43 Area west of the Mississippi
45 Regardless of
48 500 sheets
49 Visitor in "District 9"
50 Little vegetables that roll
51 Pitchfork-shaped Greek letter
54 Features of yawls or ketches
58 Essayist's newspaper piece
59 Suffix with billion
60 Fabric introduced by DuPont
61 Poetic nights
62 Use a spyglass
63 Sport with shotguns

DOWN

1 Couch
2 Part of a sneeze after "ah-ah-ah . . ."
3 Fidel Castro's brother
4 "To ___ is human . . ."
5 Indian beads used as money
6 Really bother
7 Ear-busting
8 Drunkard
9 Marine ___ (presidential helicopter)
10 Tiny slice of pie
11 Politico Sarah
12 Long jump or 100-meter dash
13 Peddlers peddle them
18 Woes
19 Fabrics with wavy patterns
23 Art ___ (1920s–'30s style)
24 Doorbell
25 Queue
26 Test the weight of
27 Swear to
28 ___ avis
29 Predecessor of bridge
31 Part of a mall
32 Italian port on the Adriatic
33 Closely related
34 Rubies, emeralds, etc.
36 Thin layer
37 "Dang!"
38 E-mail often caught in filters
42 Risks being caught in a radar trap
43 Bog fuel
44 Rodeo ropes
45 Willem of Spider-Man movies
46 Run off to the justice of the peace

by Fred Piscop

47 Patrol car wailer
48 Direct, as for information
50 Whittle down

51 Heap
52 ___ gin fizz
53 "Money ___ everything!"
55 40 winks
56 Expire
57 Noah's vessel

2

ACROSS

1 Kitchen V.I.P.'s
6 Towel (off)
10 Rock star, say
14 W.W. II German sub
15 Peak
16 Moore of "G.I. Jane"
17 Tilter at windmills
19 City NNW of Oklahoma City
20 Raised, as livestock
21 "Dee-fense! Dee-fense!" and others
23 Little article accompanying a bigger article
27 For free
28 One of golf's four majors
29 Biblical objects of multiplication
30 Sprinted
31 __ Carlo (part of Monaco)
32 "Hike!" callers in football, for short
35 Entryway
36 Fabricate, as a signature
37 Multinational currency
38 Umberto __, author of "The Name of the Rose"
39 Santa's little helpers
40 Cranium contents
41 Hire, as a lawyer
43 Industry in Las Vegas and Atlantic City
44 Plaza
45 Plaza displays
46 Psychology 101, e.g.
47 Number of calories in water
48 Nobelist Wiesel
49 Place to order a Blizzard
55 Softly hit ball in tennis
56 "Render __ Caesar . . ."
57 Eggs on
58 Writer __ St. Vincent Millay
59 Aspirin target
60 __ Gay (W.W. II plane)

DOWN

1 What a cow chews
2 "Entourage" network
3 Ages and ages
4 Online help page
5 Struck accidentally, as the toe
6 Floor finisher
7 Item with earbuds
8 Favorite
9 Detest
10 Think creatively
11 Star of "The Rookie," 2002
12 Fails to mention
13 Jar tops
18 Ahmadinejad's country
22 One who's well off
23 Increase in troop levels
24 Newton with a law named after him
25 Medicine woman of 1990s TV
26 Fencing sword
27 Pagoda instruments
29 Italian 31-Down star Sophia
31 See 29-Down
33 Salt water
34 Hymns, e.g.
36 Came back strong, as allergies
37 Bombeck who wrote "The Grass Is Always Greener Over the Septic Tank"
39 Greek H's
40 Like the works of Handel and Bach
42 "I've got it!"
43 Indiana birthplace of the Jackson 5
44 Sphere or cube
45 Argentine dictator who was ousted in 1955
46 Relinquish
47 Casserole pasta
50 "Gimme __!" (Alabama cheerleader's cry)

by Anthony J. Salvia

51 Container
at many
receptions

52 Maniacal
leader?

53 Ingredient in
some sushi
rolls

54 Intelligence-
gathering org.

ACROSS

1 Container for serving wine
7 Kindergarten learning
11 Sounds during backrubs
14 Witty
15 Lunch or dinner
16 Gift at Honolulu airport
17 *1966*
19 Norse war god
20 Treasury secretary Geithner
21 ___ guy (one who gets things done)
22 Flank
23 Drinking cup
26 With 51-Across, roles for 17-, 38- and 62-Across
28 Big part of an elephant
29 Jacob's first wife
32 Pictures at a hospital
33 City on the Black Sea
36 Actress Zellweger
38 *1989*
42 Theater walkway
43 Came out with
45 Solar phenomenon
48 Laudatory poems
50 A pair
51 See 26-Across
53 Chinese blossom
56 Big name in elevators
57 Fashionable
60 Official with a whistle
61 ___ Tin Tin
62 *2008*
66 "i" topper
67 French eleven
68 Mark slightly longer than a hyphen
69 ___-cone
70 Be overrun (with)
71 Declares emphatically

DOWN

1 Roman 300
2 Ginger ___
3 Place to pull over
4 Be of help to
5 Physicist Enrico
6 Flub
7 Bullets and BBs
8 Borscht vegetable
9 Chocolate substitute
10 ___-mo
11 Nissan sedan
12 Period of one's prime
13 Fire truck sounds
18 Double curve
22 Emphasize
23 Pooh-bah hired by a board of directors
24 Muslim's pilgrimage
25 Family groups
27 Leaps in ice-skating
30 Like parabolas
31 When doubled, a villain's chuckle
34 Close calls, perhaps
35 One taking to the slopes
37 Static, e.g.
39 Nobel Prize-winning U.N. workers' grp.
40 On empty
41 6:30 p.m. broadcast
44 Female deer
45 Norwegian coastal features
46 Skin soother
47 Like
49 Draw like Albrecht Dürer
52 Where the action is
54 Where the action is
55 Helen who sang "I Am Woman"
58 Jimi Hendrix's "Purple ___"
59 See 62-Down
62 With 59-Down, something flying off the shelves

by Mike Buckley

4

ACROSS

1 What skunks do
6 Oared racing shell
11 Harley-Davidson, slangily
14 Domed domicile
15 Book after Daniel
16 One-spot
17 "Keep going!"
19 Born: Fr.
20 Workers just for the day
21 Edgar who painted dancers
23 "Sound off – one, two . . .," e.g.
26 Square cracker
28 ___ about (roughly)
29 Neighbor of an Azerbaijani
31 Cheap seat cover material
33 Pizazz
34 Cough medicine amt.
37 Superlative suffix
38 Do impressions of
41 Garden tool
42 "I agree"
43 Donated
44 Erupts
46 Coffee liqueur brand
50 Nabisco cookie
51 Bibliophile
53 Playful puppies
55 Mumbai money
56 Baby food (whose name is an anagram of 55-Across)
57 Hostel
58 "Keep going!"
64 Prefix with tourism
65 Decorative upholstery fabric
66 Acquire information
67 Small number
68 Peevish states
69 Letters before tees

DOWN

1 Use a stool
2 Store head: Abbr.
3 Bridge writer Culbertson
4 Scratch-off game, e.g.
5 Best Actress for "Two Women"
6 Woodworking tool
7 Gear teeth
8 Where Springsteen was born, in song
9 Floral necklace
10 Noncellular phones
11 "Keep going!"
12 Atlantic or Pacific
13 Fliers in V's
18 Village People hit whose title completes the line "It's fun to stay at the . . ."
22 Seventh Greek letter
23 Small flock
24 Licorice-tasting seed
25 "Keep going!"
26 Actress Ward
27 Course related to physiology: Abbr.
30 It might go from 0 to 60 minutes
32 Easily torn bands of tissue
35 Spreader of seeds
36 Mexican money
39 Papa's mate
40 "Terrible" czar
45 Popular chain of chicken restaurants
47 Dick was his running mate in '52 and '56
48 Hardens
49 Broadcasts
51 Succinct
52 1/16 of a pound
54 "Positive thinker" Norman Vincent ___
56 Animal hide
59 Seeming eternity

by Betty Keller

60 7, to Caesar
61 "___
Rheingold"
62 Wrath
63 Coast Guard
officer: Abbr.

ACROSS

1 What some people do in an online "room"
5 Shoe bottom
9 Swift
14 Circle of light around the sun or moon
15 Bard of ___ (Shakespeare)
16 Microscopic creature
17 "So be it"
18 Nourish
19 Beckett's "Waiting for ___"
20 *Mays*
23 Zinc or zirconium
24 Home of Barack Obama's father
25 Radical 1960s org.
28 1st to 220th, in Manhattan: Abbr.
29 Israeli-made gun
31 Like hereditary factors
33 English dramatist George
35 Actress Turner
36 *Maize*
42 ___ Mountains (Asia/Europe separator)
43 What the dish ran away with, in "Hey Diddle Diddle"
44 Soda can feature
48 "___ the ramparts we watched . . ."
49 Butter serving
52 One step ___ time
53 Zones
55 Rock with a crystal inside
57 *Maze*
60 Tangle
62 "Honest to God!"
63 Place of research: Abbr.
64 With 34-Down, golf's U.S. Open champion of 1994 and 1997
65 Peru's capital
66 "Beetle Bailey" dog
67 West Pointer, e.g.
68 Toward the rising sun
69 First-year college student, usually

DOWN

1 Gorges
2 Small village
3 Native Alaskans
4 South Pacific kingdom
5 Official's call with outspread arms
6 Excess
7 Frederick ___, "My Fair Lady" composer
8 Part of a whodunit that reveals who done it
9 Overcoat sleeve
10 Mine: Fr.
11 Statue's support
12 Nigerian native
13 "Gimme ___!" (rude order)
21 Viscous
22 Soapmaker's supply
26 Flintstones' pet
27 Surgery souvenir
30 Zuider ___ (former inlet in the Netherlands)
32 North Carolina university
33 ___-mell
34 See 64-Across
36 Larva successor
37 In ___ (stuck in the same old same old)
38 Dreamy place
39 Arboreal animals with pouches
40 Anguish
41 Welsh dog
45 One of two for the Ten Commandments

by Janet R. Bender

46 Departure's opposite: Abbr.
47 Any of the Fab Four
49 Ballerina's position
50 "___ Fideles"
51 German
54 Courtyards
56 Writer T. S.
58 Singer India.___
59 Vegetarian's no-no
60 Dry, as wine
61 Gun lobbyists' org.

6

ACROSS

1 Bogged down
6 Sword handles
11 ___-Magnon man
14 High-speed train from Boston to Washington
15 Stand in a queue for, say
16 Drink with Grabbin' Grape and Smashin' Wild Berry flavors
17 College professor's mantra
20 Splenda rival
21 Short-sheeting a bed, TP'ing a house, etc.
22 2K race, e.g.
25 Bloodhound's trail
27 Yoko of "Double Fantasy"
28 Uganda's ___ Amin
30 As, chemically
34 G.P.S. offering: Abbr.
35 Highway entrances and exits, typically
37 "First, ___ harm" (medical axiom)
38 Highly collectible illustrator
42 Kuwaiti chief
43 ___ orange
44 The upper Midwest's ___ Canals
45 Hits the hay
48 Stimpy's cartoon pal
49 Ernie of golf fame
50 Penny vis-à-vis a dime
52 Gird oneself
54 Finisher of pottery or cakes
57 ___ note (dictionary bit)
59 Lafayette or Orleans
64 Bed-and-breakfast
65 Dazzling effect
66 Dull, in poetry
67 "Wanna ___?"
68 What light bulbs and bootblacks do
69 English nobles

DOWN

1 Atlas page
2 Critical hosp. area
3 Yank's foe in the Civil War
4 Aunt from "Oklahoma!"
5 Rum and lime juice drink
6 LOL, out loud
7 Mil. truants
8 Distant
9 One leaving cash on the table?
10 Backs of boats
11 It might be cut by an uppercut
12 Jeopardy
13 Adolph who was chief of The New York Times from 1896 to 1935
18 Dairy Queen order
19 Deemed not suitable for kids
22 Previous
23 Wild
24 1944 Jean-Paul Sartre play
26 One of the Wise Men
29 "Please help me with directions"
31 Boom, zoom and vroom
32 Cushiony part of a shoe
33 Matt Lauer or Meredith Vieira for "Today"
36 They have precincts: Abbr.
39 Nancy's 56-Down in the comics
40 Feature of a May-December romance
41 Deserter
46 ___ Peanut Butter Cups

by Allan E. Parrish

47 Fortify with vitamins, e.g.
51 Style of Chinese cuisine
53 ___ incognita
54 Fast-talking
55 Unaccompanied
56 See 39-Down
58 Completely fill
60 Rope-a-dope boxer
61 Suffix with cash
62 "My gal" of song
63 60-min. periods

ACROSS

1 "Uncle ___ Cabin"
5 Witches' faces have them
10 ___ vu
14 "Put a sock ___!"
15 Writer T. S. or George
16 Midterm, e.g.
17 Sicilian spewer
18 Former British P.M. Tony
19 Surprisingly lively for one's age
20 What the love of money is, they say
23 Lop off, as branches
24 RR depot
25 "The Lord of the Rings" enemy
28 "So long!"
31 Ninth-inning pitcher
33 Squealer
36 Stop a prevailing trend
38 Gillette razor
40 "I'll take that as ___"
41 30-second spot, e.g.
42 Quickly turn the pages of
47 That: Sp.
48 Mexican revolutionary ___ Villa
49 Check the fit of, as a dress
51 "___ Pinafore"
52 Hospital trauma ctrs.
54 "Oh, bushwa!"
57 Factory supervisors . . . or a hint to the starts of 20-, 36- and 42-Across
62 Old woman's home in a nursery rhyme
64 "Fear of Flying" writer Jong
65 Marco Polo crossed it
66 Simplicity
67 Contract conditions
68 Sore, with "off"
69 Arduous journey
70 Like Georgia Brown of song
71 "Put a tiger in your tank" brand

DOWN

1 It may hang out in a sports stadium
2 First in the rankings
3 17-year-old, legally
4 Condition of affairs
5 Duck features
6 ___ breve (2/2 time in music)
7 Iranian money
8 Works long and hard
9 Seventh-inning ritual
10 Arnaz of "I Love Lucy"
11 Nitroglycerin or dynamite
12 Cookie holder
13 "The Joy Luck Club" writer Tan
21 George Washingtons
22 Low-lying area
26 ___ a beet
27 Belief
29 Vintage designation
30 "I ___ amused!"
32 Hall-of-Famer Mel
33 Alice's mate on "The Honeymooners"
34 First string
35 Make lemons into melons, e.g.?
37 Go from gig to gig
39 Steelers' grp.
43 Ellington's "Take ___ Train"
44 Big stingers
45 One who mounts and dismounts a horse
46 Georgetown athlete
50 Nullify
53 Spread, as seed

by Pancho Harrison

55 Go-aheads
56 Great
Lakes Indians
58 Cousin of
an onion
59 Bog
60 Summit

61 Lead-in
to masochism
62 Filming
site
63 Part of
33-Down's
laugh

8

ACROSS

1 Chicago's ___ Planetarium
6 Country singer Brooks
11 Opposite of dis
14 Like oil directly from a well
15 Hilo hello
16 Aussie hopper
17 Ditch digging, e.g.
19 Little Rock's home: Abbr.
20 Yolk's site
21 City name before Heat or Vice
22 "Inferno" writer
24 Money borrowed from a friend, e.g.
26 Fleet
29 Bald person's purchase
30 Serve, as tea
31 "Airplane!" or "Spaceballs"
34 Flow back
37 The Dalai Lama, e.g.
41 At any time, to a poet

42 Six ___ a-laying (gift in a Christmas song)
43 Silent screen star Naldi
44 Reverse of WSW
45 Acid blocker sold over the counter
47 Slash symbol, e.g.
53 Helicopter part
54 Hotelier Helmsley
55 Address for an overseas G.I.
58 Wonderment
59 Comfily ready to sleep . . . or a hint to 17-, 24-, 37- and 47-Across
62 Moms
63 One of the Judds
64 Ryan of "The Beverly Hillbillies"
65 Tidbit for an aardvark
66 Lugs
67 Homes for 65-Acrosses

DOWN

1 Pinnacle
2 Wet blanket
3 Aqua-___
4 Univ. e-mail ending
5 Cleaned out, as with a pipe cleaner
6 Black-tie affairs
7 "Remember the ___!" (rallying cry of 1836)
8 Harbinger of spring
9 Even if, informally
10 What a serf led
11 Clog-busting brand
12 Main artery
13 Thimble or shoe, in Monopoly
18 Franc : France :: ___ : Italy
23 $2x+5=15$ subj.
24 Last name of Henry VIII's last
25 M.P.'s quarry
26 Cathedral recess
27 Hillbilly's belt

28 John who founded the Sierra Club
31 Take to court
32 Dads
33 Shout after a bull charges
34 Blue-pencil
35 Gamma preceder
36 Bric-a-___
38 Unaware
39 Many a driver's ed student
40 First name of Henry VIII's second
44 Self-esteem
45 Next-to-last element alphabetically
46 ___ Skywalker of "Star Wars"
47 Comedy's counterpart
48 Cedar Rapids native
49 Event that could be seen as far away as Las Vegas in the '50s
50 Mete out
51 "I'll do it!"
52 1930s–'40s heavyweight champ Joe

by C. W. Stewart

55 Fruit drinks
56 Pub serving
57 Small bills
60 Thai neighbor
61 Before, poetically

9

ACROSS
1 Fruit often cut into balls
6 ___ Disney Pictures
10 Actress Thompson of "Howards End"
14 Give off, as charm
15 Song for a diva
16 The North and the South, in the Civil War
17 Company-paid medical and dental coverage, college tuition, etc.
20 Controversial substance in baseball news
21 Reduce to mush
22 "___ look like a mind reader?"
24 Most like Solomon
25 Upholstered piece
30 Dorothy, to Em

32 Not so congenial
33 Poet ___ St. Vincent Millay
34 Tanning lotion abbr.
37 A sot he's not
41 Tissue layer
42 "This will ___ further!"
43 Artful deception
44 Factory
46 Pattern on a pinto horse
47 Angora goat's fleece
50 ___ Lanka
52 Ward off
53 Ireland's hue
59 Bit of attire for a business interview, maybe
63 Bowlful accompanying teriyaki
64 A slave to opera?
65 Superior to
66 Pindaric pieces
67 Hosiery spoiler
68 Identified

DOWN
1 Diner on "Alice"
2 Emergency door sign
3 Garage job, for short
4 Baltic Sea feeder
5 Wolfe of whodunits
6 Hard-to-find guy in children's books
7 Wall St. whiz
8 Tell a whopper
9 Get some sun
10 Pour forth
11 Wavy pattern on fabric
12 Apportions, with "out"
13 Liability's opposite
18 Capitol Hill helper
19 Cast-of-thousands movie
23 Hits the tab key, say
24 Grow tiresome
25 Nincompoop

26 Environmental sci.
27 Neat
28 ___ time (golf course slot)
29 Blow it
31 ___-European languages
33 School attended by princes
34 Burlesque bit
35 ___-mell
36 Gratis
38 Petri dish gel
39 "Here ___ again"
40 Macadamia, for one
44 Breaks down grammatically
45 Lo-fat
46 Actress Rogers who was once married to Tom Cruise
47 PC shortcut
48 Egg-shaped
49 "It follows that . . ."
51 Put a new price on
54 Politico Bayh
55 McEntire of country music

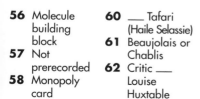

by Fred Piscop

56 Molecule building block

57 Not prerecorded

58 Monopoly card

60 ___ Tafari (Haile Selassie)

61 Beaujolais or Chablis

62 Critic ___ Louise Huxtable

10

ACROSS

1 Prom night transportation
5 Jack who once hosted "The Tonight Show"
9 Bring upon oneself
14 "Green" sci.
15 "___ upon a time . . ."
16 Drunkard
17 Seven or eight hours, typically
20 Furtively
21 When repeated, sound of disapproval
22 James who wrote "A Death in the Family"
23 Early delivery in the delivery room
27 "Hey, way to go!"
30 Kristofferson of music
31 Columbus Day mo.
32 Moon's path
33 Salon sound
34 Chop ___
35 Inventor's goal

38 180° turns, in slang
39 Removes a squeak from
40 Where 43-Across run free
41 Super Bowl stats
42 Do nothing and like it
43 Mustangs, e.g.
44 Did nothing
46 Rock's ___ the Hoople
47 Drunk motorist's offense, briefly
48 Brainy bunch
52 They rarely see the light of day
56 Martini garnish
57 "___ I say, not . . ."
58 Neither fem. nor masc.
59 A little drunk
60 Igor, to Dr. Frankenstein: Abbr.
61 Equipment at Vail

DOWN

1 Plastic block brand
2 Pic you can click
3 Not worth debating, as a point
4 Things that die hard
5 Self-confident, as a pageant contestant
6 Journalistic slant
7 Sore all over
8 Like Gen. Colin Powell: Abbr.
9 Topics of debate
10 Nick of "48 HRS."
11 Pool player's stick
12 Take advantage of
13 Dem.'s opponent
18 Make null and void
19 Prepares to streak
23 Fuel-efficient Toyota
24 Expresses great sorrow
25 Freezing period

26 Classic Jaguars
27 "Forget the excuses!"
28 Frozen potato brand
29 Diagnostic that entails sticking the forearm with a needle
30 Small, rounded hill
33 "Say cheese!"
34 Bravura performances
36 Dormmate
37 X-rated
42 Hardly ostentatious
43 "Really and truly"
45 Modern viewing options, for short
46 Flat-topped Southwestern hills
48 Old Pontiac muscle cars
49 Hide-and-___
50 Decorative needle case
51 Former fast fliers
52 Automaton, for short

by Paula Gamache

53 Yeller
in the
Yale Bowl
54 Not guzzle
55 BlackBerry
or iPhone,
briefly

11

ACROSS

1 King Kong, e.g.
4 Trailer's connection to a car
9 Highly skilled
14 Where IV's may be administered
15 Japanese automaker
16 Theatrical medley
17 Emphatic south-of-the-border assent
19 Lessen
20 Comet, say, to the impressionable
21 Mocking remark
22 After-dinner candies
23 Central American canal locale
25 In great shape
26 Beginning piano student's exercise
33 Feeds, as pigs
37 Thing to hum or whistle
38 Neural transmitter
39 Vagrant
40 Test answer you have a 50-50 chance of guessing right
41 Nevada gambling mecca
42 Demon's doing
43 Nobelist Wiesel
44 Just sits around
45 Parting words
48 Finish
49 Prickly plant
54 No longer fashionable
57 Killer whale
60 United ___ Emirates
61 A-list
62 Wind that cools a beach
64 Aviator ___ Post
65 Word said upon answering a phone
66 Suffix with rocket or racket
67 Shop
68 Woody or Gracie
69 Banned bug spray

DOWN

1 See 8-Down
2 ___ donna (vain sort)
3 Ruhr Valley city
4 Contains
5 Winter river obstruction
6 Bluefin, for one
7 Wheat or soybeans
8 Loser to a tortoise, in a fable by 1-Down
9 Fragrance named for a Musketeer
10 Quick, cashless way to pay for things
11 "___ Almighty" (2007 movie)
12 Miniature golf shot
13 Gadgets not needed in miniature golf
18 "___ pig's eye!"
24 Roast hosts, for short
25 Costing nothing
27 The Beatles' "Any Time ___".
28 Roberts of "Erin Brockovich"
29 Beginning
30 Rink leap
31 The ___ Ranger
32 Outfielder Slaughter in the Baseball Hall of Fame
33 Kenny Rogers's "___ a Mystery"
34 Zero, in tennis
35 Village Voice award
36 Leisure suit fabric
40 Hatfield/McCoy affair
44 Ill temper
46 Cyclops feature
47 Give power to
50 ___ kwon do
51 Cornered

by Fred Piscop

52 Vegged out

53 Roger with a thumbs-up or thumbs-down

54 Sunday seats

55 Touched down

56 Storage for forage

57 Workplace watchdog org.

58 Irish dance

59 Do some telemarketing

63 "Apollo 13" director Howard

12

ACROSS

1 Trap
6 Actress Stapleton of "All in the Family"
10 Way off
14 "The Goose That Laid the Golden Eggs" writer
15 The Bruins of the N.C.A.A.
16 ___ Valley, Calif.
17 "Portnoy's Complaint" author
19 Quick cut
20 Word after Web or camp
21 Geological stretch
22 Hosiery hue
23 Founder of the Christian Broadcasting Network
27 What oil cleanups clean up
30 Make ashamed
31 Silver or platinum
32 Italian and French bread?
34 Escape
37 "Duck soup!"
38 Promoters . . . or a description of 17-, 23-, 46- and 57-Across?
39 It may hold back the sea
40 Flight info
41 Twists out of shape
42 Russian revolutionary with a goatee
43 Old office note taker
45 Bank (on)
46 "Le Déjeuner des Canotiers" painter
50 Billy Crystal or Whoopi Goldberg for the Oscars, often
51 Perjure oneself
52 Currier's partner in lithography
56 "Phooey!"
57 He didn't really cry "The British are coming!"
60 Matured
61 Ferris wheel or bumper cars
62 Three wishes granter
63 Tennis do-overs
64 Poetical tributes
65 Willow for wicker

DOWN

1 Drains
2 Classic soft drink
3 With 41-Down, seemingly
4 Be a wizard or an elf, say, in Dungeons & Dragons
5 Prefix with center
6 One of 12 at a trial
7 Commercial prefix with Lodge
8 Computer key abbr.
9 "I'll pass"
10 Stock, bank deposits, real estate, etc.
11 Where winners are often photographed
12 Friend in a sombrero
13 Mature
18 No ___ Allowed (motel sign)
22 They're worn under blouses
24 The works
25 Reveals
26 Deep black
27 "Peter Pan" pirate
28 Mulching matter
29 "Mum's the word!"
32 Misplay, e.g.
33 Official behind a catcher
35 Related (to)
36 Repair
38 Window section
39 Takes away from, with "of"
41 See 3-Down
42 Luau gift
44 Stock analysts study them

by John Dunn

45 Activist
46 Piano part
47 Concern of 38-Across
48 Escape from
49 "Frasier" character

53 Start of Caesar's boast
54 Buffalo's county
55 Clairvoyant

57 Golf lesson provider
58 Relief
59 Kind of trip for the conceited

13

ACROSS

1 See 1-Down
5 Manages
10 Indolent
14 Wheel turner
15 Cognizant
16 Suffix with buck
17 "Out, damned __!"
18 Perry Mason's secretary __ Street
19 "Thumbnail" writings
20 What a broken-down car may get
21 Thick growth of trees
23 Former Ford compacts
25 Simian
26 Burden
27 Bullfighter
32 W.W. II-ending weapon, for short
34 Diamond or sapphire
35 Work __ sweat
36 Actor Gyllenhaal of "Brokeback Mountain"
37 Four-bagger
38 Despot Idi __
39 Bauxite or galena
40 Much of afternoon TV
41 Subsided
42 Voice between tenor and bass
44 Dispatched, as a dragon
45 1980s TV's "Emerald Point __"
46 Old indoor light source
49 It's more than 90°
54 Three on a sundial
55 Actress Loughlin of "Full House"
56 Harsh light
57 Sicilian peak
58 Door to the outside
59 Like certain cereals
60 Explorer Ponce de __
61 Gold's and others
62 Seize (from)
63 Words of approximation

DOWN

1 With 1-Across, Coke vs. Pepsi competition, e.g.
2 Montreal baseballers, 1969–2004
3 Crockpot
4 Asian holiday
5 West Point students
6 Country singer Buck
7 Buddies
8 Writer __ Stanley Gardner
9 Mariner
10 __ tar pits
11 1997 Indy 500 winner __ Luyendyk
12 Menageries
13 Dennis __ and the Classics IV (1960s–'70s group)
21 Beat badly
22 German-made car since 1899
24 "This round's __"
27 Home of Arizona State University
28 Has debts
29 Tray transporter
30 "The Andy Griffith Show" boy
31 Author Ayn
32 Do __ on (work over)
33 Theda of early films
34 __ of Arc
37 Lockup
38 Cain's victim
40 Depots: Abbr.
41 Women's magazine founded in France
43 Eskimos
44 Like 33-Down's films
46 Really mean people
47 Mythical king of Crete
48 Instrument for Rachmaninoff
49 Designer Cassini

by Randy Sowell

50 Hardly
streamlined,
as a car
51 Fit
52 Banned
orchard
spray

53 ___ Dogg
of
R&B/hip-hop
57 "Do Ya"
group,
for
short

14

ACROSS

1 With 66-Across, first in a series of five TV personalities (1954–57)
6 With 65-Across, second in a series of five TV personalities (1957–62)
10 "Think" sloganeer
13 Dropped flies and bad throws, in baseball
15 Sheltered from the wind
16 Teachers' org.
17 Fifth in a series of five TV personalities (2009–10)
19 With 22-Across, fourth in a series of five TV personalities (1992–2009, 2010–)
20 Football six-pointers, for short
21 Since way back when
22 See 19-Across
23 Teacher's teaching
24 Norse race of gods
25 "La Bohème" heroine
28 Closest friends
30 Free from worry
33 Two halved
34&35 Third in a series of five TV personalities (1962–92)
40 Scot's cap
42 French actress Catherine
43 Despise
48 Minor hang-up
49 Unaccompanied performances
50 Taunt
53 Desk job at 58 & 59-Across?
54 Decrease
55 Con's opposite
58&59 TV home for this puzzle's five featured TV personalities

61 Suffix with ball
62 Opening stake
63 Prompt
64 Telephone book info: Abbr.
65 See 6-Across
66 See 1-Across

DOWN

1 Religious offshoot
2 Trampled
3 Sea eagles
4 U.S. broadcaster overseas
5 Bert's "Sesame Street" pal
6 Tech talk, e.g.
7 Not consistent with, as a way of thinking
8 Middling grades
9 Author Follett
10 How quips are delivered
11 Close-fitting cap
12 City hall leaders
14 Daughters' counterparts
18 Bandleader Count ___

22 Good place to have a cow?
23 Property claim
24 "He doesn't have ___ bone in his body"
25 Not minor: Abbr.
26 "How was ___ know?"
27 Speed limit abbr.
29 Early film director Thomas H. ___
31 "Nay" sayers
32 Shade of blue
36 Observe the Sabbath
37 The Sabbath, to Christians: Abbr.
38 Eggs in a lab
39 Less than zero: Abbr.
41 Purplish tint
42 Clear of defects, as software
43 Actor Kutcher
44 [Sob!]
45 Twins Mary-Kate and Ashley
46 Bon ___ (clever remark)
47 Neater

by John Farmer

51 Bounce back, as sound
52 Insurance provider since 1850
54 Jaffe or Barrett

55 Grammy-winning Collins
56 All roads lead to this, they say

57 Wilson of "Zoolander"
59 Strike lightly
60 Letters on a Cardinals cap

15

ACROSS
1 Home (in on)
5 Arrow shooters
9 Hunk
13 Lumberjacks' tools
14 Margarine
15 Uneaten part of an apple
16 Small milk carton capacity
17 Ken of "thirtysomething"
18 Eager
19 1989 Sally Field/Dolly Parton/ Shirley MacLaine movie
22 Hold up
23 Hunk
24 Foresail
27 "Here's to you!" and others
29 Old Pontiac
32 Electrical device for foreign travelers
34 "Git!"
35 2000 Martin Lawrence movie

39 Swamps
40 Cork
41 Novelist Tan
42 Seeks blindly
45 ___ Lanka
46 With 51-Down, John Ashcroft's predecessor as attorney general
48 Legal matter
50 1992 Alec Baldwin/Meg Ryan film
56 Not imaginary
57 Jai ___
58 "To Live and Die ___"
59 The "A" in A.D.
60 Lunkhead
61 Santa's landing place
62 Part of M.V.P.
63 Pitch
64 Thing hidden in each of the movie names in this puzzle

DOWN
1 Microwaves
2 Stage direction after an actor's last line
3 Philosopher Descartes
4 Blender maker
5 Classic John Lee Hooker song of 1962
6 Earthenware pot
7 Puts on a scale
8 One of Shakespeare's begins "Shall I compare thee to a summer's day?"
9 Milan's La ___
10 Some trophies
11 Diva's number
12 They have headboards and footboards
20 Game with a $100 million prize, maybe
21 Meditation syllables

24 "Star Wars" villain ___ the Hutt
25 "Knock it off" or "get it on," e.g.
26 Hip-hop wear
28 One of an octopus's octet
30 Police stunner
31 Onetime "S.N.L." player Cheri
33 Evenings, briefly
34 Soak (up)
36 Egyptian cobra
37 Shots taken by some athletes
38 Old Testament prophet
42 Bearded beast
43 Edit
44 Verdi hero married to Desdemona
47 Apportion
49 Mini or tutu
50 Nanny's vehicle
51 See 46-Across

by Peter A. Collins

52 New Mexico resort
53 "Are you ___ out?"
54 Gin flavoring
55 Not out

16

ACROSS
1 "___ or charge?"
5 Winger or Messing
10 Suffix with song or slug
14 Rights org.
15 Go inside
16 Parisian girlfriend
17 Graham cracker pie shell
19 Binges
20 Poster paints
21 President who followed Harry
23 AOL or MSN: Abbr.
24 18-wheeler
25 Exhausted
26 Spider or worm
31 Delights in
34 Molecule part
35 Tint
36 Bog material
37 Freezer cubes
38 Spreadsheet contents
39 Bond creator Fleming
40 Lois of The Daily Planet
42 Pan-fries
44 Lending crisis

47 ___ I.R.A. (savings plan for old age)
48 Tippler
49 Engineering sch. in Troy, N.Y.
52 Fruit for a monkey
55 Common burger topper
57 All in a twitter
58 Cajun seafood dish
60 Make over
61 Friend of Fran and Ollie
62 At the peak of
63 Garden of ___
64 Exorbitant
65 "Hey, you!"

DOWN
1 Prickly plants
2 Real estate units
3 Batter's dry spell
4 Camel feature
5 Criticizes openly
6 Infuriate

7 A/C measures
8 Hi-___ monitor
9 Style of the 1920s and '30s
10 Tex-Mex treat
11 Online 'zine
12 Sound of relief
13 Try out
18 Fruit on a bush
22 Toasty
25 Computer memory measure
26 Foldaway bed
27 Harness racer
28 One of the five W's
29 Minstrel's instrument
30 Votes opposite the nays
31 The "Odyssey" or "Beowulf"
32 Close by
33 Tarzan's love
37 Ruler division
38 "Well, that's obvious!"

40 Cowardly resident of Oz
41 Blitzes
42 Year-round Alp topper
43 Cast member
45 Fire-breathing beast
46 Functional
49 Mob scenes
50 Collared pullovers
51 Bumbling
52 Like Mother Hubbard's cupboard
53 Ripened
54 Bump on a branch
55 Autumn tool
56 Twice-a-month tide
59 Dirt road feature

by Billie Truitt

17

ACROSS

1 Africa's ___ Victoria
5 Rope material
9 Letter after beta
14 ___ of March
15 Theater award
16 Bird-related
17 1971 Tom Jones hit
19 Appealingly piquant
20 Photocopier cartridge contents
21 Weeper of Greek myth
23 Perfumery emanations
25 Hot sauce brand
30 1972 Carly Simon hit
33 Items on which baseball insignia appear
37 Opposite of post-
38 Seasons or deices
39 Have ___ (be connected)
40 Bergen dummy Mortimer
43 Words of understanding
44 Windshield flip-down
46 Geese formation shape
47 Finishing 11th out of 11, e.g.
48 1966 Monkees hit
52 Photographers, informally
53 Parish leader
58 ___ chip, which might be topped with 19-Across 27-Down dip
61 Still kicking
62 ___ the Hutt of "Star Wars"
66 1962 Crystals hit
68 Martian or Venusian
69 ___ May Clampett of "The Beverly Hillbillies"
70 Suffix with concession
71 Poet Stephen Vincent ___
72 Gin flavoring
73 London art gallery

DOWN

1 Rosters
2 Kind of committee
3 New Hampshire college town
4 Krupp Works city
5 Christmas or Thanksgiving: Abbr.
6 Abba of Israel
7 Longish skirt
8 Mescaline-yielding cactus
9 Garden pavilions
10 N.Y.C.'s Park or Lex
11 Prefix with place or print
12 Yoga class surface
13 "___ takers?"
18 Pseudo-stylish
22 English majors' degs.
24 Absorbs, with "up"
26 Be of use
27 Tex-Mex preparation
28 Uses as a reference
29 Beginning stage
31 Makeshift vote receptacle
32 Superman portrayer Christopher
33 Be nitpicky
34 Japanese cartoon art
35 Native of the Leaning Tower city
36 Nose-in-the-air sorts
41 Minister's nickname
42 Animal that may be caught in the headlights
45 Carpet leftover
49 Meadow
50 Rainfall units
51 Derrière
54 Golf shoe gripper
55 Fibula's neighbor
56 Plain to see
57 C.S.A. general

by Fred Piscop

59 Satan's domain
60 Norway's capital
62 Sharp left or right, in the ring
63 Ginger __
64 Bargain basement container
65 Quilting party
67 Sailor's assent

18

ACROSS

1 In ___ land (daydreaming)
5 Boeing products
9 Path around the earth
14 Greek vowels
15 Elvis Presley's middle name
16 Battery brand
17 Succumbing to second thoughts
20 Beatnik's "Got it!"
21 "Salut!," in Scandinavia
22 Concorde, in brief
23 Performed prior to the main act
25 What it takes to tango
26 "That's all ___ wrote"
27 Neither's partner
28 Billiard sticks
31 One still in the game, in poker
33 Submit, as homework
35 Low digits
36 Succumbing to second thoughts
40 Mare's newborn
41 Colbert ___ (Comedy Central show audience)
42 Blunders
45 978-0-060-93544-3, for Roget's Thesaurus
46 U.K. record label
49 Genetic material
50 Hunky-dory
52 Sailor
54 ___ and downs
55 How Santa dresses, mostly
58 Anatomical passages
59 Succumbing to second thoughts
62 Start of the Spanish calendar
63 Biblical captain for 40 days and 40 nights
64 Golden ___ (senior citizen)
65 Two-door or four-door car
66 Friend in war
67 Unfreeze

DOWN

1 Veterans' group, informally
2 Returning to the previous speed, in music
3 Agitated state
4 Actor/ brother Sean or Mackenzie
5 Dutch painter Steen
6 Energy units
7 Tick-___
8 High-hatter
9 Fewer than 100 shares
10 Fight adjudicator, for short
11 "Gesundheit!"
12 Arctic covering
13 Walks unsteadily
18 Drug used to treat poisoning
19 Statutes
24 Easy two-pointer in basketball
29 Genesis garden
30 Mount ___, where the Commandments were given to Moses
32 Loads
33 Largest city on the island of Hawaii
34 Tiny criticisms
36 Dixie bread
37 Pestered
38 Writing points
39 Entered
40 Old schoolmasters' sticks
43 Ruin, as one's parade
44 Any one of the Top 40
46 Come out
47 ___ Comics, home of Spider-Man and the Fantastic Four
48 Add with a caret, e.g.

by Mark Milhet

51 Swedish coin
53 Starting group of athletes
56 Certain alkene

57 Order to the person holding the deck of cards
60 Author Levin
61 Not camera-ready?

19

ACROSS
1 Part of a Halloween costume
5 Rich soil component
10 Get an ___ effort
14 "Do ___ others as . . ."
15 Not appropriate
16 Duo plus one
17 Mark left from an injury
18 Refuse a request
19 Detained
20 Separate grains from wheat, e.g.
22 Valentine candy message
24 Animated TV character whose best friend is Boots
28 Suffix with access
29 Young dog or seal
30 China's Mao ___-tung
31 ___ Jima
32 Casey of "American Top 40"
34 Main port of Yemen
35 2008 campaign personality
40 Like paintings and some juries
41 As a result
42 Fruity cooler
43 Animal pouch
46 Plane takeoff guess: Abbr.
47 Chicken ___ king
50 Norman Rockwell painting subject of W.W. II
54 Fix permanently, as an interest rate
55 Helmet from W.W. I or W.W. II
56 "Beauty ___ the eye . . ."
58 Semiconductor giant
60 Idiot
61 Tenth: Prefix
62 Hospital attendant
63 Kuwaiti leader
64 Business V.I.P.
65 Velocity
66 Say "No, I didn't"

DOWN
1 High-priority item
2 Katie Couric, for one
3 Like the night sky
4 Seoul's home
5 Top-secret
6 Italian article
7 Answer that's between yes and no
8 Coming immediately after, as on TV
9 Leaves in a huff, with "out"
10 Prefix with -centric
11 Something for nothing, as what a hitchhiker seeks
12 OPEC product
13 Fishing pole
21 March 17 honoree, for short
23 ___ de France
25 Sword of sport
26 Fancy pitcher
27 Politico ___ Paul
32 Beer blast centerpiece
33 Measure of a car's 65-Across: Abbr.
34 Lincoln, informally
35 Cousin of karate
36 Minimum pizza order
37 Lusty look
38 Like the Beatles' White Album
39 The year 1406
40 Part of a guffaw
43 1/60 of a min.
44 Diet doctor
45 "Don't let it get you down!"
47 Comfortable (with)
48 Go right at it, as work
49 Vein's counterpart

by Joe Krozel

51 Kind of column, in architecture

52 ___ nous (between us)

53 Kaput

56 Suffix with chlor-

57 It sells in advertising, they say

59 180° from WNW

20

ACROSS
1 Knights' competition
6 Baby kangaroo
10 Kid around
14 Winfrey who said "I still have my feet on the ground, I just wear better shoes"
15 Feminine suffix
16 Length × width, for a rectangle
17 Brother outlaw in the Wild West
19 Spick-and-span
20 Suffix with pay
21 "___ happy returns"
22 Imbeciles
24 Ones with caws for alarm?
25 Some boxing wins, for short
26 Humiliate
28 Cause for a mistrial
32 Not taut
33 "Tell ___ lies"

34 Prime draft status
35 Googly-eyed Muppet
36 Retail clothing giant . . . or a description of 17- and 54-Across and 10- and 24-Down?
37 Color for baby girls, traditionally
38 L.B.J. son-in-law Charles
39 Things inflated with hot air?
40 Cabalists' plans
41 Mexican beans
43 Makes progress
44 Up to the task
45 19th-century educator Horace
46 Politico Milk of "Milk"
49 Bo : Obama :: ___ : Roosevelt
50 "___ Baba and the 40 Thieves"

53 Jai ___
54 White Sox outfielder nicknamed "Shoeless"
57 Injured
58 Choir voice
59 Discover by chance
60 Home of Iowa State University
61 Back end
62 Midterms and finals

DOWN
1 "___ left his home in Tucson, Arizona" (Beatles lyric)
2 Autobahn auto
3 With 45-Down, home of the Big Dipper
4 Carrier to Copenhagen
5 1994 Jim Carrey film
6 Levi's, e.g.
7 "Time Is ___ Side" (Rolling Stones hit)
8 Opposite of WSW

9 "So you've said"
10 "Me and Bobby McGee" singer, 1971
11 Nabisco cookie
12 Chair or sofa
13 Bowlers that don't bowl
18 "The Gong Show" panelist ___ P. Morgan
23 Hound
24 Longtime New York senator for whom a center is named
25 iPod downloads
26 "It's ___ nothing"
27 Thumper's "deer friend"
28 Give a ___ welcome
29 The "U" in A.C.L.U.
30 Payments to landlords
31 Talks, talks, talks
32 Feudal worker
33 Fibber of old radio

by Randall J. Hartman

36 Smucker's container
40 Flair
42 U.K. award
43 Black-tie affair
45 See 3-Down
46 "That's rich!"
47 Homecoming attendee, in brief
48 Once in a blue moon
49 Greek cheese
50 Dashiell Hammett hound
51 Tapestry device
52 Places to stay the night
55 Bullring cheer
56 Spherical breakfast cereal

21

ACROSS

1 Best-selling computer game of the 1990s
5 Players in a play
9 Unwanted e-mail
13 Helicopter blade
15 "___ your thirst" (former Sprite slogan)
16 Therefore
17 Myanmar, once
18 Al Capone, for one
20 Mentalist Geller
21 Little devil
23 Breadth
24 Not heeding danger
27 Apartment that's owned, not leased
28 Nick at ___
29 Computer whiz
32 ___ Antonio, Tex.
33 Jobs at Apple
35 Corridors
37 Widespread Internet prank involving a bait-and-switch link to a music video
41 Reason for engine trouble, perhaps
42 Christmas carols
45 ___ and eggs
48 Metal that gave its name to a shade of blue
51 Writer Harte
52 Caribbean vacation spot
54 Mick Jagger or Bruce Springsteen
56 Prayer beads
58 Parisian "yes"
59 Studio that made "Notorious"
60 Packs for bikers and hikers
63 Young pigeon
65 52-Across, e.g.
66 Cry while careering downhill
67 Bulrush, e.g.
68 Fortuneteller
69 Stop or Do Not Pass
70 Almost-failing grades

DOWN

1 Owner of the Springfield Nuclear Power Plant on "The Simpsons"
2 Shout in tag
3 Less forgiving
4 ___ Sawyer
5 Body in a whodunit
6 "The ___ Daba Honeymoon"
7 Fraction of a min.
8 Little fella
9 Fight that might include fisticuffs
10 Prettifies oneself, as in a mirror
11 Order of business at a meeting
12 "When it rains, it pours" salt brand
14 Train travel
19 Be great at
22 Encountered
25 Bandleader Eubanks of "The Jay Leno Show"
26 Learned one
30 "2001" computer
31 Running a temperature, say
34 High-m.p.g. vehicles
36 Hoity-toity sorts
38 Hootchy-___
39 "Spare" part of the body
40 She says "The lady doth protest too much, methinks" in "Hamlet"
43 Problem with pipes
44 Disco lights
45 Joel Chandler ___, creator of Uncle Remus
46 Excite
47 What a bodybuilder builds

by Natan Last

22

ACROSS

1 Iditarod vehicle
5 Money for the poor
9 In a stupor
14 Skunk ___ Le Pew
15 Jacob's wife
16 President sworn in on Lincoln's Bible
17 They can be stroked or bruised
18 "Othello" character who says "Who steals my purse steals trash"
19 Bearer of gold, frankincense or 66-Across
20 Speaking with lofty language
23 Cunning
24 "Do ___ others . . ."
25 Riddle
29 Ginger ___ (Canada Dry product)
30 Droop
31 ___ Luthor of "Superman"

32 Withholding nothing
37 Jazz's Fitzgerald
38 October 31 shout
39 Luau garlands
40 What a fresh ad campaign helps combat
45 History segment
46 Auditor's org.
47 Like carrots that crunch
48 Calm
50 Campbell's product
52 Damage
55 Holder of the first-in-the-nation presidential primary
58 "Dancing With the Stars" airer
61 Help in crime
62 Tolkien creatures
63 One getting one-on-one instruction
64 Egg on
65 Sainted fifth-century pope
66 Gift brought to Bethlehem

67 Pb, in chemistry
68 Its cycle is indicated by the starts of 20-, 32-, 40- and 55-Across

DOWN

1 Shoots, as lava
2 Permissible
3 Strong bond
4 Arnaz of "I Love Lucy"
5 Like celestial bodies exhibiting syzygy
6 Pounced (on)
7 Nearsighted Mr. of cartoons
8 What a cobbler works on
9 Santo ___, Caribbean capital
10 Beaded counters
11 Zig's partner
12 Cousin of an ostrich
13 Prosecutors, briefly
21 ___ and void

22 Blue-winged duck
26 3-Down and others
27 Earn
28 x and y, on a graph
29 Jai ___
30 Sean Connery, nationally speaking
32 Airborne signal
33 Like a bone from the elbow to the wrist
34 Bird seen in hieroglyphics
35 Bush 43, to Bush 41
36 Large amount
37 Rams' mates
41 Ancient Assyrian capital
42 Sprouted
43 Blew, as a volcano
44 Notorious B.I.G. releases
49 Key in
50 Buffalo hockey player
51 "Phi, chi, psi" follower
52 Actor Sal of "Exodus"

by Dustin Foley

53 "Star Wars" droid
54 Plant exudation
56 Lug
57 Captain's place
58 Dispenser of 20s
59 Totally accept, as an idea
60 Midpoint: Abbr.

23

ACROSS

1 Side of a doorway
5 1928 Oscar winner Jannings
9 ___ and dangerous
14 Actor Morales
15 Western locale called the Biggest Little City in the World
16 Late hotel queen Helmsley
17 Small hotel room specification
20 Modern workout system
21 Fan sound
22 "Hel-l-lp!"
23 Capone and Pacino
25 Sticky stuff
27 1944 thriller with Fred MacMurray and Barbara Stanwyck
36 ___-bitty
37 Falco of "The Sopranos"
38 Ad ___ per aspera (Kansas' motto)
39 Former AT&T rival
40 Princess Diana's family name
42 Suffix with president
43 Eagle's nest
45 Trojan War hero
46 Years, in Latin
47 Baked dessert with lemon filling, maybe
50 Partner of long. in a G.P.S. location
51 Small pouch
52 "___ sells seashells by the seashore" (tongue twister)
54 Bulletin board fastener
58 Oliver's love in "As You Like It"
62 Serious heart surgery
65 Brink
66 Continental money
67 Author Morrison
68 Words to live by
69 TV's warrior princess
70 Former jets to J.F.K.

DOWN

1 Words said in fun
2 Where India is
3 Lion's hair
4 Chronic whiner
5 Before, poetically
6 Cat's plaint
7 $\frac{1}{12}$ of a foot
8 Graph points
9 Swiss peak
10 Deduces
11 Not stereo
12 Letter attachments: Abbr.
13 When the sun shines
18 Laze about
19 Impulse
24 Ooze
26 Poet Khayyám
27 Probe persistently
28 Stream critter
29 Wombs
30 Like a score of 10 for 10
31 Japanese fighter
32 Go bad, as teeth
33 Singer Turner's autobiography
34 Drug that calms the nerves, slangily
35 New Haven collegian
40 Actress Ward
41 Old flames
44 Start of a daily school recital
46 Opposite of refuses
48 "___, Brute?"
49 Bordering on pornographic
52 Litigant
53 Tortoise's race opponent
55 Peak
56 Word in many a Nancy Drew title

by Andrea Carla Michaels

24

ACROSS

1 Point the finger at
6 Impudent
10 Jail unit
14 Parts to play
15 One putting finishing touches on a cake
16 Light greenish blue
17 Worker for 15%, say
18 "Meet Me at the ___"
19 Japanese wrestling
20 Fix part of dinner with lettuce, carrots, peppers, etc.
22 Large part of a waiter's income
23 A.B.A. member: Abbr.
24 Game company behind Sonic the Hedgehog
26 Play a part
29 Go off like Mount St. Helens

31 Sailor's "Stop!"
35 Writer Harte
37 Put ___ good word for
38 Words cried before "No hands!"
39 Activity with bubbles
40 Retail giant selling dog food, birdcages and such
42 Knots
43 Islands west of Portugal
45 ___-Magnon man
46 Coup d'___
47 Church council
48 Food Network stars
50 "___ you ready?"
51 Take a 39-Across
53 Boneheads
55 ___ California
58 Prepare to camp
63 Minnesota's St. ___ College

64 What "video" means literally
65 Bit part
66 Sitarist Shankar
67 In tatters
68 Perrier competitor
69 Pesky flier
70 Lighted sign over a door
71 Bush's 2004 opponent

DOWN

1 Kid with frequent temper tantrums
2 Golden arches, for McDonald's
3 Pub draughts
4 High-I.Q. group
5 Billionaire's home
6 Petty
7 Environmental sci.
8 Meal
9 Swap
10 Participate on Election Day
11 Prefix with lateral
12 It's in your throat when you choke up

13 Vientiane's land
21 Bacon units
25 Fed. auditing agcy.
26 The P.L.O.'s Mahmoud ___
27 Touched in the head
28 Wyoming's ___ Range
30 Where watermelons grow
32 Japanese dog
33 Mascara mess
34 Important sense for a gourmet
36 Show childish anger
38 Sponge used in a 39-Across
41 Moon shape
44 Psychologist/ writer LeShan
48 Longtime Comiskey Park team, informally
49 Sissy of "Carrie"
52 Ill will
54 Prevent, with "off"

by Randy Sowell

55 Tennis's Bjorn
56 Astronaut Shepard or Bean
57 Coffee, slangily
59 Garr or Hatcher
60 Mideast bigwig
61 Close
62 Broadway honor

25

Note: The answers to the eight starred clues all have something in common, each in a different way.

ACROSS
1 China's ___ Zedong
4 ___ and sciences
8 Wrist, elbow and ankle
14 Reach
16 Shook hands (on)
17 *Fraternity with a sweetheart of a song
18 *Drink that often comes with an umbrella
19 Afternoon socials
20 "My bad!"
22 Cold war foe, for short
23 Info on a W-2 form: Abbr.
24 *Like some socks
26 "Après ___ le déluge"
28 Ready for skinny-dipping
29 Rx signers
32 Bryn Mawr graduate
35 Cause of a clock change twice a yr.
36 Paint layer
37 *Smart aleck
39 *Salon supply in a bottle
41 "___ go bragh!"
42 Cold and blustery
44 Attach with Elmer's
45 Cul-de-___
46 "___ Was a Rollin' Stone"
47 "Bad" cholesterol, for short
48 *Good picnic forecast
51 Opposite of post-
54 "The Simpsons" girl
56 Lt. Kojak
57 Plenty
58 *Chocolaty ice cream dessert
60 *Second-generation senator from Indiana
62 Away from the coast
63 Faith
64 Insurance sellers
65 Exam given face-to-face
66 Snaky swimmer

DOWN
1 Sail holders
2 First sign of the zodiac
3 Hymn accompaniment
4 ___ Gardner, Mrs. Sinatra #2
5 Military info-gathering
6 Sierra Nevada resort lake
7 Grad student's income, often
8 Smucker's product
9 Track choice for Lionel trains
10 Like many St. Patrick's Day celebrants
11 Meshes
12 Rip
13 U.S. Star Wars program
15 AOL chitchat
21 "Be quiet!"
24 Queen's mate
25 Dangler on a dog collar
27 Broken mirror, to some
29 Small replica of the Spirit of St. Louis, e.g.
30 Harry Belafonte catchword
31 Brit's W.W. II gun
32 Fills with wonder
33 Franc : France :: ___ : Italy
34 Saintly glows
36 Gunk
38 Talk to persistently and with a big mouth
40 Badly
43 Purple Heart recipient
46 Lament
48 Network showing Capitol Hill proceedings
49 Cut off
50 Australian eucalyptus eater

by Lynn Lempel

52 Rolls-___ (car)
53 Jazzy Waters
54 Where inhaled air goes
55 No longer working
57 Lawyers' org.
58 ___ Farrow, Mrs. Sinatra #3
59 Bradley and Begley
61 Zilch

ACROSS

1 Early calculators
6 What it takes not to say "I see you've put on a little weight"
10 Arabian Peninsula land
14 Georgia Music Hall of Fame city
15 Workplace watchdog org.
16 Fashion line named for a sport
17 Conceals, as a card
18 Golda of Israel
19 Just slightly
20 Residential area of California [think Chevy]
23 In the style of
24 Clumsy sort
25 Fresh talk
26 Start of a stampede, maybe [think Ford]
32 "The Simpsons" storekeeper
33 Commuter's option
34 Realm of Tolkien's Middle-earth
37 Subtle flavor
39 Sonora snacks
42 Elbow
43 Locale of many outsourced jobs
45 Altar exchange
47 Be sociable
48 Part of a peace treaty [think Honda]
52 Blue shade
54 Tot's "piggy"
55 Letter-shaped cross
56 Cars suggested by 20-, 26- and 48-Across?
62 Surface figure
63 Trevi Fountain throw-in, once
64 Colonel North, informally
66 Put on the line
67 Dr. ___ (Mike Myers character)
68 The Beav's big brother
69 Rose who surpassed Cobb
70 Religious offshoot
71 Soda shop order

DOWN

1 Roadie's load
2 Meadow calls
3 Rights org.
4 Front-line action
5 Isolated, as a people
6 Mummy's locale
7 On a cruise
8 Casual slacks
9 Takeoff or touchdown site
10 Gem mined in Australia
11 It might have a "wide load" sign
12 It's good when airtight
13 Still in bed
21 Charged
22 At a distance
26 Hawaiian fish, on menus
27 ___ arms (indignant)
28 Going-to-church clothes
29 Actress ___ Scala
30 Conqueror of Valencia, 1094
31 Much Top 40 music
35 Closely related
36 Barbershop call
38 Quirky habit
40 "___ to Billie Joe" (1967 #1 hit)
41 Sir Georg of the Chicago Symphony
44 Play opener
46 Dugongs or manatees
49 Lots and lots
50 Bring back, as a fashion
51 Islamic leader
52 Quick-witted
53 "___ eleison" ("Lord, have mercy")
57 Do some yard work
58 Idle of "Life of Brian"

by Bob Johnson

59 Sentry's order
60 Jazz's Fitzgerald
61 Symbol of smoothness
65 Check out

27

ACROSS
1 Short
7 Hideout
11 General on a Chinese menu
14 Plugs
15 Right-hand person
16 Help in a heist, say
17 Fountain treat
19 Bearded beast
20 Bearded bloom
21 "Just watch me!"
23 Type size used in typewriters
27 Tangy pie filler
30 Goes postal
32 Penlight batteries
33 Patty Hearst kidnap grp.
34 He flew too close to the sun, in myth
35 "___ du lieber!"
36 Abbr. on an envelope
37 Relative of a certain cobbler
41 Idiosyncrasies
43 Batman and Robin, e.g.
44 Game keeper?
47 Setting for TV's "Newhart"
48 Sharif of "Doctor Zhivago"
50 A little scared
51 Candy bar with maraschinos
54 Big stingers
55 Show deep respect (to)
56 Make
58 Vermeer's "Woman With a ___"
59 Popular Fanta-like soda
66 Those, in Toledo
67 "___ Cop"
68 Robert Ludlum hero searching for his identity
69 Hideout
70 Carriers of Lyme ticks
71 Balloons

DOWN
1 Alert, for short
2 Thing with cups and hooks
3 Harry Potter's best friend
4 Actress Thurman
5 Pays what's due
6 Peter I, II or III
7 Run out, as a subscription
8 Feel ill
9 Uganda's ___ Amin
10 Eye part
11 Rib-eye alternatives
12 Natural seasoning
13 Club chair companion piece
16 Biology lab supply
18 Buildup at a river's mouth
22 IV amounts
23 Yale student
24 Tone ___ (early rapper)
25 Scientist who experienced a great fall?
26 Maryland squad
28 Lens type
29 Diamond Head locale
31 Archipelago unit: Abbr.
35 Lexus competitor
36 Big name in metal foil
38 Dutch dairy product
39 Aid in locating a pirate's treasure
40 Root beer float with chocolate ice cream
41 Amused
42 Not farmed out
45 Passbook abbr.
46 Masthead contents, briefly
48 ___ y Plata (Montana's motto)
49 "Dear me!"
50 Thick carpet
52 66 and others: Abbr.
53 Guadalajara guy
57 Confederate soldiers, for short

by Tony Orbach

60 ___ v. Wade
61 Actor Vigoda
62 Lament
63 http://www. yahoo.com, e.g.
64 Skit-filled NBC show, for short
65 "For ___ a jolly . . ."

28

ACROSS

1 Loss of heart
7 Mardi Gras wear
11 Go for it
14 "Seinfeld" woman
15 Prefix with potent
16 Go fast
17 Prison for soda jerks?
19 Simile center
20 When prompted
21 Proofer's mark
22 MapQuest suggestions: Abbr.
23 "What's Going On" singer Marvin
24 Prison for bishops?
26 La-la lead-in
28 Patches, as a fairway
29 Sweep's heap
32 Modern means of relaying jokes
36 Shut down

39 Prison for vintners?
42 Islamic equivalent of kosher
43 Bandleader Skinnay ___
44 Part of a journey
45 Lady of the Haus
47 10-digit no.
49 Prison for corny humorists?
54 Ayatollah's land
58 Has
59 Melt ingredient
60 Cartoon art genre
61 A fire sign
62 Prison for gardeners?
64 Doc with a tongue depressor, maybe
65 Creole cooking pod
66 "Good comeback!"
67 Draft org.
68 Call for
69 Slow movers

DOWN

1 Clear up, as a windshield
2 Massey of old films
3 Smart-mouthed
4 Stately dance in 3/4 time
5 It may be upped
6 Roll-call call
7 "Haystacks" artist Claude
8 More than enough
9 Shows derision
10 Thanksgiving guests, often
11 "Over and out"
12 Affected by 13-Down
13 Bakery supply
18 Infamous Amin
22 Its competitors may be thrown
24 Singer Michelle or Cass
25 Full of merriment
27 Slo-mo footage, perhaps

29 Oktoberfest "Oh!"
30 Doo-wop group ___ Na Na
31 Macramé ties
33 Census datum
34 Travel guide listing
35 Spy novelist Deighton
37 "Didn't I tell you?"
38 Fraction of a joule
40 Horses that produce milk
41 Nancy in France, e.g.
46 Slow on the ___
48 ___ franca
49 They may be punched
50 1936 Olympics star Jesse
51 Bizarre
52 Work, as dough
53 The "E" in 64-Across
55 Christina of "Monster"
56 Menotti title role
57 Spanish babies

by Jeffrey Wechsler

60 Like most bathroom graffiti: Abbr.
62 Took the cake
63 "___ been real!"

29

ACROSS

1 Performed on Broadway, say
6 Cry like a baby
10 Invitation request, for short
14 Actress Christine of "Chicago Hope"
15 Madame Bovary
16 Its license plates say "Birthplace of Aviation"
17 Envision in one's sleep
19 Yawl or yacht
20 Bad thing to have on one's face
21 List ender: Abbr.
22 Transition
24 NPR newsman Adams
26 Where to run some tests
28 Like some bad film scenes
31 Sleepwear component
34 Vegas intro?
35 Scoreboard figure
36 Tombstone letters
37 ___ salts
40 Hog's home
41 Dishful near a restaurant door
43 "How stupid of me!"
44 Nickname for Hemingway
46 Krazy ___ of the comics
47 The Chattahoochee River forms part of it
51 Classic family name in Florence
52 Street caution near a school
53 Sunday service
56 Schindler of "Schindler's List"
58 Genetic letters
60 2006 Verizon purchase
61 Former speaker Gingrich
63 Arrive on the Enterprise via transporter
66 Done
67 Molten flow
68 "Live Free ___" (New Hampshire motto)
69 Take from the top
70 Noted garden site
71 President whose name can be found backward in 17-, 31-, 47- and 63-Across

DOWN

1 John on the Mayflower
2 Freight
3 Clothing retailer starting in 1969
4 Pilot's announcement, for short
5 It's smaller than a penny
6 Online video equipment
7 Start of a Latin conjugation
8 Big name in morning radio
9 Sometime in the future
10 Hearty
11 Squeeze (into)
12 By way of
13 One calling the kettle black, in a phrase
18 Collection of plates
23 Sees red
25 Circle of angels?
27 What some drinkers run up
29 Skip
30 Recipe amts.
32 Fill to capacity and then some
33 Pick up, in a way
37 Dutch cheese
38 Gondolier's need
39 Tailed
40 Rejuvenation location
42 Part of an agenda
45 Friendly
46 Money from Sweden
48 European-style cafe
49 Subject of a Hemingway title

by Alan Arbesfeld

50 Holiday Inn alternative

54 Fabric for theater curtains

55 Part of a record getting the most airplay

57 Peruse

59 Bug chaser?

61 Hide-hair connector

62 Threshold

64 Cry in old Rome

65 Sphere

ACROSS

1 Tight-lipped
4 "Stat!"
8 Seven-up and crazy eights
13 Lennon's second wife
14 Jane of "Monster-in-Law"
16 Disco-era suffix
17 "Sure thing"
20 Note in an E major scale
21 Word before sheet or music
22 Loughlin of "90210"
23 Bygone despot
25 Outfielder's asset
28 "Chances are good"
33 "___ Said" (Neil Diamond hit)
34 ___ Lama
35 "It could go either way"
41 Like dessert wines
42 Water co., e.g.
43 "Doubtful"
50 Turned on
51 Studio constructions
52 Close by
53 Gitmo mil. branch
54 Counselor's clients, perhaps
56 "Forget it!"
62 Perfect
63 Fluctuates wildly
64 Ill temper
65 Apt to pout
66 Had a bawl
67 Ballpark fig.

DOWN

1 "The Jungle Book" hero
2 Oneness
3 Insect monster of Japanese film
4 Get an ___ effort
5 Borscht, e.g.
6 Amazon ___ (aggressive insect)
7 "Stat!"
8 Shocked reaction
9 F.B.I. worker: Abbr.
10 "You don't mean ME?!"
11 Self-esteem
12 Sequel title starter, sometimes
15 Surrounding glows
18 Precipitation that may be the size of golf balls
19 Banjoist Scruggs
23 The so-called fourth dimension
24 Attire on the slopes
25 Melville's obsessed captain
26 Thing to play
27 Haunted house sound
29 More than deceive
30 Put down
31 Pastoral poems
32 God, in Roma
35 AOL alternative
36 Whom an M.P. hunts
37 Hulking Himalayan of legend
38 Asteroid area, e.g.
39 Range units: Abbr.
40 Bailed-out co. in the news
44 ___ buco
45 "South Park" boy
46 "Movin' ___" ("The Jeffersons" theme)
47 Cheech or Chong persona
48 Gawking sorts
49 Where one might see "OMG" or "TTYL"
53 Hideous
54 Dojo blow
55 Brewery dryer
56 Deadeye's skill
57 Words said after ". . . so help you God?"
58 Keanu's "The Matrix" role
59 Wee bit
60 "Stat!"
61 Floor vote

by Tony Orbach

31

ACROSS

1 Almost half of U.S. immigrants in 1840
6 Male tabbies
10 O.K. Corral figure
14 Actress Thomas
15 Smell ___ (be suspicious)
16 Console used with the game Halo
17 Like stadiums after touchdowns
18 Places to put briefs
20 New York Times headline of 7/21/69
22 Letters that please angels
23 Clumsy boat
24 Hoagy Carmichael lyric "___ lazy river . . ."
25 1988 Dennis Quaid/Meg Ryan movie
28 Subject of a photo beneath 20-Across
32 La ___ vita
33 Old-time Norwegian skating sensation
34 Soprano ___ Te Kanawa
37 Loses traction
40 D-Day vessels
41 Desktop symbols
43 The Dapper Don
45 With 55-Across, message left by 28-Across for future explorers
49 Peeve
50 Geom. prerequisite
51 "Aladdin" hero
52 Little Red Book writer
55 See 45-Across
59 Even more certain: Lat.
61 Diacritical squiggle
62 Sight in the Arctic Ocean
63 When morning ends
64 "Silas Marner" author
65 Whirling water
66 Anglo-Saxon laborer
67 Opportunities, metaphorically

DOWN

1 Mosque leaders
2 Less common
3 Like some patches
4 Cabbage dish
5 Whom Hamlet calls "A man that Fortune's buffets and rewards / Hast ta'en with equal thanks"
6 Sass, with "to"
7 McFlurry flavor
8 Large wine bottle
9 They may come in sheets
10 ___ 67 (onetime Montreal event)
11 Forsakes
12 Reel's partner
13 Stores for G.I.'s
19 Reluctant
21 Respites
26 Handling the matter
27 Matures
29 Minneapolis suburb
30 Have the throne
31 Archaeologist's find
34 Fuzzy fruit
35 Cupcake finisher
36 1970s James Garner TV title role
38 Pleasure-associated neuro-transmitter
39 Inscribed pillar
42 Natty
44 Not pure
46 Julia's "Seinfeld" role
47 Inuit homes
48 Estevez of the Brat Pack
53 Choice words
54 "Waiting for Lefty" playwright
56 Bacchanalian revelry
57 "Dianetics" author ___ Hubbard
58 D.E.A. seizure, maybe
59 The Rail Splitter
60 G-man

by Donna S. Levin

32

ACROSS

1 Partner of punishment
6 John Irving title character
10 Leftovers from threshing
15 Dwelling section whose name comes from the Arabic for "forbidden place"
16 Kind of exam
17 Oscar winner Berry
18 Dickens novel with the 56-Across as its backdrop
21 Not an elective: Abbr.
22 Like hen's teeth
23 Features of the Sierras
24 Venue
25 Nickelodeon explorer
27 Declaration attributed to Marie Antoinette just before the 56-Across

33 Oyster eater in a Lewis Carroll verse
34 Fraternal group
35 Stale Italian bread?
37 "___ Irish Rose"
38 Catch sight of
39 Miserly Marner
40 ___ Pahlevi, last shah of Iran
41 Launder
42 Without profit
43 Song of the 56-Across
46 Butter slices
47 Indian tourist mecca
48 109, famously
52 "Yikes!"
53 To's opposite
56 Event that began in 1789
60 Play caller
61 "Milk's favorite cookie," in commercials
62 Unguent

63 Binge
64 Volunteer State: Abbr.
65 Grove constituents

DOWN

1 Scorch
2 Assign stars to, say
3 With 33-Down, topic in the 2008 presidential campaign
4 ___ B or ___ C of the Spice Girls
5 Retired
6 Get out of jail
7 Johnson of "Laugh-In"
8 Unprocessed
9 Negotiating partner of Isr.
10 Sarkozy's presidential predecessor
11 Loathe
12 Landed
13 Leave, as out of fear
14 Admit, with "up"
19 Solemn promises

20 Vehicles on the links
24 Dam site
25 Oracle site
26 Like some chardonnays
27 Arista or Motown
28 "My Fair Lady" role
29 Tinkers (with)
30 Singer Keys
31 Drug units
32 Wipe out
33 See 3-Down
36 Superlative suffix
38 Big ___ Conference
39 Hoagy Carmichael classic
41 Anger
42 Like some pond life
44 Geronimo, e.g.
45 Middle of an atoll
48 Gomer Pyle and platoonmates, by rank: Abbr.
49 Classic Vegas hotel, with "the"

by Donna S. Levin

33

ACROSS
1 500 sheets
5 Cuts down
10 Panty raid prize
13 It takes a hammering
15 Roundup rope
16 It might make a ewe turn
17 Late-arriving TV detective?
19 Puppy's bark
20 Nimble circus performer
21 Short-term govt. securities
23 Like a wallflower
24 Alpha's counterpart
27 Lesser-used PC key
28 Late-arriving actor of old?
32 Classroom jottings
35 Home for Adam and Eve
36 Campus e-mail letters?
37 Verve

38 Former U.N. head Kofi ___
40 Fish with only minute fins
41 Harrison of "My Fair Lady"
42 Work monotonously
43 Like some needs
44 Late-arriving singer/actress of old?
48 ___ of Good Feelings
49 Parcel out
50 Blackball
53 Knack
56 Region of pre-Roman Italy
58 ___ Lilly & Co.
59 Late-arriving disco singer?
62 "Act your ___!"
63 Many Conan O'Brien lines
64 Down the hatch
65 U.K. fliers
66 Word next to an arrow in a maze
67 Screen star Lamarr

DOWN
1 Indian royalty
2 Tennyson title hero ___ Arden
3 New York's ___ Fisher Hall
4 Kind of soup at a Japanese restaurant
5 Having decorative grooves
6 Obstacle for a barber
7 Source of a hippie's high
8 Exam for A.B.A.-approved schools
9 Protein-rich legume
10 "A little dab'll do ya" brand
11 Complain bitterly
12 Concert blasters
14 Feats for Hercules
18 Docile
22 AOL, for one

25 Monster defeated by Beowulf
26 Slave entombed with Radames
28 Swamp
29 100 years: Abbr.
30 Just loafing
31 The hots
32 Jock's counterpart
33 Margarine
34 Government's gift to I.R.S. filers
38 Drink from a stein
39 Star of changing brightness
40 Official lang. of Guyana
42 Manners
43 Erroneous
45 Fury
46 Atlanta Braves' div.
47 Tiny bit
50 "Et tu, ___?"
51 Got ready to shoot
52 Kids' caretaker
53 Shred
54 Sea lettuce, e.g.
55 Talk up

by Lynn Lempel

34

ACROSS

1 Senate page, e.g.
5 Island neighbor of Tonga and Tuvalu
9 Places of interest?
14 Sea dog's libation
15 North African port
16 "Take this job and shove it!"
17 *Informal greeting
19 Like undercooked eggs
20 New wing
21 Credit union's activity
23 It may be stacked or cut
26 Knock over, so to speak
27 "Eureka!"
30 *At times
36 PC video gear, for short
38 Take it on the ___
39 Lion-colored

40 Exercise in pronunciation . . . like the first words of the answers to the starred clues
44 Scout's mission, for short
45 Hide-hair link
46 One of TV's Mavericks
47 *One not using the company cafeteria, maybe
51 U.F.O. crew
52 Fall back
53 Stone for many Libras
55 Mocks
59 Were in accord
63 PC-less Internet hookup, once
64 *Bay Area concert venue
67 More than sore
68 Newton or ohm
69 Liniment target
70 Fan mags

71 Sonic the Hedgehog's company
72 Black belt's blow

DOWN

1 Ottoman Empire V.I.P.
2 Hotel room amenity
3 Elevator direction half the time
4 Prodded, with "on"
5 "Friend or ___?"
6 Org. with a code
7 One corner of a Monopoly board
8 Worker for free, often
9 Small pool site in a yard
10 Here, in Honduras
11 Former Georgia senator Sam
12 Piece moved in castling
13 Pig's home
18 Plow team
22 Affirmative action

24 Revolver inventor
25 "The Bridge on the River ___"
27 Sharp-tongued
28 More vigorous
29 BP gas brand
31 In the midst of
32 Clothing
33 Clued in
34 Boxed-off map section
35 Kremlin denials
37 Garbage hauler
41 Rattles
42 Scrapped, as a mission
43 Get ready for an exam
48 Small ammo
49 Device you can count on
50 Big Indian
54 Pale shade of violet
55 Ryan of "Boston Public"
56 Israel's Abba
57 Suffix with kitchen or room
58 TV color adjustment

by Steve Dobis

35

ACROSS

1 Place for an oath
6 It's bugled on a base
10 Elevs.
14 Electron tube with two elements
15 Loads
16 Asia's shrunken ___ Sea
17 "Sharp Dressed Man" band
18 1970 Kinks song
19 TV explorer of note
20 Slapstick puppet show
23 Didn't bother
26 Guthrie at Woodstock
27 Baseball's Young and others
28 The Monkees' "___ Believer"
29 Kind of tide
31 Impress permanently
33 "I'm ready for anything!"
37 Centers of circles
40 Room at the top of stairs
41 Mideast fed.
42 Tacitus or Tiberius
43 Not a mainstream religion
44 Go get some shuteye
46 Prefix with pad
48 Mermaid's realm
49 Mail carrier's assignment: Abbr.
50 State of shock
52 Custard ingredients
55 Drink said to prolong life
57 Yuletide tune
60 Mercury or Saturn
61 Wise to
62 da-DUM, da-DUM, da-DUM
66 Tied
67 Je ne sais ___
68 Like redheads' tempers, supposedly
69 Villain in 2009's "Star Trek"
70 Bygone barrier breakers
71 Mystery writer's award

DOWN

1 Carpenter's tool with a curved blade
2 Eight-times-married Taylor
3 Tyke
4 Take on
5 Form of government Plato wrote about
6 Baby powder ingredient
7 Lei giver's greeting
8 ___ opposites
9 Co-creator of the Fantastic Four
10 Journey to Mecca
11 He said "Here's to our wives and girlfriends . . . may they never meet!"
12 Arriving after the bell, say
13 Wows at a comedy club
21 Classic brand of hair remover
22 E, in Morse code
23 Simpson and Kudrow
24 Ham it up
25 Magazine staffer
30 It has many needles
32 Bus. honchos
34 Toy you might enjoy while running
35 Basis for a Quaker cereal
36 Citi Field team
38 They have many needles
39 Worker on a comic book
42 Actuality
44 140 and up, say
45 Cad
47 Tennis umpire's cry
50 Some Madison Ave. workers

by Caleb Madison

51 Drive drunkenly, perhaps
53 The "Homo" in "Homo sapiens"

54 "Tell me"
56 "In case you didn't hear me the first time . . ."

58 Casino game with Ping-Pong-like balls
59 Spanish liqueur

63 Computer unit, informally
64 Cup holder?
65 Leb. neighbor

36

ACROSS

1 Leave in a hurry
7 Toothed tools
11 Where a truck driver sits
14 Swingline item
15 Field yield
16 Corrida cheer
17 *Impervious to picking, as a lock
19 Telecom giant acquired by Verizon
20 Legal ending
21 Leisure
22 Air apparent?
23 "Liquid diet" devotee
25 *Engraver's surface
28 Piled carelessly
30 Superlative suffix
31 Seized vehicle
32 High-rise apartment garden site
36 *Motto of the U.S. Coast Guard
40 Playful kissing
41 Middle-earth creatures
43 Catherine, the last wife of Henry VIII
45 Nestles
47 *Routine-bound bureaucrat
51 Online communications, for short
52 Notable times
53 Start the kitty
54 Tibetan beast
56 Rocker Ocasek
57 *Countries with big militaries
61 Part of a tuba's sound
62 Vietnam's continent
63 Naturally illuminated
64 Petal plucker's pronoun
65 Remain undecided
66 Compliment heard in the dress department

DOWN

1 Q–U connection
2 Hagen of Broadway
3 Camp clothing identifier
4 Antonyms: Abbr.
5 Lamb's coat
6 Not agin
7 Bit of fabric
8 Got out of bed
9 Affection seeker
10 Tanning lotion letters
11 ,,,,,
12 "Little Women" author
13 It's darker than cream
18 Jalapeños and chilies
22 Rained pellets
23 Knight's title
24 Bills in tills
26 Hall's singing partner
27 Type size
29 Men of La Mancha
33 Sch. in Troy, N.Y.
34 Owner of a brand?
35 Debate the pros and cons
37 Sign of a contented cat
38 Improbable
39 Flower holder
42 Deflation sound
43 Persona non grata
44 Geronimo's tribe
46 Recover from a soaking
47 Those "walking" through the answers to the starred clues
48 YouTube button
49 Remove, as a corsage
50 Lieu
55 Barley beards
57 Knucklehead
58 Letter before omega
59 ___ Grande
60 "The ___ Erwin Show" of 1950s TV

by Paula Gamache

37

ACROSS
1 Breezes through
5 Andrews and Edwards, for two: Abbr.
9 Wall supports
14 Blockhead
15 Zoo barrier
16 One getting one-on-one help
17 *Movie starring a cross-dressing John Travolta
19 Having a lot to lose?
20 In base 8
21 *Big writing assignment
23 Enjoyed Bazooka, e.g.
25 Carillon sounds
26 Lowly worker
28 ". . . ___ thousand times . . ."
29 Step up from dial-up
32 Not at rest
36 Driver's license feature
38 Lab container

39 Word that can precede the starts of the answers to the eight starred clues
42 Lowell and Tan
43 The "A" in WASP
45 Is on deck
47 Most apts. have them
48 Strike caller
51 Wizard's stick
52 Places to serve slop
54 Flea market deal, perhaps
58 *Very easy tasks
62 Unable to retreat, as an animal
63 Fine fiddle
64 *Electric Slide, for one
66 Introductory TV episode
67 Author Bagnold
68 Not e'en once
69 Idyllic places

70 B'way booth in Times Square
71 Temperance supporters

DOWN
1 Like some committees
2 Alternative to first-class
3 Cream of the crop
4 *Nonbinding vote
5 Sound booster at a concert
6 Siege site
7 Called to a lamb, say
8 "Sophie's Choice" author
9 *Like a band-aid solution
10 Instruments in military bands
11 Lone Star State sch.
12 Dis and dis
13 Palm reader, e.g.
18 Winter driving hazard

22 6 on a telephone
24 The Everly Brothers' "All I Have to ___ Dream"
27 Japanese drama
29 Capitol feature
30 River of Hades
31 Not grasping the material, say
32 Lendl of tennis
33 Padre's boy
34 Rack purchases, briefly
35 Yuletide quaff
37 *Heels-over-head feat
40 Column crosser
41 Sign of sorrow
44 *Defeats mentally
46 Golf's Slammin' Sammy
49 Actress Farrow
50 Bit of shotgun shot
52 Determined to achieve

by Steve Dobis

38

ACROSS

1 Recorder input: Abbr.
4 "Beloved" author Morrison
8 Run through
14 All __ day's work
15 "What __ for Love" ("A Chorus Line" song)
16 Setting for C. S. Lewis's "The Lion, the Witch and the Wardrobe"
17 Mountain shelter
19 Travels like a flying squirrel
20 Parched
21 Time off, to a sailor
23 Optometrist's concern
25 Poet Khayyám
26 Lawman Wyatt
28 Disfigure
29 Sound from a terrier
32 Endangered feline
36 Name before Cool or Camel
37 Office setting?
38 "Holy Toledo!"
39 Spring time: Abbr.
40 Supped
41 "Arabesque" actress, 1966
46 Lad
47 Rainbow component
48 Surmounting
49 Elusive Himalayan creature
50 99 and 86, on "Get Smart"
54 Highway posting
59 Like Hotspur's horse in "King Henry IV, Part I"
60 Where Hudson Bay is
61 Where rupees are spent
63 The Carnegie of Carnegie Mellon University
64 Dorothy __ of "The Wizard of Oz"
65 Apostrophized preposition
66 Abbr. preceding multiple surnames
67 Places for play things?
68 TV staple for over 30 years (and a hint to 17-, 21-, 32-, 41-, 54- and 61-Across)

DOWN

1 "Divine" showbiz nickname
2 One way to sing
3 Egypt's capital
4 Spanish uncle
5 "Most likely . . ."
6 Near
7 Prefix with logical
8 Former heavyweight champion Johansson
9 Duck type
10 Snoop
11 Shave __ haircut
12 Schreiber of the "Scream" films
13 Leisure
18 Cartoon skunk Pepé __
22 Birthplace of Elie Wiesel
24 Suffix with different
27 Italian archaeological locale
29 Cracked open
30 Lariat
31 Bit of green in a floral display
32 Try
33 Alliance since '49
34 Do as told
35 Cry of disbelief
41 Cat or dog, especially in the spring
42 Jesse James and gang
43 Cocked
44 What an andiron holds
45 Wagner composition
49 Sentence units
51 They're verboten
52 Spoken for
53 Complicated situation
54 Hustle
55 Glazier's sheet

by Patrick Blindauer

56 Extremities
57 In-box fill: Abbr.
58 "Dies ___" (hymn)
62 "___ Liaisons Dangereuses"

39

ACROSS

1 With 67-Across, an appropriate title for this puzzle?
5 Second of two sections
10 Beaver's project
13 Competed in a regatta
15 Formal answer to "Who's at the door?"
16 Vein contents
17 Where to learn a vocation
19 Earl Grey, for one
20 Set as a price
21 Ornery sort
22 Fictional salesman Willy
24 "Remington ___" of 1980s TV
26 "Who's the Boss?" co-star
28 Basis for a moneyless economy

33 When repeated, exuberant student's cry
36 Put pen to paper
37 Vitamin bottle info, for short
38 Go across
39 Artemis' Roman counterpart
40 "Veni, ___, vici"
41 Intraoffice PC hookup
42 Stately home
43 When some morning news programs begin
44 Two dollars per pound, say
47 Radiohead singer Thom
48 Yanni's music genre
52 Got a C, say
54 Drink with sushi
56 Drink with Christmas cookies
57 Palme ___ (Cannes prize)

58 "On/off" surrounder
62 Completely impress
63 Torpedo launcher
64 Emma of "Dynasty"
65 Go off course
66 Guilty feelings, e.g.
67 See 1-Across

DOWN

1 Spanish counterparts of mlles.
2 Beat in a match
3 Open-eyed
4 ___ Xing
5 Snaps
6 Sports players: Abbr.
7 Carnaval city
8 General on a Chinese menu
9 TV's Science Guy
10 Early printer type
11 Realm
12 Intend
14 Remove the nails from, as a cat
18 Plaintiff

23 Parts of lbs.
25 Black, in verse
26 One who goes on and on
27 Nick and Nora's pooch
29 Sudden, sharp pain
30 Render blank, as a floppy disk
31 Old Norse work
32 Incapacitate
33 Tropical vacation spot
34 Title planet in a 2001 Kevin Spacey movie
35 Character who first appeared in "The Secret of the Old Clock"
39 Like dungeons, typically
40 Feature of a house in the hills
42 Annotates, as a manuscript
43 Soaks in hot water, as 19-Across

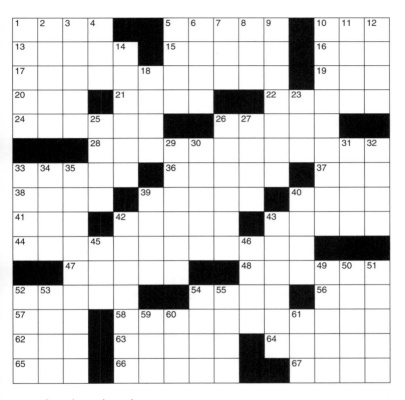

by Mike Nothnagel

45 "Yoo-___!"
46 Egyptian cross
49 "What's in ___?"
50 "Dunno"

51 Discharge
52 "It's now or never" time
53 Home of the Hawkeyes of the Big Ten

54 How some people go to a party
55 Romans preceder

59 Org. for heavyweights
60 Chloride, for one
61 On the ___ (fleeing)

40

ACROSS

1 Industry honcho
5 "Do the ___!"
9 Suffix with beer or fun
13 Move, in Realtor lingo
14 Sirius XM ___
15 In the old days
16 Lunchbox dessert item
17 Jump for joy
18 "The Good Earth" heroine
19 Tom Collins or Rob Roy
21 Turkic people
23 Grass bought in rolls
24 End of an exhaust system
26 Beehive State athlete
29 Guitar pioneer Paul
31 Paddler's target
32 Unrealistic idea
35 Hold back, as a news story
39 Salon sound
40 In a foxy fashion

42 "Uh-uh"
43 Regatta entry
45 1992 U.S. Olympic hoopsters, with "the"
47 Peseta's replacement
49 La-la lead-in
50 ___-mo
51 Basketball or baseball
55 Ike's monogram
57 Tangle in a net: Var.
58 Fighting rooster
63 Hair removal brand
64 Take forcibly, old-style
66 Tom Wolfe novel "___ in Full"
67 Bigger than mega-
68 Elizabeth of cosmetics
69 After-beach wear
70 Supersecure airline
71 Name on toy fuel trucks
72 Two caplets, say

DOWN

1 Swamp menace, for short
2 Total loser
3 Guinness or Waugh
4 Corner pieces, in chess
5 Ankle-length dress
6 X-rated
7 Up to, in ads
8 Real babe
9 Evidence washed away by the tide
10 China's Zhou ___
11 Bluff formed by a fault
12 In need of a rubdown
14 Blogger's audience
20 Ratted (on)
22 "Sad to say . . ."
25 Decorative band
26 "___-daisy!"
27 Fey of "30 Rock"
28 Huge in scope
30 Only now and then

33 Short-lived
34 Firth of Clyde town
36 The "ten" in "hang ten"
37 Stone for many Libras
38 Nautilus skipper
41 Landscaper's crew
44 Harbor workhorses
46 Showed up in time for
48 Gung-ho
51 Trace of color
52 Messages that may contain emoticons
53 Old computer
54 "Zounds!"
56 Paperless birthday greeting
59 Birds, collectively
60 1847 Melville work
61 Some urban rides
62 "Trick" body part
65 Before, to a bard

by Damon J. Gulczynski

41

ACROSS
- **1** Get some sun
- **4** Blow one's stack
- **9** Kid-lit pachyderm
- **14** Naked ___ jaybird
- **15** Sine, cosine or tangent
- **16** Tourist mecca off the coast of Venezuela
- **17** "Beat swords into plowshares"
- **20** Way off
- **21** Parasol's offering
- **22** Cathedral area
- **23** Grazed, say
- **25** Silver of the silver screen
- **27** "Ignore the red, white and blue"
- **35** Marx Brothers-like
- **36** Meat favored by Sarah Palin
- **37** With 44-Across, a traditional Catholic prayer

- **39** Ring decisions, for short
- **40** Chuck who sang "Maybellene"
- **41** Petty quarrel
- **42** Moray, for one
- **43** "Peachy keen!"
- **44** See 37-Across
- **45** "Oust from practice, then interrogate"
- **48** Take steps
- **49** The "A" in MoMA
- **50** Shi'ite leader
- **53** Typical John Wayne film
- **57** Stir up
- **61** "Scatter while fleeing"
- **64** Neptune's realm
- **65** Word before city or tube
- **66** Etiquette guru Vanderbilt
- **67** Smallest possible
- **68** Has to have
- **69** Masseur's place

DOWN
- **1** Bit of verbal trumpeting
- **2** "A likely story"
- **3** Shuttle org.
- **4** Pull a boner
- **5** Any of several Egyptian kings
- **6** Six-sided state
- **7** ___ colada
- **8** Rocker Rundgren
- **9** Ovine sound
- **10** Giorgio of fashion
- **11** Fist ___ (modern greeting)
- **12** Lincoln and others
- **13** Like proverbial hen's teeth
- **18** A Musketeer
- **19** Rejection of church dogma
- **24** Behavioral quirk
- **26** Rich rock
- **27** Palm fruit
- **28** Put one's John Hancock on

- **29** Vodka brand, informally
- **30** Makeup mishap
- **31** Main artery
- **32** Mental midget
- **33** Blue Grotto's isle
- **34** To no ___
- **38** List-ending abbr.
- **40** Bang, as a drum
- **41** "No Exit" dramatist
- **43** "30 Rock" network
- **44** Dugout V.I.P.: Abbr.
- **46** Rio dances
- **47** Moved like a hummingbird
- **50** Miley Cyrus, to teens
- **51** Owls' prey
- **52** Where pirates go
- **54** Score after deuce
- **55** Mute, with "down"
- **56** Feminine suffix
- **58** Portfolio holdings, briefly
- **59** Sugar unit

by Wayne and P. K. King

60 One-named
New Age
singer
62 Tiny
colonist
63 Four-baggers:
Abbr.

42

ACROSS

1 Cheney's successor as vice president
6 Prize in the ad biz
10 ___ irregular basis
14 Hersey's "A Bell for ___"
15 Prefix with nautical
16 Count (on)
17 Decide against reorganizing the pet store?
20 Mediterranean tree
21 Geog. or geol.
22 Stagehands' items
23 Picked out of a lineup
25 Ankle-related
28 Announcement from a cockpit, for short
30 Doughnut-shaped
32 Very chocolaty, say
33 Finish shooting a movie
34 Bathroom fixture
36 Break in the day
37 Cousin of beige
38 Conversation-filled places in a restaurant?
42 Oscar winner Winslet
43 ___ Aviv, Israel
44 Evil computer in "2001"
45 Mother of Horus
46 Sign of the future
48 Come up again and again
52 Computer connection choice
53 Massless particle
55 A MS. might come back in it
56 Make a connection with
58 "Au Revoir, ___ Enfants"
60 Pre-___ (undergrad study)
61 What chicks have?
65 "Deutschland ___ Alles"
66 "Windows to the soul"
67 Amazingly coincidental
68 Zero
69 Certain conifers
70 "The Devil Wears ___"

DOWN

1 Mismatch
2 Musical whose opening song is "All the Dearly Beloved"
3 What a flashing red light may indicate
4 Suffix with differ
5 Jules et Jim, par exemple
6 Expensive eggs
7 Washington and ___ University
8 Certain savings plan, for short
9 Sound from a 38-Down
10 Very small pasta
11 Pacific Northwest tribe
12 Baseball V.I.P.'s
13 Comedian Louis
18 When Canada celebrates Thanksgiving: Abbr.
19 Web address
24 Airheads
26 Hair curl
27 Nonsense singing
29 Clerk on "The Simpsons"
31 Since, slangily
33 "Citizen Kane" director
35 Nestlé candy
38 Low-pitched instrument
39 Availed oneself of
40 Whom Marlin sought in a 2003 film
41 Tavern
42 Young goat
47 Amazingly enough

by Trip Payne

49 Cell phone feature, often
50 Computer handle
51 Sudan/Saudi Arabia separator

53 Sch. group
54 Largest U.S. labor union: Abbr.

57 Old Testament book
59 Dance lesson
61 Enjoyment
62 Hide the gray, say

63 Many's opposite
64 "How Stella Got ___ Groove Back"

43

ACROSS

1 They put the frosting on the cake
6 Grant's is in New York
10 ___ as a post
14 Pacific archipelago nation
15 "Young Frankenstein" role
16 Golden State sch.
17 Fix the hair just so, say
18 Bind with a band
19 Actress Singer of "Footloose"
20 ___ as an arrow
22 Jug capacity
24 ___ as a pin
25 ___ as a fox
26 ___ as an ox
29 Outlaw Barrow
30 "Bingo!"
31 Newton's Black Panther Party co-founder
33 Barbecue remnants
37 ___ as an owl
39 Command to a dog
41 ___ as a dog
42 Some chips, maybe
44 Less loony
46 4 on a telephone
47 Bottom dog
49 Some chips
51 Theme of this puzzle
54 Eric who played 2003's Hulk
55 Like, with "with"
56 ___ as an eel
60 Chowderheads
61 Sparkling wine locale
63 Indoor trees may grow in them
64 Words after "woe"
65 One end of a hammer
66 ___ as a judge
67 ___ as a doornail
68 ___ as a diamond
69 The way things are going

DOWN

1 AOL and others
2 Auto denter in a supermarket parking lot
3 Leader in a robe
4 Italian cheese
5 Latin for 37-Across
6 ___ as a drum
7 Doing the job
8 Apartment bldg. V.I.P.
9 The Joker in Batman movies, e.g.
10 Tedium
11 Gastroenteritis cause, maybe
12 Baseball All-Star every year from 1955 to 1975
13 Impulsive indulgence
21 Light green plums
23 Lawrence Welk's "one"/"two" connector
25 ___ as a whistle
26 Fellers in the woods?
27 ___ as a rail
28 Literally, "scraped"
29 ___ as a bell
32 Cathedral recesses
34 ___ as a kite
35 Repetitive reply
36 Nordic runners
38 Overshadowed
40 Alaskan peninsula where Seward is located
43 Nut for caffeine?
45 Told to in order to get an opinion
48 Angelic figure
50 Prisoner's opposite
51 ___ as a rock
52 Busy
53 Volcanic buildup
54 ___ as a bat

by Matt Ginsberg

44

ACROSS

1 Soft or crunchy snack
5 Like a 52-Across
10 Start of an incantation
14 The "A" in Chester A. Arthur
15 Rudely assertive
16 When repeated, Road Runner's call
17 1908 Cubs player and position
20 How fame comes, sometimes
21 Friars Club event
22 The Braves, on a scoreboard
23 "Pants on fire" person
25 1908 Cubs player and position
33 Chutzpah
34 Put an edge on
35 Hydrotherapy locale
36 "How sweet ___!"
37 Barbers' touch-ups
39 Polish's partner
40 U. of Miami's athletic org.
41 Baseball analyst Hershiser
42 Command to an attack dog
43 1908 Cubs player and position
47 Salt Lake City athletes
48 Ike's W.W. II command
49 "Yes we can" sloganeer
52 2006 Ken Jennings book . . . or the author himself
57 What 17-, 25- and 43-Across were, famously
60 Virginia ___ (noted 1587 birth)
61 The Dapper Don
62 Fountain order
63 Polaris or Sirius
64 Jimmy of the Daily Planet
65 They're splitsville

DOWN

1 "Toodles"
2 Touched down
3 Water-to-wine site
4 Peeling potatoes, stereotypically
5 Mast extensions
6 Bodyguard's asset
7 Only African-American male to win Wimbledon
8 P, on a fraternity house
9 Norse war god
10 Work like paper towels
11 Software test version
12 Vintage autos
13 Date with an M.D.
18 Clear, as a tape
19 The "t" in Nafta
23 Machine with a shuttle
24 Rustic lodgings
25 1946 high-tech wonder
26 Climbing plant with pealike flowers
27 Novelist Jong
28 Homes on wheels, in brief
29 Hot dog topper
30 Humane org. since 1866
31 Black-clad and white-clad Mad adversaries
32 Wonderland cake phrase
37 Logic diagram
38 Flag tossers, for short
39 Bro or sis
41 Of base 8
42 Showing no emotion
44 "Sorry, Wrong ___"

by Ronald J. and Nancy J. Byron

45 Add a star to, say
46 Not leave the house
49 They may be stacked against you
50 Dinghy, e.g.
51 Surrounding glow
52 Nonkosher diner offerings
53 Iditarod terminus
54 Huge-screen format
55 Up to it
56 Hotel room roll-ins
58 Part of Freud's "psychic apparatus"
59 Vote seeker, for short

45

ACROSS

1 Go 50 in a 30-m.p.h. zone, e.g.
6 Joyful tune
10 Enthusiasm
14 Similar
15 "Are you ___ out?"
16 Utah ski resort
17 1985 Glenn Close/Jeff Bridges thriller
19 Saint Barthélemy et d'autres
20 German's "Dear me!"
21 Mail service made obsolete by the transcontinental telegraph
23 Fish stew containers
25 Slowly, in music
26 Most Little Leaguers
27 Hay unit
30 Hardly a little angel
32 Simple swimming stroke
37 In a Kinks hit s/he "walked like a woman and talked like a man"
38 Waiters' handouts
39 Mob scene
40 Widening in a highway, maybe
42 Lenin's "What ___ Be Done?"
43 River of Spain
44 Eisenhower and Turner
46 "When You Wish Upon ___"
50 Groveled
53 1970s Robert Young TV role
57 "Gloria in excelsis ___"
58 Farm team
59 What the long Across answers with circles have
61 Go here and there
62 Actress Hathaway
63 "Evil ___" (comics series)
64 Oklahoma city
65 Bat, ball, glove, etc.
66 Number of hills in Roma

DOWN

1 Pat of "Wheel of Fortune"
2 Come in second
3 It's last to be sunk
4 Heart test readout: Abbr.
5 Very much
6 Property claims
7 Four-time Harrison Ford film role
8 Second-level seating
9 Fearsome display at a natural history museum
10 Congo's name before 1997
11 TV's DeGeneres
12 Mushroom producer, for short
13 Rodeo rope
18 Bucks' partners
22 Appeal
24 General Mills brand
27 "Bedtime for ___" (Reagan film)
28 Contents of the Spanish Main
29 8-track alternatives
30 Deli sandwich, for short
31 Kanga's baby
32 Honeybunch
33 Like raisins vis-à-vis grapes
34 Andrei Sakharov in the Soviet era, e.g.
35 Film studio locale
36 W.W. II command
38 World Series org.
41 Where Simón Bolívar was once president
44 The Beatles' "Let ___"
45 Economist John Maynard ___
46 Love, Italian-style
47 The "S" in WASP

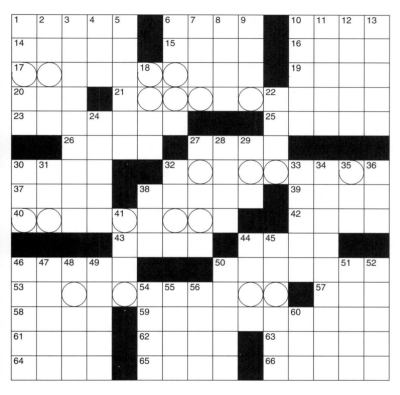

by Barry Boone

ACROSS

1 Pat down
6 Lead character on "Saved by the Bell"
10 On a cruise
14 Neopagan belief
15 Second word of many fairy tales
16 Extremist sect
17 Red Sox Hall-of-Famer Bobby
18 ___ Strauss jeans
19 Spelunker's hangout
20 Valuable discoveries
23 Prevailed
24 Most enlightened
25 Cry while holding a bag
31 Exploding stars
32 Loud chuckles
33 Married mlle.
36 Sch. on the bank of the Rio Grande
37 East ___ (nation since 2002)
38 Billy who sang "We Didn't Start the Fire"
39 Lean-___
40 Ebbed
41 The time it takes mountains to rise
42 Proven to work
44 Cirque du ___
47 Diplomat's bldg.
48 Semi
54 Impulsive
55 Home of Città del Vaticano
56 Less common
58 Letter-routing abbr.
59 Actor McGregor
60 Brilliant display
61 South-of-the-border currency
62 "Well, gosh darn!"
63 Timetables, informally

DOWN

1 Subject line starter on many an e-mail joke
2 Hilarious act
3 Cake decorator
4 Twist-off bottle top
5 Word derived from Japanese for "empty orchestra"
6 Last letter of a pilot's alphabet
7 Imitator
8 Sheltered inlet
9 Sweaters and such
10 Approach aggressively
11 Debonair
12 Dwellers in Middle-earth
13 "This is only ___"
21 ___-cone
22 Narrow inlets
25 Letter-shaped fastener
26 ___-Rooter
27 Currier and ___
28 Riesling wines are produced in its valley
29 Having dams at various locations, as a river
30 Spinoff of "The Mary Tyler Moore Show"
33 What boats may do in an inlet
34 File, Edit or Help
35 "That's something ___"
37 Made to order, as a suit
38 Not just dark
40 Habeas corpus, for one
41 Looks up to
42 Electronic dance genre
43 Teacher's union: Abbr.
44 Amusement park ride feature
45 Hold forth
46 Endures
49 Prime seating spot

by Joon Pahk

ACROSS

1 Internet address starter
5 Shoe part
9 Shoe mark
14 Where Donegal Bay is
15 Declare frankly
16 "The Yankee Years" co-writer
17 Word after "ppd." on a sports page
18 Like a 1943 copper penny
19 Desilu co-founder
20 Bitter-tasting vegetable
23 Steps nonchalantly
24 Common commemorative items
28 Mobile's state: Abbr.
29 Garfield's foil
31 The Eiger, for one
32 "Young Indian brave" in a 1960 Johnny Preston #1 hit
36 Even up
37 Arguing loudly
38 Abbr. in a help wanted ad
39 Essen's region
40 "Kid-tested, mother-approved" cereal
41 Least acceptable amount
45 Prefix with tourism
46 Resistance units
47 Unit of RAM, for short
48 Actress Bullock
50 Morphine and codeine, for two
54 Country singer with a hit sitcom
57 Dwelt
60 ___ & Chandon Champagne
61 Village Voice award
62 Baja buddy
63 Munich Mrs.
64 Make out
65 More than a twitch
66 Macy's department
67 S.&L. offerings

DOWN

1 Rosemary and thyme
2 Princess' topper
3 The Dixie Chicks and the Dixie Cups
4 Strong liking
5 "The Human Comedy" novelist William
6 Cameo shapes
7 Actress Loughlin of "90210"
8 Vessel by a basin
9 Less likely to collapse
10 Jazzman Chick
11 Subject of a Keats ode
12 Monk's title
13 Shriner's topper
21 Colombian city
22 Samoan port
25 10-year-old Oscar winner O'Neal
26 Peace Nobelist Root
27 ___ whale
29 Slender woodwinds
30 Consider
32 Landscapers' tools
33 City in New York's Mohawk Valley
34 "Frost/___," 2008 nominee for Best Picture
35 Listerine target
39 Tubular pasta
41 Yawn inducer
42 Melville's obsessed whaler
43 Driving force
44 Deutschland denial
49 Bottom-of-the-barrel stuff
50 Great blue expanse
51 River of Rome

by Allan E. Parrish

52 Author Jong
53 Is in the market for
55 Like most car radios
56 Oliver Twist's request
57 ___ Cruces, N.M.
58 Handful for a baby sitter
59 Itinerary word

48

ACROSS

1 Wrote an ode to
7 China's Chou En-___
10 Captain Hook's henchman
14 Cause of weird weather
15 Press worker's stain
16 Brighton bye-bye
17 Augments
18 Wine servers
20 Adolescent boy's growth
22 Recurring Woody Allen theme
23 Have a go at
24 What oil helps dissolve
25 "I Pity the Fool" star
26 Brother of Little Joe on '60s TV
27 "Jingle Bells" starter
31 Little green man
34 Soldier's period of service
36 Isaac's eldest

37 Cocoon occupants
38 Little green men, for short
39 Target competitor
40 Where a tab is inserted
41 Joan of the Blackhearts
42 "Biography" network, once
43 King Cole was a merry one
45 "Death in Venice" author Thomas
47 Demolition aid
48 "The Witches" director Nicolas
49 Some Super Bowl Sunday highlights
52 Africa's largest city
55 Bargains for leniency
57 Dukakis in 1988 and Dole in 1996
59 (0,0) on a graph
60 Reach a high
61 Grampa Simpson

62 They can be found in 20- and 55-Across and 10- and 26-Down
63 Lap dog, informally
64 Window units, briefly
65 Electrician's alloy

DOWN

1 Did an axel, e.g.
2 Tree with catkins
3 It's observed on Oct. 24
4 Wink in tiddlywinks, e.g.
5 Make king or queen
6 Goofball
7 "Hungarian Rhapsodies" composer
8 Animated bug film of 1998
9 Clanton at the O.K. Corral
10 Musial's nickname
11 Helgenberger of "CSI"

12 LAX postings
13 American League division
19 Some are declared
21 J. P. Morgan co.
25 Scratch
26 Dehydration may help bring this on
27 Housecleaning aid
28 "This ___ outrage!"
29 Source of a fragrant oil
30 "___ Nacht" (German words of parting)
31 Lhasa ___
32 Temporary calm
33 Popular MP3 player
35 Mel in Cooperstown
39 Emblem on the Australian coat of arms
41 Protrude
44 ___ about (circa)
46 "___ Fables"

by Pancho Harrison

49

ACROSS

1 Comprehend
6 Contemptible
10 Shade of many a swimming pool basin
14 Surgeon's tool
15 Web addresses
16 Parts of a tea set
17 Sprightly
18 Politician's goal
19 Give the heave-ho
20 1940s hit radio show featuring the bartender Archie
23 Salad additive
24 Marveled audibly (at)
28 1939 James Joyce novel
33 Second-smallest state: Abbr.
34 Instrument held with two hands
35 Pakistani leader, 1977–88
36 1960s sitcom about a group of castaways
41 G.I. entertainers
42 X ___ xylophone
43 Work unit
44 1946 Bing Crosby hit
49 Blog messages
50 Sculler's item
51 1960s sitcom set in a P.O.W. camp
59 On the briny
62 "Am ___ late?"
63 ___ cotta
64 Wimbledon surface
65 Head for
66 Jew traditionally dressed in a black coat and hat
67 Canned
68 Period of time
69 Solo

DOWN

1 Delighted
2 Prego competitor
3 "Yeah, right!"
4 "To thine own ___ be true"
5 Victimize
6 Ado
7 Geographical datum
8 Czech, e.g., but not a Hungarian
9 Ferrara ruling family
10 Ad exhortation
11 Status ___
12 Good times
13 Numbskull
21 Transgress
22 Kentucky Derby prize
25 Sand trap, e.g.
26 Barely making, with "out"
27 Defunct
28 Prison population
29 Needing a doctor's attention
30 "___ Fly Now" ("Rocky" theme)
31 Tummy muscles
32 "___ won't!"
33 Establishment with a revolving mirrored ball
36 Forrest ___, 1994 Oscar-winning role
37 Schoolyard retort
38 Fed. property overseer
39 Publicize
40 Novelist Deighton
45 Available
46 "Already?"
47 "Rubbish!"
48 First name in soul
52 Play dates?
53 Surmounting
54 ___ bene
55 Down-to-earth
56 Roughly
57 Land that's saluted in this puzzle
58 Marquis de ___
59 Menu phrase
60 Instrument famously played by Bill Clinton on "The Arsenio Hall Show"
61 One catching a ram's eye

by Richard Chisholm

50

ACROSS

1 Org. for boomers, now
5 Smooth-talking
9 Cause of something going up?
14 Iranian money
15 The last Mrs. Charlie Chaplin
16 London line
17 Food-stamping org.
18 Do a cashier's job
19 Tech callers
20 Attack helicopter
22 "___ Lay Dying"
23 Raptor's roost
24 Sister of Rachel
26 Snack machine inserts
29 Abode, informally
31 Do a cashier's job
33 Day-___ colors
34 "Just a ___" (1931 hit)

37 Director Kazan
38 Pick on, in a way
39 WWW bookmark
40 Often-joked-about professionals
42 Summer on the Seine
43 Ellington's "Prelude ___ Kiss"
44 Will-___-wisp
45 Walk unsteadily
47 U.S.N.A. grad
48 Portuguese king
49 Zeus, to the Romans
50 The Big Board, for short
52 Cornell or Pound
54 Make rhapsodic
58 Where to read about the 50-Across: Abbr.
60 In the altogether
62 Gaucho's rope

64 Baseball's Moises
65 "Holy cow!"
66 "Over the Rainbow" composer Harold
67 Lincoln's state: Abbr.
68 Sons of ___ (group promoting Irish heritage)
69 Far from faithful
70 Determination
71 Root beer brand

DOWN

1 Tourist mecca off Venezuela
2 Seating option
3 Weather forecaster's tool
4 Tenor Domingo
5 "Holy cow!"
6 Many subway trains
7 Blown away
8 Sure to bring in money
9 Pastel hue
10 Costner's "Tin Cup" co-star

11 Really steamed
12 Wilder's "___ Town"
13 Classic game console letters
21 Radio host Garrison
25 Buzz, bob or bangs
27 Select few
28 Unloaded?
30 Colonel Sanders facial feature
32 Appliance with a pilot
34 Word before "Morgen" or "Tag"
35 O. Henry literary device
36 See-through partition
37 Word that can follow each half of 20- and 60-Across and 11- and 36-Down
41 Super-duper
46 Stuck in traffic, say
49 Derek of "I, Claudius"

by Thomas Takaro

51 ___ Park, Colo.
53 Kaiser or czar
55 Director Kurosawa
56 Not so hot
57 Idyllic spots
59 Girl with the dog Spot
61 Quarterback Warner
62 Luftwaffe foe: Abbr.
63 Portfolio part, for short

ACROSS

1 Hurts
7 3, 4 or 5, typically, in golf
10 Best-selling computer game from the early 2000s, with "The"
14 When Hamlet says "To be or not to be"
15 Payment promise
16 "I'm ___!" ("Will do!")
17 "___, please" (diner's request)
19 Endangered state bird
20 PC capacity, for short
21 "Full" sign
22 Shot using one's noggin
24 Beethoven dedicatee
27 "___, please" (announcer's request)
29 What to do at a crossroads
31 Postpone yet again
32 Vehement speech
35 Roman household god
36 "___, please" (awards show presenter's request)
40 G.I.'s mail drop
42 "Twelfth Night" duke
43 Malodorous critter
47 Mexican revolutionary played by Brando
51 "___, please" (operator's request)
54 18 oz., maybe, on a cereal box
55 Hardware store boxful
56 Springsteen's birthplace of song
58 Gerber eater
59 Old salt's direction
60 "___, please!" (Henny Youngman's request)
64 Past the golf pin, say
65 Direction from L.A. to K.C.
66 Band with the 1975 #1 hit "One of These Nights"
67 Ferrara family name
68 Blazed a trail
69 Dada, to many

DOWN

1 With 45-Down, something not to criticize
2 Ernest Borgnine title role
3 ___ FireBall (hot candy)
4 Job for a tailor
5 Rejoinder to "'tain't!"
6 Collects splinters, so to speak
7 Embroidery loop
8 Just fine
9 Fraternity hopeful
10 Beethoven keyboard work
11 Like poisonous mushrooms
12 Seat of Nassau County, N.Y.
13 Less lenient
18 401(k) alternative
23 Fangorn in "The Lord of the Rings," e.g.
25 Jedi enemy
26 Falco who played Carmela on "The Sopranos"
28 Familial diagrams
30 Bard's before
33 "I can't sing ___"
34 TiVo, for one
36 Broad-minded
37 Taylor who said "I do" eight times
38 ___ equal footing
39 Wearer of a triple tiara
40 Last Supper guest
41 Some rainwear
44 Come into prominence
45 See 1-Down
46 Dutch brew
48 The Scourge of God
49 Get-one-free deal

by Gary Cee

50 Swear (to)
52 Microwaved, slangily
53 "The Waste Land" monogram
57 Grace ender
61 "I'd like to buy ___, Pat"
62 Hoopster ___ Ming
63 Chicago Cubs' station

52

ACROSS

1 ___ unto itself
5 Brown fur
10 Is shy, in a way
14 Game Gear company
15 Philanderer, in slang
17 Our genus
18 Madre's hermanos
19 To this point, in verse
20 Intravenous hookup
21 Hamid Karzai, starting in 2004
24 Uppity type
25 Org. concerned with firing practices?
26 One of four generations in a photo
34 Iranian cash
35 Occasion for a proctor
36 Overly
37 "Must've been something ___"
38 Like "King Lear"
41 Keep an appointment
42 When juillet and août occur
43 Get rid of
44 Vacant, in a way
45 Driver's electric convenience
50 Old Ford model
51 Like 26-Down
52 Frances Hodgson Burnett kid-lit novel . . . and a hint to 21-, 26- and 45-Across
59 Piltdown man, notably
60 Longtime label for 38-Down
61 Like a hottie
62 Rocker Quatro
63 Father ___, leper priest of Molokai
64 "Ain't it the truth!"
65 Siesta time, maybe
66 Has-___ (ones who are washed up)
67 Like some sums

DOWN

1 Wirehair of film
2 Son of Eric the Red
3 All worked up
4 Stock transaction made to claim a tax deduction
5 Court worker, for short
6 Sluggishness
7 Mobster's code
8 Dots over eyes?
9 New Mexico skiing locale
10 "Mercy!"
11 Dog-eared
12 Discharge
13 Conciliatory bribe
16 Promo container that's a twofer
22 See 39-Down
23 Apothecary weight
26 "Peer Gynt" composer
27 Gaucho's gear
28 What "-vore" means
29 Like some ions: Abbr.
30 Early sixth-century date
31 Patriot Allen
32 Nary a soul
33 Air controller's place
38 Jerry Garcia's band, for short
39 With 22-Down, stinging insects
40 Hubbub
41 Shows disdain for
43 Snorkel and colleagues: Abbr.
44 Res ___ loquitur
46 "Dynasty" vixen
47 Infant's bodysuit

by Peter A. Collins

53

ACROSS
1. Cause for an eyelift
4. Playground shout
9. With 59-Across, novel of 1851
13. Benzoyl peroxide target
14. Bitter
15. Shield border
16. Complain
17. Frigid temps
18. Head of the Egyptian god Thoth
19. Take the lead
21. Sig Ep and others
22. Fish tail?
23. At sea
24. Stable display
25. Stylize anew, as a car seat
27. Rushed (by)
29. Warhol associate ___ Sedgwick
30. Israel's Barak and Olmert
31. Character in 9- & 59-Across
36. Chills, so to speak

37. Sorvino of "Mighty Aphrodite"
40. Cordial offering?
44. "___ is gained as much by good works as by evil": Machiavelli
46. St. Stephen, notably
47. Pronoun in the starts of many letters
49. Netflix offering
50. Simon Says players, say
51. Displays
53. Designate "commercial" or "single-family," e.g.
54. Incline (and a hint to the location in this completed puzzle of the first line of 9- & 59-Across)
55. Recipe direction
56. Hollywood's Kazan
57. Lumberjack competition

58. Change of address, for short
59. See 9-Across
60. Does what a good dog does
61. Halftime features

DOWN
1. Searched high and low
2. ___ Geometry (college course)
3. Four-star leader: Abbr.
4. Grasp
5. They're served with spoon-straws
6. 9- & 59-Across
7. Rear
8. QBs' coups
9. Shimmery fabrics
10. Jerry of "Law & Order"
11. Carefree
12. Assented
13. Eponymous French physicist
20. 1960 Olympics boxing gold medalist

21. High-school class, informally
24. Musical conclusion
26. "Fool (If You Think It's Over)" singer Chris
28. Onetime Asiatic nomads
30. New York's ___ River
32. Hunts, with "on"
33. Numerical prefix with oxide
34. Qty.
35. What a swallow may swallow
38. Displays
39. Supplements
40. Blown away
41. "In ___, where love is king" (start of "That's Amore")
42. Peaceful
43. Word with hot or blue
44. Reading for home mechanics

by Peter A. Collins and Joe Krozel

45 Rambler maker, once: Abbr.

48 Baklava ingredient

51 One whose shirttail is always untucked, maybe

52 Start of an incantation

54 Sign of success

ACROSS

1 Did a dog trick
6 ___-Ball (game on an incline)
10 "Mamma Mia" quartet
14 Renault 5, in North America
15 Rain cats and dogs
16 Film critic Pauline
17 First few bars
18 Mrs. Dithers in the comics
19 "This ___ joke!"
20 America's so-called Third Coast
22 Clementine's shoe size
23 Playboy or Playgirl-caliber model
24 Item with a magnetic strip, nowadays
26 Tyler of "The Incredible Hulk"
27 What Hail Mary passes rarely result in, briefly

28 One who must be above suspicion, in a saying
32 Ex-governor Palin
33 Hero maker's aid
34 Crèche trio
37 Whole bunch
39 Prefix with normal
40 Hunky sort
43 One who tries
46 Many an autobiographer's need
48 Early Beatle Sutcliffe
51 Original Luddite ___ Ludd
52 Oklahoma's ___ Tree National golf course
53 Like Bill O'Reilly's "zone" on Fox News
55 Clearance rack words
57 Character known for exclaiming the first words of 20-, 28- and 46-Across

60 Like certain sums
61 Ballet bend
62 Perfect Sleeper maker
63 Smooth
64 "___ Enchanted" (Anne Hathaway movie)
65 Range extending to the Arctic Ocean
66 Huge quantities
67 Gray no more, say
68 Longtime CBS boss William

DOWN

1 Cold-shoulder
2 Booth Tarkington title tween
3 Largish combos
4 Unit of purity
5 Racy reading
6 Pet welfare org.
7 Wack job
8 "That's it!"
9 Blackboard accessories

10 Closely related
11 St. Peter's, e.g.
12 Affleck/Lopez as a tabloid twosome
13 Important plant in alternative medicine
21 Father of Goneril
25 Fashion inits.
29 Mother's cry at a dinner table
30 Japanese sliding screen
31 Disposable cleaning aid
32 Lust and envy, for two
34 Ones in high places
35 Post-it component
36 Brainstorming result, perhaps
38 Wack job
41 "Who am ___ say?"
42 Out of order, in a way

by Donna S. Levin

44 Refuse to grant
45 Matures
47 Singer with the 1994 #1 hit "Bump N' Grind"
48 Form of a well-thrown pigskin
49 Y. A. known for well-thrown pigskins
50 On edge
54 Mattel's Princess of Power
56 Roget offerings: Abbr.
58 Anger
59 Interpret

55

ACROSS

1 Clinks
6 Way out
10 Baseball star in Senate steroid hearings
14 Sheltered water
15 Repetitive routine
16 It may be pumped
17 Argue forcibly
20 South American cruise stop
21 Finish lacing up
22 ___ fly (run producer)
25 Catch red-handed
27 Royal Navy drink of old
28 Pesticide spreader, e.g.
32 Brian of ambient music
35 Prefix with sphere
36 Arthurian times, say
37 Name in 2001 bankruptcy news
39 Knoxville sch.
41 Grizzlies' org.
42 "Call it!" call
43 Lehmann of opera
44 Damage, so to speak
46 Con man?
47 Chaotic place
48 Terse
51 "Don't ___ me, bro!"
53 Dark half of a Chinese circle
54 G.P.S. heading
55 Like a Möbius strip
59 Class with the periodic table on the wall, often: Abbr.
61 Where Olaf I or Olaf II sat
66 "___ la Douce" (1963 film)
67 Fish-eating raptor
68 Moves gingerly
69 Cold war propaganda disseminator
70 Rink fake
71 Like Yogi Berra, physically

DOWN

1 Huck's raftmate
2 Bibliophile's suffix
3 Sort
4 Lounge lizard's look
5 Discolorations
6 Works in a gallery
7 Snow structure
8 Yours, in Tours
9 Bridge no-no
10 2007 Michael Moore documentary
11 Juicer remnants
12 Eh
13 Work without ___ (be daring)
18 Needing a rinse
19 "La Bohème" setting
22 Charles who created Peppermint Patty
23 "Am not!" response
24 Shake hands
26 It's most useful when it's broken
29 Blood drive donation
30 Shady retreat
31 Like bread dough or beer
33 Actor Nick and family
34 Like some football kicks
38 Tandoor-baked bread
40 Storied monster, informally
45 Dance for Chubby Checker
49 Counter-balanced, as bets
50 What some races are won by
52 ___ the custom (traditionally)
55 "Get ___!" ("Stop procrastinating!")

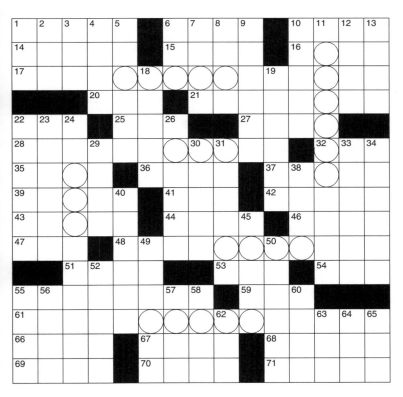

by Tim Wescott

56 "The Thin Man" detective
57 Mayo's land
58 Dungeonlike
60 Modern home of ancient Ur
62 Alumna bio word
63 Columbus sch.
64 Teachers' org.
65 1970s self-improvement program

56

ACROSS

1 It's found in chambers
5 Moves quickly
10 It was dropped in the '60s
14 Just watch TV, say
15 Historic San Francisco theater, with "the"
16 Dame ___ Everage (Barry Humphries character)
17 Olympic boxing gold medalist of 1964
19 It may be down at the heel
20 For the nonce
21 Was in a no-win situation?
23 Under the table
24 King in "Jesus Christ Superstar"
25 Hero of Super Bowl III

27 Run out of gas, say
29 Tooth trouble
30 47th U.S. vice president
35 Cheri of "Scary Movie"
38 Abrasive soap brand
39 While away, as time
42 Trampled (on)
43 Wipe
45 Oscar winner of 1990
47 Pockets of dough?
50 Light hair color
51 Singer on day three of 1969's Woodstock
54 Handy
59 Scand. land
60 "No, mein Herr"
61 Egyptian god with the head of a jackal
62 "'Tis a pity"
64 School cafeteria fare . . . and a hint to this puzzle's theme

66 Commend, as for outstanding service
67 More sick, in dialect
68 Bibliophile's suffix
69 Archie or Veronica
70 Winter Palace figures
71 Canine order

DOWN

1 Jewish leader?
2 Roger who played the same role seven times
3 Paramount
4 "___ the races!"
5 Disney World transport
6 Cartoonist Chast
7 Nitrous ___
8 Steering system component
9 Composed
10 1950s political inits.
11 Sound system staples

12 Indigenous Canadian
13 Title before Sidious or Maul
18 ___-wip
22 Steve Martin's birthplace
25 Cherokee, for one
26 Certain finish
28 Bouncers check them, briefly
30 Cheer for a matador
31 Candy holder
32 Disappear
33 Meat-and-potatoes
34 Three-time Keanu Reeves character
36 "Arabian Nights" bird
37 Uganda's ___ Amin
40 By
41 Wedding reception hirees
44 Neighbor of Slough
46 Like the 28-Down of underage drinkers

by Patrick Blindauer

48 Gets 100 on a test
49 Learned things
51 Pass
52 Half of Brangelina

53 ___ Gay (W.W. II bomber)
55 Some apples
56 W.W. II menace

57 ___ College, north of Albany, N.Y.
58 Lamb piece
61 Loan figs.

63 Committee member, maybe: Abbr.
65 Word in a price

57

ACROSS

1 It may be hand-picked
6 Not express
11 "The word"
14 Deep blue
15 Earthy tone
16 Brian who produced or co-produced seven U2 albums
17 Feeling of nonfulfillment
19 "Wait Wait . . . Don't Tell Me!" network
20 Went for, at an auction
21 Playing marbles
23 Case of bad spelling?
24 Frequent home acquisition
26 Fill in for
29 Big ___
30 Friend of Falstaff
31 Szyslak of Springfield
32 "Come on, pack your stuff . . . !"
35 Signs
38 Statement about 17-, 24-, 49- and 59-Across

41 "Baseball Tonight" network
42 Hall-of-Fame QB/kicker George
43 With 45-Down, "Trust No One" series
44 Fandango offerings, slangily
46 "___ Dalloway"
47 Arterial implant
49 Burgers and fries, often
52 Orch. section
53 Aggrieved person's cry, maybe
54 Bill & ___ Gates Foundation
58 "My Big Fat Greek Wedding" actress Vardalos
59 Item that may have a date stamp
62 Comprehended
63 Like 36 piano keys
64 Original Thanksgiving fare

65 Cosine of 2π
66 Where Moses received the Law
67 Kingly title in Spanish

DOWN

1 Big Broadway hit
2 It might be a lot
3 Neither masc. nor fem.
4 Violinist Heifetz
5 Surreptitiously
6 Whites or darks, say
7 Mo. of Indigenous Peoples Day
8 Christogram part
9 Bellowing
10 Extent
11 Internal memo?
12 Let off the hook?
13 Robert who won a Tony for "How to Succeed in Business Without Really Trying"
18 Kingly title in Latin

22 Another time
24 Colonel suspected of murder
25 Hearts, e.g.
26 French girlfriend
27 Barracks lineup
28 Maybe takes one risk too many
29 Sailor's patron
33 Recede
34 Rubber-stamped
36 Former baseball commissioner Bowie
37 "Leave it in" mark
39 "Clear Light of Day" author Desai
40 Town near New London, Conn.
45 See 43-Across
48 Like "Survivor" councils
49 Bat used for fielding practice
50 Chloride or carbonate
51 Graceful African antelope

by Joon Pahk

58

Note: When completed, this puzzle grid will contain an unusual feature that appears nine times. Can you find it?

ACROSS

1 Steal from
4 Go on a jag
9 "Beat it!"
14 "O Henry, ___ thine eyes!": Shak.
15 "In an ___ world . . ."
16 Boorish
17 Spell-off
18 Just learning about
19 "I've ___ up to here!"
20 Make arable, perhaps
22 Ants, archaically
23 Acts the shrew
24 ___ Penh, Cambodia: Var.
25 Is compassionate
30 Half a flock, maybe
34 Sisters' org.
35 Dues payer
36 Hindu god
37 What a cow chews
38 Style of truck with a vertical front
40 Mule of song

41 "101 ___ for a Dead Cat" (1981 best seller)
43 Multi-act shows
44 "The Closer" cable channel
45 1978 Yankees hero Bucky
46 Remains of a felling
48 "So satisfying!" sounds
50 Louis XIV, Louis XVI et al.
52 Deep divides
55 Bacardi concoction, perhaps
59 "___ lost his mind?"
60 Yam or taro
61 Fish-to-be
62 Pale with fright
63 Ohm's symbol
64 "A Chorus Line" song
65 Casts off
66 Alternative to roll-on
67 Bard's nightfall

DOWN

1 Batcave figure
2 Diva's workplace
3 Place for a pilsner
4 Cherry variety
5 "Aha!" elicitor
6 "Winning the Future" author Gingrich
7 Event receipts
8 "Xanadu" band, for short
9 Dorky sort
10 Pulled an all-nighter
11 Like cutting in line, e.g.
12 Mine opening
13 "Amazin'" team
21 Mag. copy
22 Followers of appetizers
24 Sneak peek, informally
26 ___ Theaters (national cinema chain)
27 Fireplace floors

28 Fireplace remains
29 Higher-ranking than
31 Louisiana city named for the fifth U.S. president
32 Big name in women's apparel since 1949
33 Margarita glass rim coating
34 Gulf war missile
39 Run after Q
42 Squirreled away
47 Montevideo's land: Abbr.
49 Church chorus
51 Unwashed hair may have it
52 Cartoonist Addams
53 "Slung" dish
54 Arthur who wrote "A Hard Road to Glory"
55 Beef cut
56 Super, slangily

by Tim Wescott

57 Prefix with
vitamins
58 Do penance,
say
60 How-___
(do-it-yourself
books)

59

ACROSS

1 City SW of Syracuse
7 Ripoff
11 First word of 10-/25-Down's "Billie Jean"
14 Richie who wrote "We Are the World" with 10-/25-Down
15 1982 blockbuster by 10-/25-Down
17 Moviegoer's chocolate bite
18 More honest
19 Kind of cheese
21 Its symbol is omega
22 Right away
24 Trek to Mecca
26 Zero
30 Give the slip to
32 1991 hit album by 10-/25-Down
35 "Yum!"
37 Air-conditioned

38 Dir. from Gary, Ind., to Sault Ste. Marie
39 Grates on
40 "Don't you ___ for no favors" (42-Down lyric on 32-Across)
42 Joan of rock
43 Middle of the second century
44 Ziegfeld and others
45 Deluges
47 Nickname for 10-/25-Down
50 Romeo's love?
51 Popeye creator Elzie ___
52 Zero
54 Old spy grp.
55 Vitality
57 Juan's uncle?
59 Skin cream ingredient
64 Less than wholesale
67 Vocal style of 10-/25-Down, at times
68 First record label of 10-/25-Down

69 "Farewell"
70 Stink up the joint
71 Small piano

DOWN

1 Some urban rails
2 Writer ___ Yutang
3 Classic part of a 10-/25-Down stage act
4 Atahualpa, for one
5 Gets to
6 Greek leader?
7 City grid: Abbr.
8 ___-Town (Midwest hub)
9 River under the Ponte Vecchio
10 With 25-Down, this puzzle's honoree
11 Certain camera, for short
12 Laugh syllable
13 Miss the mark
16 Ring-tailed primate

20 Quirky
22 Old fast-food chain
23 Be positioned above
25 See 10-Down
27 Song on 32-Across
28 Bird dogs, say
29 Flies over Africa?
31 Bad-mouth
33 Jean Valjean, e.g.
34 Takes off
36 Either 50 of 50-50
41 Appeasement
42 First song on 32-Across
44 With 10-Down, 1975 album by 10-/25-Down
46 Handheld device
48 Goggles
49 Bit of wordplay
53 Rich soils
56 Rose family member
58 Play starter
59 Vance in Okla., e.g.
60 Minstrel's song

by David J. Kahn

61 Arena cry
62 Itinerary part: Abbr.
63 Just dandy
65 Riksdag locale: Abbr.

66 Cable channel with the slogan "We Know Drama"

ACROSS

1 "60 Minutes" correspondent starting in 1991
6 It may be run up
9 Hunky-dory
12 More delicate
14 "I don't believe this!"
15 Many-armed org.?
16 Talking like a junkie?
18 Be discordant
19 Rock's David Lee ___
20 Canapé topper
21 "The Hot Zone" virus
23 Agnostic's display?
26 Vanessa Williams/ Brian McKnight duet
29 Be nosy
30 Sunbathing at Ipanema, e.g.?
34 Plaza locale: Abbr.
37 Suffix with psych-

38 With 22-Down, recliner brand
39 ___-dieu
40 Widower of Maude on "The Simpsons"
41 Rink jewelry?
45 Female whale
46 E-mails from Nigerian princes, e.g.
47 Letter carrier's uniform?
53 The 40 of a "back 40"
54 Targets of a Moe Howard poke
55 ___ operandi (methods)
59 Cote call
60 Promote one's business, maybe . . . or a hint to 16-, 23-, 30-, 41- and 47-Across
63 Barrister's abbr.
64 Group with a Grand Lodge in Chicago

65 "Fiddler on the Roof" setting
66 Wahine's offering
67 Indian novelist Raja ___
68 Tanning element

DOWN

1 Baghdad's ___ City
2 Newbie: Var.
3 Stuck, after "in"
4 Buccaneers' place
5 Set the tempo
6 Fence supplier
7 Mayo is part of it
8 Parched
9 Pear variety
10 Name in dental hygiene
11 Unit of purity
13 Fencing thrust: Var.
14 Uniformed comics dog
17 Call from a farm field
22 See 38-Across

24 Blazin' Blueberry drink brand
25 Just right
26 Scientology's ___ Hubbard
27 Chantilly's department
28 Tear up, so to speak
31 Off one's feed
32 Batman after Michael
33 Suffix with final
34 Fare "for kids"
35 ___ tar (baseball team supply)
36 Things to tap
39 Device with a flat panel
41 Whoop it up
42 Part of M.Y.O.B.
43 What "Rh" may stand for
44 A.L. East team, on scoreboards
45 A.L. Central team, on scoreboards
47 Normand of old movies
48 Make ___ for (support)

by Corey Rubin

49 Operation ___ Freedom
50 Gordon ___ ("Wall Street" role)
51 Shoemakers' supplies
52 Flying Cloud of 1927–36
56 Lollapalooza
57 What's spread on a spreadsheet
58 Way to stand by
61 Tuskegee U. locale
62 Day after so-called "hump day": Abbr.

61

ACROSS

1 Sub for
6 Jungfrau or Eiger
9 Campaign against Troy, e.g.
14 Word after "thou"
15 Lighter maker
16 Bow, the "It Girl"
17 "Rikki-___-Tavi"
18 Mid 10th-century year
19 Tiny bits
20 Feature of a Las Vegas "bandit"
22 April 1 cigar sound
24 George Harrison's "___ It a Pity"
25 Do a Sherpa's work
27 24-line verse form
29 Toy on a layout
32 Water cannon target
33 Patch up
34 Nutrition label units
36 Branded beast
38 Lard holder
39 Kiltie's instrument
44 Huskies' sch.
46 Thing depicted by this puzzle's circled letters
47 "Night" novelist
51 Jet fuel component
54 Software buyer, usually
56 Kidney-related
57 "That was ___ . . ."
58 Tool at Henley
60 It beats the alternative, in a saying
63 Radio letter after sierra
65 Here-there link
67 Like porridge
68 Like SEALs
69 "That's not fair!"
70 Blast from the past
71 Architectural Digest topic
72 Pay stub abbr.
73 Items in a 46-Across, often

DOWN

1 Concerning
2 Place for a Vandyke
3 "Bye, now"
4 High-pH
5 Add while cooking
6 Multiple-choice choices
7 Life's partner
8 Place for a programming class, perhaps
9 Poli ___
10 Philippine seaport
11 Bothers no end
12 Starbucks size
13 Egg roll time
21 Ruler divs.
23 Old-time schoolteacher
26 "I ___ differ"
28 Daffy Duck trademark
29 One might pass for these, briefly
30 One down in the dumps?
31 Magician's prop
35 Daisy Mae's guy
37 Wishes undone
40 "Meet you then!"
41 Church dignitaries
42 Dark time, to a bard
43 Drop in on
45 '63 Liz Taylor role
47 Licked, e.g.
48 Yoga instructor's direction
49 Like paradise
50 Serenaded
52 Flying Cloud automaker
53 Like the art in some exhibits
55 Told in order to get a quick opinion
59 Cheer (for)
61 Heroic deed
62 Docs who might treat sinusitis
64 Key contraction
66 Axle, e.g.

by Peter A. Collins and Joe Krozel

62

ACROSS
1 This and that
6 Locale of famous playing fields
10 Start of the 13th century
14 Top of some forms
15 Whole lot
16 Obsessed mariner
17 Encyclopedia volume
18 Element number 55-Across
20 Bygone compact
21 Go carefully (over)
22 Dryer remains
23 Atlanta Brave who wore the number 55-Across
26 Done in
28 Halloween candy
29 Justification
30 Promising
34 Chemical suffix
35 President number 55-Across

38 It's a wrap
40 Cousin of a camel
41 Turn "this" into "— ···· ·· ···," e.g.
44 Earl Grey holder
48 Prefix with -hedron
49 Feb. 7, 2010, the date of this event's number 55-Across
52 Group of courses
53 Times in want ads
54 Cell material
55 See 18-, 23-, 35- and 49-Across
57 Steamy
59 Lake ___, discovery of Louis Jolliet
60 Lord over
61 Senseless
62 Absolutely
63 Melodramatic cry
64 Fireplace tool

DOWN
1 Snub
2 Musical liability
3 Brought to ruin
4 Charge
5 Transmit electronically
6 Calculator message
7 Bullish beginning?
8 A lot
9 Nonacademic degree
10 Capital founded by Spanish invaders, 1571
11 Sight from Taiwan
12 Admonishment
13 ThinkPad developer
19 If not
21 Music section
24 "American Idol" judge DioGuardi
25 Suffix with liquid
27 Santa Fe-to-Colo. Spr. direction
29 Sale sweeteners

31 Euro predecessor
32 Abbr. on a blotter
33 Truck scale unit
35 Study of Louis Pasteur
36 Stellar server
37 Old Dead Sea kingdom
38 Red or black, at a gaming table
39 Bar request
42 Held the floor
43 Tony winner Tyne
45 Apollo astronaut Frank
46 Deck cover
47 Forest clearings
49 1988 Olympics host
50 Palate part
51 Shimon of Israel
55 Ness, for one
56 Term of address in a monastery
57 Any of the Billboard Top 40
58 Game with Skip cards

by Richard Silvestri

63

ACROSS
1 Like some fevers
9 Title role for Ben Kingsley
15 Tiny, as a town
16 It's north of the Strait of Gibraltar
17 Some long flights
18 Teeming, as with bees
19 Fabric amts.
20 Letter sign-off
22 Diminutive endings
23 Restaurateur Toots
25 Stewart and Lovitz
27 Florida theme park
29 X-rated stuff
30 Garment line
33 "___ Gold" (Fonda film)
34 Banned apple spray
35 Actress Rogers
36 What this puzzle's perimeter contains abbreviations for

39 "Must've been something ___"
40 Visa alternative, for short
41 Early Mexican
42 Chemical in Drano
43 Make a snarling sound
44 In pursuit of
45 Hockey's Jaromir ___
46 Eau, across the Pyrenees
47 Dealer's wear
50 Wile E. Coyote's supplier
52 It's measured in minutes
55 Class clown's doings
57 Winter warmer
60 Farsi speakers
61 Summer cooler
62 Drink of the gods
63 Retired Mach I breaker

DOWN
1 When repeated, a Billy Idol hit
2 Give ___ to (approve)
3 Monocle part
4 Sounds from a hot tub
5 Hogwash
6 2004 Will Smith film
7 "___ your instructions . . ."
8 More, in a saying
9 1970s–'80s supermodel Carangi
10 Playing hooky
11 Colorful salamanders
12 "Curses!"
13 Bring on board
14 Pet food brand
21 Discount apparel chain
23 Part of a shoot
24 Parasite's home
26 Sharer's pronoun

27 Former QB John
28 Former QB Rodney
29 More artful
30 Blackjack player's request
31 Mideast bigwig: Var.
32 Like items in a junk drawer: Abbr.
33 Gas, e.g.: Abbr.
34 Eritrea's capital
35 Mediter-ranean land
37 Yin's counterpart
38 Vegan's protein source
43 Deadhead icon
44 What many fifth graders have reached
45 Like some tax returns
46 BP gas brand
47 Self-absorbed
48 Concerning
49 Opposite of legato, in mus.

by Samuel A. Donaldson

51 In vogue
52 Big name in desktop computers
53 Map line
54 Showed up
56 Ukr., once, e.g.
58 New Deal inits.
59 Conquistador's prize

64

ACROSS

1 One-two part
4 Cattle-herding breed
9 Playground retort
14 Draft pick?
15 Keats title starter
16 Stands at wakes
17 Diam. × π
18 Get on
19 Daisy type
20 Words of encourage-ment to a Brit?
23 Up to
24 Abu Dhabi's fed.
25 Little jerks
28 "Hey, over here!"
29 Group of dancing Brits?
32 One way to think
34 Dark horse's win
35 Eggs Benedict need
38 With 30-Down, kind of clause
39 Aramis, to Athos

41 Causes for stadium cheers, for short
42 Extract with a solvent
44 Give off
46 British smart alecks?
49 Favor one side, perhaps
53 Dresden denial
54 Sail through
55 Wedding memento
56 Sleep like a Brit?
60 When doubled, a wolf's call
62 Turbine part
63 Sacha Baron Cohen character ___ G
64 On ___ (hot)
65 Money in la banque
66 Net judge's call
67 iPhone display unit
68 Piece in the game of go
69 Method: Abbr.

DOWN

1 Hike, as a price
2 Vulcans and Romulans
3 Left Bank toppers
4 Computer language in Y2K news
5 Take too much of, briefly
6 True-to-life
7 Bout
8 Clad like some Halloween paraders
9 Bernstein/ Sondheim's "___ Like That"
10 Have a tussle
11 Hardest to see, perhaps
12 Direct conclusion?
13 Sugar suffix
21 Hummus holder
22 "The Crying Game" Oscar nominee
26 Like some actors going on stage

27 Things some designers design
29 Friday, notably
30 See 38-Across
31 British pound, informally
33 Leopold's partner in a sensational 1924 trial
35 Rough-___ (unfinished)
36 Get caught in ___
37 It may have a spinning ballerina
39 Pink-slip
40 Lambda followers
43 Like a solid argument
44 Just manages
45 Monarch crowned in 1558: Abbr.
47 Geneva's ___ Léman
48 Earth tones
50 Worthy principles
51 This-and-that concert per-formance
52 Puts forth

by Corey Rubin

55 Chapter's
partner
57 Seven-foot,
say
58 Other, in
Oaxaca

59 Provide with
a rear view?
60 Chance,
poetically
61 Ocean
State sch.

65

ACROSS

1 Actor Assante
7 Imprison
12 Mil. rank
15 Oregonian
16 Frost lines
17 Netscape acquirer
18 Entrance requirement, maybe
20 Meter-candle
21 Barack Obama, 2005–08, e.g.
23 Part of Santa's bagful
24 ___ Enterprise
25 1950s White House resident
27 Rookie's superstition
32 Skier's wish
34 Archaeological find
35 "Just kidding!"
36 Texas city . . . and a hint to the starts of 21-, 27-, 45- and 56-Across
42 ___-wop
43 Bum ___
44 To be, to Brutus
45 Subsidiary member of a firm
51 Blockage remover
52 Actress ___ Ling of "The Crow"
53 Fool
56 Some restaurant and pharmacy lures
62 Feel awful
63 French Academy's 40 members
64 Classic British two-seaters
65 Vapid
66 Ogle
67 Like Dvořák's "Serenade for Strings"
68 Philosopher Kierkegaard
69 Gauge

DOWN

1 Toward the stern
2 Not an original
3 "Ahoy, ___!"
4 Company with the stock symbol CAR
5 Belg. neighbor
6 Solicit, as business
7 Still
8 Subway Series participant
9 "Desperate Housewives" role
10 Part of PTA: Abbr.
11 Bring back to domestication
12 Gold-colored horses
13 Multipurpose, somehow
14 160, to Caesar
19 Place for a gauge, informally
22 Persian for "crown"
26 Bus. card info
27 Tijuana tanner
28 Pooh pal
29 High school dept.
30 Little bit
31 Messenger ___
32 Half-salute
33 Only you
37 Make a clanger
38 Clothing retailer since 1969
39 Air monitor, for short
40 Shirt to wear with shorts
41 Mideast land: Abbr.
42 CD players
46 Days ___
47 Ear inflammation
48 Ones who drive people home?
49 Australian island: Abbr.
50 San ___, Christmas figure in Italy
53 Entrap
54 World record?
55 Attention getters
57 [Gasp!]
58 Tail end
59 Sup
60 Tram loads
61 Shoshone speakers
62 Ennemi's opposite

by Ashish Vengsarkar

66

ACROSS

1 Windy City team
5 "Me, me, me" sort
9 Like a teddy bear
14 Summer Games org.
15 Radiate
16 Steinbeck migrants
17 Certain mortgage, briefly
18 All over
19 Successfully defend
20 Spicy bar fare
23 Turns, in a way
24 It may have orchids or plumerias
25 Ceremonial utterance
28 Yellow
32 Author Ferber
36 Kiltie's turndown
37 Wipe out
38 Cape Cod town
40 Baseball bigwigs, for short
42 Largish combo
43 Lacking melanin
45 Where It.'s at
47 "Dear" ones
48 Game to 11 points
51 Milk source
52 Crew leader
53 Place for pampering
58 Easy preparation instruction . . . or a hint to the starts of 20-, 28- and 48-Across
61 Big cheese
64 Form of silica
65 Group of thousands, maybe
66 Muscat native
67 Comstock's find
68 Scoreboard tally
69 One, for one
70 Sail support
71 2004 Brad Pitt film

DOWN

1 Cuts back
2 Finish off
3 Super, in showbiz
4 "Futurama" genre
5 Buys and sells
6 "___ expert, but . . ."
7 Op-ed's offering
8 Freely
9 Pardoned
10 Luau strings
11 Mail aid
12 Zuider ___
13 Fashion monogram
21 Tide competitor
22 Frau's "forget it"
25 Certain Oriental rug maker
26 Ward off
27 "Golden Boy" playwright
29 Internet annoyance
30 Red Sea land
31 They may clash
32 Les ___-Unis
33 1964 Tony Randall title role
34 Having a rough knotted surface
35 Seed covering
39 18 inches, give or take
41 Radiation source
44 Siouan speakers
46 "Batman" villain, with "the"
49 Sings the praises of
50 Go back and forth in the woods?
54 America's Cup entrant
55 Flight part
56 Green topping
57 Too-too
58 Mitchell who wrote and sang "Chelsea Morning"
59 Per unit
60 Jean Arp's movement
61 Signal at Christie's
62 "___ losing it?"
63 Avocation, slangily

by Nancy Kavanaugh

67

ACROSS
1 No. crunchers
5 Haute cuisine it's not
9 Places for links
14 Rope material
15 Audiophile's concern
16 Of service
17 307 for Wyoming and 907 for Alaska
19 El Líder of Argentina
20 Not paying immediately at the bar
22 100 or so, e.g.: Abbr.
23 Use a prie-dieu
24 Adoptee in Genesis
26 2002 Adam Sandler title role
29 Building beams
30 Through the uprights
31 Hams it up
34 "Whew!"

35 Google search need . . . or a hint to the ends of 20- and 49-Across and 11- and 28-Down
38 Satisfied sound
39 Like drinks with umbrellas
41 Fraternal letters
42 Sax type
43 "A diamond is forever" sloganeer
46 Lower oneself
47 Deduces, with "out"
48 Pewter component
49 Go ballistic
54 "Socrate" composer Erik
56 1978 Cheech & Chong movie
57 "It's the end of ___"
58 "Holy ___!"
59 Line of rotation
60 Less typical

61 Morel morsel
62 Duma dissent

DOWN
1 Burn on the grill
2 Machu Picchu's land
3 "You said it!"
4 Punished with a wooden spoon, say
5 Like Cheech & Chong, typically
6 41-Across meeting places
7 Center Shaq
8 Annoying type
9 China's place
10 Beehive State native
11 Apartment building feature
12 Dental hygienist's advice
13 In the mail
18 Cannes film
21 ___ Alert (abduction bulletin)
25 Majorca Mrs.
26 Those in charge: Abbr.
27 Crowd sound

28 Road sign warning
29 1961 Literature Nobelist Andric
31 Harry Potter's pet Hedwig, e.g.
32 Hammer-wielding god
33 "___ All That" (Freddie Prinze Jr. film)
35 Cordelia's father
36 Low-budget prefix
37 Yevtushenko's "Babi ___"
40 Louvre pyramid architect
41 Reception toast giver
43 Easily managed
44 Penn, to Pennsylvania
45 Uncle ___ rice
46 Paul Anka #1 hit
47 Greyhound stop
48 Autocrat until 1917
50 Bottom lines

by Michael Callaway Barnhart

51 Classic Manhattan theater

52 Dust Bowl migrant

53 For fear that

55 Ill temper

68

ACROSS

1 *Start of a 38-Across
5 "The Good Earth" heroine
9 So last year
14 ___ about
15 *Small part of a spork
16 Recyclable item
17 Prayer wheel user
18 *Musical quality
19 Strike down
20 Cockpit announcements, briefly
21 Millstone
22 *Made tracks
23 Strength
25 Cord unit
27 Good name for an investment adviser?
29 Permanently attached, in zoology
32 Early MP3-sharing Web site
35 *Teed off
37 Up-to-date

38 Hint to the word ladder in the answers to the starred clues
43 ". . . and that's final!"
44 *Put into piles
45 Canal site, maybe
47 Showing irritation
52 Last in a series
53 Toxic pollutant, for short
55 Sweet, in Italy
56 *Locale in a western
59 Many Christmas ornaments
62 Holly
63 Crossword maker or editor, at times
64 *It may precede a stroke
65 Rat Pack nickname
66 Dirección sailed by Columbus
67 *Ax

68 Change components, often
69 Dag Hammarskjöld, for one
70 Some cameras, for short
71 *End of a 38-Across

DOWN

1 At minimum
2 How baseball games rarely end
3 Kind of land
4 Undoes
5 Camp Swampy dog
6 Symbol of courage
7 Undo
8 "Kinsey" star, 2004
9 Orkin victim
10 Survivalist's stockpile
11 Full of energy
12 "The Way of Perfection" writer
13 Word after red or dead
24 Solomon's asset
26 In profusion

28 Pseudo-cultured
30 Stockpile
31 Muff one
33 Like some men's hair
34 Nasdaq buy: Abbr.
36 Wynn and Harris
38 Quick drive
39 Tried out at an Air Force base
40 Theater for niche audiences
41 Medical research org.
42 Doo-___
46 Shows scorn
48 Lacking
49 "Fighting" athletes
50 Part of an act, perhaps
51 Simple sugar
54 Range setting
57 On Soc. Sec., say
58 Trap, in a way
60 Winter exclamation
61 Goes with
63 Orgs. with "Inc." in their names

by Barry C. Silk

When this puzzle is done, the nine circles will contain the letters A through I. Connect them with a line, in alphabetical order, and you will form an illustration of the puzzle's theme.

ACROSS

1 A Morse "I" consists of two
5 Penultimate fairy tale word
9 Deadly snake
14 "Climb ___ Mountain"
15 Long skirt
16 Break point
17 With 59-Across, A-B-C-A in the illustration
18 Ship in "Pirates of the Caribbean"
20 Stop ___ dime
21 Half of a mountaineering expedition
22 Dressed like a certain keg party attendee
24 Prefix with lateral
25 F-G
29 Ship's christening, e.g.
30 C-D
31 "___ expert, but . . ."
32 Certain California wines
34 Pirating
36 "Top Hat" dancer
39 Does some electrical work on
40 Counterpart of un ángel
41 Santa-tracking org.
42 End in ___
43 A-B
45 Send, as payment
49 E-F-G-H-E
50 Part of U.C.L.A.
51 Brainstorm
52 People in fierce snowball fights
54 Yearbook sect.
55 Ship to the New World
59 See 17-Across
60 Ancient theater
61 Makeup of some little balls
62 Response to a charge
63 Stethoscope users, at times
64 Away from the wind
65 Lava lamps and pet rocks, once

DOWN

1 Bump down but keep on
2 Chekhov play or its antihero
3 "M*A*S*H" procedure
4 Lexico-graphical abbr.
5 Incorporate, as a YouTube video into a Web site
6 Actor Kilmer and others
7 Horse-race bets on win and place
8 Kitchen gadgets
9 Hook or Cook: Abbr.
10 Tribute with feet
11 Deadly snake
12 1921 play that introduced the word "robot"
13 One of the oceans: Abbr.
19 One who may put you in stitches?
21 Part of a larger picture
23 Poe's "___ Lee"
25 "Don't Go

Breaking My Heart" duettist, 1976
26 Mideast V.I.P.
27 Cousin of -trix
28 Old shipbuilding needs
30 Writer Rita ___ Brown
33 Leak on a ship, e.g.
35 Tournament wrap-up
36 Wife of Esau
37 In ___ (as found)
38 Following detective
39 CD-___
41 It may be flared
44 "Yowie, zowie!"
46 "Mississippi ___" (1992 film)
47 Words of resignation
48 Magnetic induction units
51 Livid
52 D-reviews
53 Aachen article
55 ___ sauce
56 Suffix with many fruit names
57 Minus:

by Daniel A. Finan

Abbr.
58 Dress (up)
59 Number
on a
bottle at
the beach

70

ACROSS

1 Booker T.'s bandmates in '60s R&B
4 San Diego Zoo attractions
10 [fizzle]
14 "Can't Get It Out of My Head" grp.
15 "Peter and the Wolf" musician
16 View from Buffalo
17 Have surgery
20 Great time
21 Actress Polo of "Meet the Parents"
22 RR stop
23 ___ David
24 With 37- and 50-Across, privileged
26 Colorful glacier layer
29 Bubble contents
30 Family girl
31 Family girl
34 Dolt
37 See 24-Across
41 Co. acquired by Verizon in 2006
42 Sturdy building material
43 Court figs.
45 D.C. influence wielder
48 Designer's starting point
50 See 24-Across
55 "Keep ___ alive!"
56 Geisha's accessory
57 Diamond legend, with "the"
58 "Bowling for Columbine" documentarian
60 "Gimme!"
64 Mine, in Marseille
65 ___ Palace, French presidential residence
66 Seventh in a series of 24
67 It may be caught in a trap
68 Sure
69 Rogers who was elected twice to the Country Music Hall of Fame

DOWN

1 Sister in "Little Women"
2 Doctrine that deemphasizes regional interests
3 Barry White's genre
4 Some marine herds
5 Help in a bad way
6 ___'easter
7 "Likewise"
8 One of the 12 tribes of Israel
9 Chest protectors
10 Slammer
11 Bill passed many times on the Hill, formerly
12 It may be taken in court, with "the"
13 Pop/R&B singer ___ Marie
18 Kitty's pickup point
19 Fuzzy fruit
23 "Numb3rs" network
24 They may come in a round
25 Modern locale of ancient Persepolis
27 Accts. payable receipt
28 French bus. firm
32 Winter Minn. hrs.
33 Pleistocene, e.g.
35 Fries, often
36 Began paying attention
38 They may be licked or smacked
39 "Vas ___ Vas" (former derivative Spanish-language game show)
40 Wine: Prefix
44 Geneviève, e.g.: Abbr.
46 Prefix with dextrous
47 Actress Phyllis of "I Was a Teenage Frankenstein"
49 Comrade of Mao
50 Butcher's discards
51 Feminist Wolf who wrote "The Beauty Myth"

by Michael Vuolo

71

ACROSS

1 Venetian who explored for England in the 15th century
6 Paints gently
10 Mattress filler during a recession, maybe
14 Last Oldsmobile car
15 Palindromic magazine name
16 "A pity"
17 Tail-less Old World mammal
18 Land of the descendants of 67-Across
19 "Step right up!"
20 An Olympic swimmer needs a big one
23 50+ org.
24 Royal family
28 Less than 1%
31 It may be over a window
35 Tricks
37 Not so common
38 The Greatest

39 Son of, in Arab names
40 Akihito's wife, e.g.
42 Rebelling Turner
43 ___ pooped to pop
44 Shire of "Rocky"
45 Treaty signing
47 Sound practical judgment
50 After 2004, the only way to buy a 14-Across
51 Slander
52 Modern way to put out an album
54 Fateful event for the Titanic
61 Diamond group
64 Runner in Pamplona
65 Like spoken n's
66 It turns a hundred into a thousand
67 Jacob's twin
68 Makes like the Cheshire Cat

69 Element that can precede the starts of 20-, 31-, 47- and 54-Across
70 Where the crew chows down
71 "Poor Richard's Almanack" bit

DOWN

1 Give a ring
2 Baseball's Felipe or Jesus
3 Capital of Switzerland
4 Art form that commonly depicts a swan
5 Puccini opera
6 Group with the 1968 hit "Hush"
7 2006 Emmy winner for "The West Wing"
8 Congressional Black Caucus, e.g.
9 Rest stop sight
10 Echo location

11 Stout, e.g.
12 "Harlem Nocturne" instrument
13 1940s–'50s White House inits.
21 Part of a circle
22 Common companion of a dry throat
25 Astronomical discovery of 1781
26 Grief relief
27 Ready to be typeset
28 Paul Revere and others
29 Big bang
30 Turn a deaf ear to
32 ___ to go
33 Spying against one's own country, say
34 He ran to succeed 13-Down: Abbr.
36 Et ___
41 More, on Mallorca
46 Author Kipling

by Joey Weissbrot

48 Biblical strongman
49 Part of S.A.S.E.: Abbr.
53 Line dance
55 Hot pair
56 A teaspoonful, maybe
57 Reconstruction and the Roaring Twenties
58 Indian's home
59 Club familiars
60 End of a warning
61 Gun produced by Israel Military Industries
62 La Méditerranée, e.g.
63 Whiz

72

ACROSS
1 Frog-dissecting class: Abbr.
5 "Ship of Fools" painter
10 Riot queller
14 Pink, maybe
15 Lawn care brand
16 "Such a pity"
17 Slate, e.g.
18 Where was the Battle of Bunker Hill fought?
20 Makes invalid
22 California Indian tribe: Var.
23 Seminary teaching
24 Drain
25 Cousin of a cat's-eye
29 What animal does a bulldogger throw?
30 Drop ___ (moon)
32 Soprano Gluck
33 Get copy right
35 Money

37 In what country are Panama hats made?
41 What is George Eliot's given name?
42 It'll keep the home fires burning
43 Queens's ___ Stadium
44 Seed cover
45 Golfer Ballesteros
47 From what animals do we get catgut?
52 Smallest
54 Soft shoe, briefly
55 Part of São Paulo
56 Column style
58 Putting up the greatest affront
59 In what country are Chinese gooseberries produced?
63 Times to call, in some want ads
64 Unoccupied

65 Deejay's interest, typically
66 Port opener?
67 Family dogs, for short
68 Very funny happenings
69 The "I" in M.I.T.: Abbr.

DOWN
1 Challah and baguettes
2 "You are so!" preceder
3 What color is the black box in a commercial jet?
4 Pea, for one
5 Short cuts
6 Bruins' retired "4"
7 What is actor Stewart Granger's family name?
8 For next to nothing, in slang
9 Brick carriers
10 Reddish brown
11 Clay, today
12 "Silent" prez
13 Adult ed. class, often

19 ___ Na Na
21 Rio Grande port
24 Recipe verb
26 "M*A*S*H" star
27 Eliot Ness and others
28 Bring home
31 The California gull is the state bird of which state?
34 For what animals are the Canary Islands named?
36 1974 Mocedades hit
37 Not différent
38 ___ package
39 Former Voice of America org.
40 Nobody too big or too small, on a sign
41 Fraction of a tick: Abbr.
43 What kind of fruit is an alligator pear?
46 Actor Estevez

by Ed Stein and Paula Gamache

73

ACROSS
1 Tree trunk
5 Some HDTVs
9 Heartbreaker who's "back in town" in a 1980 Carly Simon hit
14 Feature of mesh fabrics
16 The Carolinas, e.g., to the French
17 Debugs computer programs, e.g.
19 Two of racing's Unsers
20 Neighbor of B.C.
21 San ___, Marin County
22 La ___ Tar Pits
23 Bird feeder fill
24 Responds to rashes
31 Like Papa Bear's porridge
32 Collect splinters, so to speak

33 Tuskegee's locale: Abbr.
34 Nutmeg State sch.
35 Ore suffix
36 "What ___" ("Ho-hum")
38 Rap sheet entries, for short
39 Messenger ___
40 Record label owned by Sony
41 Does some mending
45 Cellular construction
46 Overlook
47 One of the Leeward Islands
50 Hesitant sounds
51 Mexicali Mrs.
54 Lines up the sewing
57 Coral creation
58 Blood type historically considered the universal donor
59 Only beardless Disney dwarf

60 Have a knish, say
61 Orbiting telescope launcher

DOWN
1 Florida city, for short
2 Australian gem
3 "Sure, why not?!"
4 Business letter abbr.
5 Return to one's seat?
6 Quarter of Algiers
7 Batter's fig.
8 Ethiopia's Haile ___
9 Glitterati
10 Blah, blah, blah, for short
11 Satirist Mort
12 Skier's turn
13 Gas brand in Canada
15 Prestigious business school
18 Umiak passenger
22 Road, in the Rheinland
24 Speech spot

25 Tiramisu topper
26 Place to rule
27 Business sign abbr.
28 Like Siberian winters
29 Give a lift
30 Long tales
35 What oysters "R" during "R" months
36 Da Vinci or Michelangelo, to Romans
37 Wordsmith's ref.
39 Florenz Ziegfeld offering
40 Set a lofty goal
42 Raw material for Wrigley's, once
43 To a great degree
44 MapQuest offerings
47 Make ___ dash
48 Brussels-based alliance
49 'Vette roof option
51 Islamic sect
52 Amps up

by Jerry E. Rosman

53 On the main

55 ___-Cat (winter vehicle)

56 Doz. eggs, commonly

74

ACROSS

1 Parroting sorts
6 Stud on a stud farm
10 Good name, casually
13 Venue for some clowns
14 Word before city or child
15 Basis for some discrimination
16 Mystery desserts?
18 Thing to roll over, in brief
19 East ___, U.N. member since 2002
20 Central part
22 Oscar winner Sorvino
25 Acquired relative
27 Musical with the song "Mr. Mistoffelees"
28 Equal to, with "with"
30 O.K. to do
32 Orange feature
33 Bates's business, in film
35 Video shooter, for short
38 Direction from K.C. to Detroit
39 Stir up
41 ___-Ida (Tater Tots maker)
42 Top end of a scale
43 Miming dances
44 Visibly frightened
46 Bucky Beaver's toothpaste
48 High-hats
49 Soprano Gluck
51 Refrain syllables
54 "Spare me!," e.g.
55 Place for a lark
57 Winter coat feature
59 Diamond corner
60 Sculler's affliction?
65 Time of anticipation
66 First-rate
67 Many an art film
68 ___ judicata
69 Hebrides isle
70 Take as one's own

DOWN

1 Flight board abbr.
2 Samoan staple
3 Byrnes of TV's "77 Sunset Strip"
4 Reason for a long delay in getting approval, maybe
5 Arias, e.g.
6 Motorist's headache
7 Calligrapher's buy
8 Period of seven days without bathing?
9 Gaelic tongue
10 What the sky might do in an inebriate's dream?
11 Everglades denizen
12 Belfry sounds
14 Pic to click
17 Mideast V.I.P.
21 Zenith competitor
22 "Impression, Sunrise" painter
23 Cockamamie
24 Illustrations for a Poe poem?
26 Choir voices
29 Leader of the pack
31 Pick up bit by bit
33 Place for a crown
34 In vitro items
36 Mountain ridge
37 Group with a meeting of the minds?
40 Employment in Munchkin-land?
45 Choir voice
47 Inflate, in a way
48 Spilled the beans
49 Honey-hued
50 Take a powder
52 Sitcom with the catchphrase "Kiss my grits!"

by Robert A. Doll

53 ___ sausage
56 Tolkien beasts
58 "Beowulf," e.g.
61 Modus operandi
62 Courtroom vow
63 Barely beat
64 The "all" in "Collect them all!"

75

ACROSS

1 Ohio town called the Bicycle Capital of the Midwest
6 Sitcom father of Mearth
10 Longest-serving senator in U.S. history
14 Sing ___
15 "The ___ Love"
16 Be biased
17 Wedding flower girl, maybe
18 Librarian's imperative
19 It's below the elbow
20 *Bush cabinet member who resigned in 2006
23 Wall Street earnings abbr.
24 Monopoly token
25 ___ Grand
26 *Her "Rehab" won a Grammy for Song of the Year
31 Out

34 Leaves after dinner?
35 Actress Naldi of the silents
36 All day every day
39 Friend from way, way back
41 Opening for outside?
42 Spread
44 Places for hops
45 *Best Actor winner for "The Champ," 1931
49 First P.M. of Burma
50 Proto-matter from which the universe was made
51 Real ending?
54 *"Star Wars" actress who's a Harvard grad
58 New member of la familia
59 Simple quatrain form
60 Al-Qatif, for one
61 ___ Sea, outlet of the Amu Darya

62 Small songbirds
63 New Mexico county
64 Glowing
65 Old pump name
66 Livia, to Tiberius

DOWN

1 2005 #1 album for Coldplay
2 Poet who wrote "This is the way the world ends / Not with a bang but a whimper"
3 Incessantly
4 Ancient Peruvian
5 What some amusement park rides have
6 Rob of "Numb3rs"
7 A pint, typically, at a blood bank
8 Chew out
9 Restaurant offering that might come with a toy

10 1957 Fats Domino hit
11 Holler
12 Pretoria money
13 Strand material
21 Towel off
22 String after E
26 "No doubt!"
27 Prefix with liberal
28 180's
29 Factoid for fantasy baseball
30 "I'm all ___"
31 Fresh
32 "Livin' La Vida ___"
33 Worldwide: Abbr.
37 Kiss
38 "The Bells" writer
40 Stereo-typically messy digs
43 "The Second Coming" poet
46 Tennis's Ivanovic
47 City on the Rio Grande
48 Want ad abbr.
51 "No more for me"

by Caleb Madison

52 Congo, once
53 Artist James
54 "I, Claudius" figure
55 "Down with . . . !": Fr.
56 Relative of a stork
57 "Ciao"
58 Judging by their names, where the answers to the four starred clues might be found?

76

ACROSS

1 Revenue / Result
6 Many a holiday visitor / Bandit
10 Welcome, as a visitor / Try to make a date with
14 Comedian George
15 1980s Geena Davis sitcom
16 Locale for a seat of honor
17 1985 Kate Nelligan title role
18 Chickadee's perch
19 Up to the job
20 Condor's claw
21 College asset
23 Glean
25 Oldest U.S. civil liberties org.
26 At a lecture, say / Surpass in quality
29 Steel helmets with visors
34 Daughter of 28-Down
35 Genesis victim
37 Gawk
38 Priest's garb
39 Choice for a dog, as well as a hint to this puzzle's theme
41 Half a score
42 Has rolling in the aisles
44 Trick ending?
45 Gist
46 Lacking inflection
48 Sub / Excel
50 D.C. bigwig
51 False god
52 Grand Canyon material
57 Doritos dip
61 "Uh-huh"
62 What a surveyor surveys
63 Govt. security
64 ___ Bora, wild part of Afghanistan
65 The Box Tops' "___ Her in Church"
66 Painter's prop
67 Soon to get / Trying to get

68 Ushered / Showed the door
69 Attract / Protract

DOWN

1 Fjord / Bargain locale
2 Mixer
3 Autobahn auto
4 Holiday display
5 Periodicals not brought by a postal carrier
6 Foot part / Go beyond
7 White House adjunct
8 Parched
9 They may be covered and circled
10 Unwavering
11 Kemo ___
12 Brick baker
13 Map feature / Start
22 Watch location
24 ___ example
26 Arriving at the tail end / Survive

27 It has four strings
28 Brother of Rebecca, in the Bible
29 Some Muppet dolls
30 Burn balm
31 Consumed
32 Tire feature
33 Submitted, as an entry / Emitted
36 Honcho
39 Antilles, e.g.
40 ___ Major
43 Spouse's response
45 India's ___ Coast
47 Necessitate
49 Tried
51 Hit so as to make collapse / Win over
52 '60s protest / Skip, as a dance
53 From
54 Peter at the ivories
55 "It's either you ___"

by C. W. Stewart

56 Poverty
58 Marge's TV
daughter
59 What
Cain did
to 35-Across
60 Tired / Total

77

ACROSS

1 Base coat
7 "More than I need to know," in modern lingo
10 Turn over
14 U.S./Mexico border city
15 Games org.
16 Tiny bit
17 Is nuts for
18 Chart shape
19 Littlest sucker
20 Component of bronze
21 Pulitzer Prize entries
24 Big lug
25 Web-footed animal
26 Ride with runners
28 ___ Zion Church
29 Makes evolutionary changes
34 Brand of clothing or energy drink
36 Tickle
37 Stand that a speaker might take
39 Randomizing device
41 Burgers on the hoof
42 Meal on a blanket
43 Even chance
45 Old spy org.
46 Resistance units
49 Muhammad's pugilistic daughter
51 Some jazz
52 They may be served at the beach
58 ". . . ___ quit!"
59 ORD or LAX figs.
60 Above, to bards
61 Indian encountered by Columbus
63 When tripled, a 1970 war film
64 My ___, Vietnam
65 "___ Nacht" (German carol)
66 Boarding pass datum
67 Pro-___ (some tourneys)
68 Dissed verbally

DOWN

1 "___ Republic"
2 Michelin offering
3 Some ornamental barriers
4 Fruits de ___ (menu heading)
5 Scene of a fall
6 Sommelier's selection
7 One with the inside track at the track?
8 Like a towelette
9 Summer cooler
10 Singer Vikki
11 Place for a thimble
12 Ready to serve
13 Rescue crew, briefly
22 John's ode to Yoko
23 Make a father of
27 Spoils, with "on"
28 ___ Lingus
30 Prenatal test, for short
31 Party servers
32 Philosopher Lao-___
33 Sun. speech
35 Schoolmaster's rod
37 W.W. II transport: Abbr.
38 Arena where 37-Downs were used: Abbr.
39 Rope fiber
40 CD burners
42 Star in Ursa Minor
44 Radio no-no
47 It may need boosting
48 What 21- and 52-Across and 3- and 31-Down might be
50 Construction girder
52 Checks out thoroughly
53 Oklahoma tribe
54 Zhivago's love
55 Aspiring atty.'s exam
56 Bonny one
57 Mex. miss
62 Grafton's "___ for Alibi"

by Kelly Browder

ACROSS

1 Hits with bug spray
5 Jaguar, e.g.
8 With 61-Across, a possible title for this puzzle
13 It may be bright
14 Ex-politico with a Nobel and an Emmy
15 The Beatles produced it
16 New entrepreneur's need
17 Cadets' org.
18 English county on the North Sea
19 Home of the Sundance Film Festival
22 Dipstick coating
23 King, in Portugal
24 Debussy subject
25 Foofaraw
28 Corporate action that increases the par value of its stock
31 "And I ___ . . ."
33 Wordsmith's ref.
34 Sari-clad royal
35 Fencing move
36 Dickensian cry
37 Makes fun of, in a way
38 Right hand
39 Monk's title
40 Like gnats
41 Bone, for one
44 Grazed, e.g.
45 One of the Manning brothers
46 Noted convert to Islam in 1964
47 Semi part
50 1999 Melissa Joan Hart movie
53 Parting word
56 Poverty, pollution and such
57 Have ___ to one's head
58 Closet filler
59 Look out for?
60 "Quo Vadis" role
61 See 8-Across
62 Mosquito protection
63 Mushroomed

DOWN

1 Nada
2 First name in 1950s politics
3 ___ onion
4 Brought to ruin
5 Bug-building game
6 Pseudo-cultured
7 Shawnee chief at the Battle of Tippecanoe
8 Artists' boo-boos
9 Beanery fare
10 Favored bunch
11 "For shame!"
12 Cigarettes have it
14 Show sorrow
20 Minos's land
21 Ticked (off)
25 Word of woe
26 Awfully small
27 Porter's regretful "Miss"
28 Physician/synonymist
29 Gads about
30 Plain English
31 Library sign
32 Excessive, as force
35 Clark's crush on "Smallville"
36 From Sucre, say
37 Battlefield shout
39 "The Persistence of Memory" painter
40 Most likely to sunburn
42 Off-season offerings
43 Shake-spearean soliloquist
47 Hoops player
48 Like a clear sky
49 At this point
50 Animal on XING signs
51 Hamburg's river
52 Summoned, in a way
53 Subj. with unknowns
54 Go kaput
55 "___ pig's eye!"

by Susan Gelfand

79

ACROSS

1 Moccasin adornment
5 Faux pas
9 Took ___ (went swimming)
13&14 Nancy Lopez and Annika Sorenstam have each won this several times
16 Russo who co-starred in "The Thomas Crown Affair"
17 Literary lead role for Gregory Peck in 1956
18 Run ___ of
19 Clinched
20 Alphabet trio
21 Keyboard key
22 Boot feature
24 Singer Corinne Bailey ___
25 Bring into being
27 Intros

29 New York's ___ Institute (art school)
32 Straying
33 Brother-and-sister dancing duo
36 Out on the water
37 $C_7H_5N_3O_6$
38 Foolish chatter
41 Educ. course in which grammar and idioms are taught
42 Verified, in a way
44 Most merciless
46 Stereo component
49 Those against
50 Joins
52 *First row*
56 Online gasp
57 "You're the ___" (Cole Porter classic)
58 Popular ISP
59 Brazilian hot spot
60 ___ Beach, Fla.
62 Muscle connector
64 *Fourth row*
65 Paradise lost

66 Have a hankering
67 Suffix akin to -trix
68 Comedic star Martha
69 Many August babies
70 Guinea pigs, maybe

DOWN

1 Mont ___
2 Ancient Spartan magistrate
3 Wide open
4 *Fifth row*
5 Result of poor ventilation
6 Boost
7 Japanese butler in "Auntie Mame"
8 Mickey Mouse's puppy pal
9 Shipping magnate Onassis
10 Shrinks
11 Passionately
12 Support for the arts?
15 Act without the parents' blessings, say

21 "Don't go in there! It's ___!"
23 Always, poetically
26 Fitting
28 Lobby in a D.C. building?
30 ___ II razor
31 Neon ___
33 Gene Roddenberry-inspired sci-fi series
34 Metallic shade, in Sheffield
35 Knock out
37 Upsets
39 Disappoint-ments
40 Architect Saarinen
43 *Third or sixth row*
45 Suffix akin to -trix
47 Intersected
48 Like plain text
51 *Second row*
53 Classic Broadway musical with the song "Alice Blue Gown"

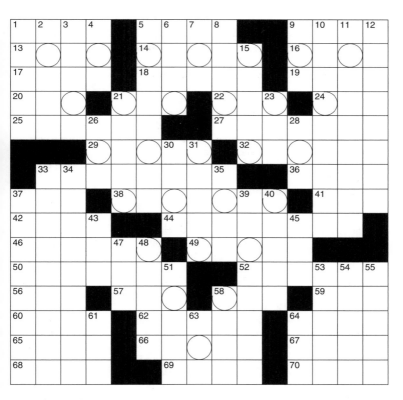

by Derek Bowman

54 Bigger
than big
55 Intersecting
points
58 Aviation-
related

61 *Seventh
row*
63 Edinburgh
refusal
64 Up on things,
daddy-o

80

ACROSS

1 Big name in oil
7 Easter flower, in Issur-Tille
10 Butterfly wings, e.g.
14 The fool in "A fool and his money are soon parted"
16 Tabula ___
17 Excuse given for asking for a ride
18 Humanoid trees in Tolkien
19 Ticks, say: Abbr.
20 Toddler's attire
21 Time for potty training, maybe
22 Rests
25 Chorus line opener
27 Handel cantata "___ e Leandro"
28 Promgoers, e.g.: Abbr.
29 Burning
32 Not shaky
34 Jagged
35 Clinks overseas
36 What's revealed by connecting the special squares in this puzzle in order
39 Start of the United Negro College Fund slogan
40 Kosher
41 ___ Szewinska, Olympic sprinting gold medalist of 1964, 1968 and 1976
42 Want from
43 Ab ___ (from the top)
46 Partisan leader?
47 Tube top
49 Daze
51 Nice kind of workweek
53 G.M., Ford and Chrysler
56 Setting for an Agatha Christie novel
57 Proctor's call
58 Advice for essay writers
61 Dickens creep
62 Eight producers?
63 Payroll dept. figs.
64 Wiring experts: Abbr.
65 Paris palace

DOWN

1 Middles that are often too big
2 Ingratiate
3 Has on hand
4 Intuit
5 When Canada celebrates Thanksgiving: Abbr.
6 Washington in the Songwriters Hall of Fame
7 Hawaiian strings?
8 You might get one before a party
9 Direct
10 Neck of the woods
11 Tony-winning "Frost/Nixon" actor
12 Constellation
13 Best Director of 1992 and 2004
15 Be an utter bore?
23 Beer from upstate New York
24 Like the symmetry of a starfish
26 Free of charge
30 Part of some chains: Abbr.
31 Walks unsteadily
33 ___ cloud (region of comets far beyond Pluto)
34 Celtic land
35 "Beauty and the Beat" band
36 P.D.Q. Bach's "Sanka Cantata" and such
37 Final words of Numbers 5:22
38 Albanian coin
41 How mini-pizzas are usually cut
42 Each
43 Sounds off

by Elizabeth C. Gorski

44 1958 #1 song with the lyric "Let's fly way up to the clouds"

45 Bully's warning

48 Old comic strip "___ an' Slats"

50 Concord

52 O.K.'s from the O.K. Corral?

54 Exits

55 School basics

59 Presidential nickname

60 Square dance partner

81

ACROSS

1 "A peculiar sort of a gal," in song
4 Muddy
8 Themed events
13 Actor Tognazzi of "La Cage aux Folles"
14 Seaside raptor
15 Allen Iverson's teammates till '06
16 Ingredient in some gum
18 Gossip
19 Request that often follows "Please"
20 Inceptions
21 Chow
22 Oscar Wilde or Bill Maher, for example
25 Some car roofs
27 Like some announcements that have been lost
28 Sister who's won the U.S. Open three times
30 Grafton's "___ for Innocent"
31 Curly shape
32 Starts of some games . . . and of the answers to 16-, 22-, 48- and 56-Across?
36 R.B.I. producer, sometimes: Abbr.
39 Holder of le trône
40 Minnesota college
44 "Hold on!"
47 Hot, after "on"
48 Like some passes
51 Mambo king Puente
52 Contravenes
53 They give you control
55 Fang
56 Cedar and hemlock
57 Lightly sprayed
58 Mathematician Post or Artin
59 Riddle-me-___
60 Foreign thoughts
61 Kind of column
62 New Left org.

DOWN

1 Hackneyed movie endings
2 Perturb
3 G.P.S. device, e.g.
4 Part of AARP: Abbr.
5 Small African antelope
6 "Back ___" (1974 Genesis song)
7 Family name of about 15% of Koreans
8 Big bomb
9 Runs out
10 Having a dividing wall, in biology
11 Locks
12 Map abbr. until 1991
15 TV Guide info
17 How many writers work
20 Buck ___, first black coach in Major League Baseball (Cubs, 1962)
23 Opening
24 Patriot's concerns, briefly
26 ___-Cat
29 What machmeters measure
33 Songs from rosy-cheeked singers, maybe
34 Moms and dads belong to it: Abbr.
35 Rather
36 Bad record, for short
37 Not a long-term solution
38 Certain plate
41 Overstays?
42 Not the same anymore
43 Gets ready to brush, maybe
45 This evening, on posters
46 Organic compounds with nitrogen

by Patrick McIntyre

49 Step heavily (on)
50 Start of a counting rhyme
54 Like Clark Kent's manner

55 Third year in the reign of Edward the Elder
56 Corp. honcho

82

ACROSS

1 Commercial name that literally means "to the skies"
5 Shouts while shaking pompoms
9 Break
13 "___ 18" (Leon Uris novel)
14 "Law & Order: S.V.U." actor
15 Insurance figure
16 Opposite of hinder
17 *Privilege
19 *No matter
21 Milch : German :: ___ : Italian
22 Common seal
25 Virgil described its "roar of frightful ruin"
28 New Deal org.
29 Use the answer to any of this puzzle's starred clues in ordinary conversation?
31 *And so forth
35 Lady of the Haus
36 *Ways things are said
40 All ___
41 *Sign to look elsewhere
42 Check out
43 Comedian Margaret
46 Some fund-raisers
47 One side in Mideast talks
50 Peak for Zeus, in Homer
54 *Stumbled upon
57 *As it's widely believed
60 Morales of "NYPD Blue"
61 Stocking caps, e.g.
62 Rock's Mötley ___
63 24-Down replacement
64 Ammonium particles, e.g.
65 Gets ready, with "up"
66 Rick with the 1976 #1 hit "Disco Duck"

DOWN

1 Modern letters
2 Scales seen at night
3 Ready
4 Age range for most first-year college students
5 TV host Kelly
6 One-hit wonder?
7 Range rovers
8 Hot
9 Much, slangily
10 News inits.
11 John
12 Cause of some skin burns
15 Conspirator against Caesar
18 Backpack fill
20 Really irk
23 "Vive ___!"
24 Coin with a laurel branch on the back
26 Modern: Ger.
27 Son of Prince Valiant
30 Kennedy's secretary of state
31 Individual and team event at the Olympics
32 Imaging lab output
33 Actor Feldman
34 Here, to Javier
35 Tournament favorite
37 Suffix with sex
38 Had
39 Juan's words of affection
43 Informal byes
44 Unlikely Oscar nominees
45 Without a break
48 Sales slips: Abbr.
49 New York hockey player
51 Put out
52 "The Wreck of the Mary ___"
53 Informal bye
55 Object under a magnifying glass, maybe
56 Some whiskeys

by Dan Naddor

83

ACROSS

1 Facility
5 ← What this is, on a calendar
8 Signals
12 Jiltee of myth
14 Yamaha offering, in brief
15 Perform acceptably
16 Profanities (and a hint to this puzzle's anomalies)
19 Peer group?
20 Razz
21 Liverpool-to-Portsmouth dir.
23 Buzzers
25 Some exchanges, quickly
28 Arrives
30 Mean mien
32 Scale range
33 Do what Jell-O does
34 Alley of Moo
35 Patient responses

36 Geisha's accessory
37 Like
38 Many "Star Wars" fighters
40 Blood, e.g.
42 Forward
43 Some people in a tree
44 Division of an office bldg.
45 Wasn't straight
46 Carry-___
47 Garden sights
49 Is behind
51 Record holders? (and a punny hint to this puzzle's anomalies)
58 Sluggish
59 Whistle blower
60 Former "American Idol" judge
61 "Man oh man!"
62 ___ admin (computer techie)
63 Hip

DOWN

1 Voltaic cell meas.
2 Abbr. in a help-wanted ad
3 E-mail address ending
4 Like H. P. Lovecraft among all popular writers?
5 Show types
6 Part of a 2005 SBC merger
7 Actress Mimieux of "Where the Boys Are"
8 Offering, as a price
9 12 or 15 min.
10 Rx abbr.
11 Peck parts: Abbr.
13 Iranian supreme leader ___ Khamenei
15 100 lbs.
17 Some musical notes
18 Football linemen: Abbr.

21 They may have niños and niñas
22 Exit
24 Royal son of the comics
26 Nuclear unit
27 Merchants
28 Stuff on a shelf
29 Kowtower
30 Squeals
31 Cans
33 Courtroom identification
36 Starts of some sporting events
39 Big chip off the old block?
40 Health supplement chain
41 Defended
43 Pergolas
45 Dance grp. at the Met
48 It goes over a plate
50 ___ leash
51 Horse and buggy
52 Official lang. of Barbados
53 Part of a violin

by Ashish Vengsarkar

54 Hardly macho

55 Actress Williams of the 1960s–'70s

56 ___ Lopez (chess opening)

57 On the ___

84

ACROSS

1 Show-off
4 Manx cries
9 U.S. Marine
14 "Wheel of Fortune" purchase
15 Leader of the pack
16 Like some flocks
17 Neurotic cartoon character
18 End of the line, e.g.
19 Auto debut of 1989
20 Bullet train type
22 Go for
24 Hosp. locations
25 Innards
27 Common sports injury site
28 Certain occupation
31 Milo's canine pal
32 See 4-Down
33 "Star Trek" empath
34 Animal control officer
36 Folded corner
37 Trail

38 1927–31 Ford
42 Alexander ___, Russian who popularized a chess opening
44 Hibernia
46 G.I.'s ID
47 Person who raises and sells pups
49 City containing a country
50 Big rig
53 "Get ___!"
54 Plotted for urban uses
55 Cans
56 Entertains
58 "Holy moly!"
59 20 places?
60 Cry that may accompany pounding
64 Using base 8
66 Steal
68 ___ Miss
69 One bit
70 One falling into good fortune
71 NBC-TV inits.
72 Old sailor
73 Animal in a lodge
74 Cutthroat

DOWN

1 Damage
2 Ready to serve
3 Kraft Foods drink
4 With "the" and 32-Across, describing an old Matryoshka doll
5 Hgts.
6 Antonym: Abbr.
7 Hit song from 2000 . . . and a hint to 10 symmetrically arranged Across answers
8 Mocking, in a way
9 Loser to Clinton
10 The 31st vis-à-vis the 1st, e.g.
11 She-foxes
12 Habituates
13 Inferior
21 Super Bowl of 2023
23 K2 locale
26 Mac, e.g.

27 Many a Kirkuk resident
28 Dance bit
29 "Dies ___"
30 Injury, in law
34 Lascaux paintings, e.g.
35 Long, long time
37 With 48-Down, for example, south of the border
39 Cornwallis's school
40 Pricey fabric
41 Yellowing, maybe
43 Parts of box scores: Abbr.
45 Sitcom with the character B.J.
48 See 37-Down
49 Shot up
50 Some Girl Scout cookies
51 First-and-second bet
52 A little nuts
54 Feature of a pleasant summer day

by Gary and Stephen Kennedy

57 "Two Treatises of Government" writer
59 Friend
61 It has two holes
62 Arms runner?
63 Stone, e.g.
65 PC key
67 Not delay

85

ACROSS

1 Recreating
7 Commercial prefix with vision
10 Election night figs.
14 Ships whose rudders don't touch water
16 Sounds heard in a bowl
17 35-Across of 57-Across that equals 12-Down
18 Medical suffix
19 Bobsled challenges
20 Aesthete
22 The Big East's Panthers, for short
23 They travel through tubes
24 Winter driving hazards
26 Start of a Hemingway title
28 Less affluent

29 French novelist Robert ___, upon whose work the 1973 thriller "The Day of the Dolphin" is based
31 Philosopher Zeno of ___
32 Signature piece?
35 See 17- and 57-Across
38 Nav. rank
39 Container for folding scissors
41 Something a chair may hold
42 Pie crust pattern
45 Rubber gaskets
49 Endocrinological prefix
50 Status follower
51 Tolkien villains
53 Destination of Saul when he had his conversion, in the Bible

55 Reader of someone else's diary, say
56 Sparkling wine source
57 35-Across of 17-Across that equals 12-Down
59 Mideast's Gulf of ___
60 Neither high nor low
61 Half-dome construction
62 Govt. ID
63 First arrival

DOWN

1 "Take ___ breath"
2 Swiss cheese
3 Cry just before a rabbit appears?
4 Dwells in the past?
5 So, so long
6 Feminine side
7 Extraordinary
8 Red-spotted ___
9 Singer of the Wagner aria "Liebestod"
10 Be a breadwinner

11 Detective's work record
12 Either 17- or 57-Across
13 Snake's warning
15 3.3 in a transcript, maybe
21 Lead from a mountain?
23 Brickmaking need
25 Women of Andalucía: Abbr.
27 Drs.' org.
28 With clammy hands, say
30 N.Y.C. airport
32 Gymnastics coach Károlyi
33 Possible title for this puzzle
34 Deep discounts
36 Britain's Royal ___ Club, for plane enthusiasts
37 1051, on a monument
40 Complete the I.R.S.'s Schedule A

by Elizabeth C. Gorski

43 ___ fog
44 Bob at the Olympics
46 Puzzled
47 Dig, with "on"
48 Servings at teas
50 Doyenne
52 Like L-O-N-D-O-N
54 100-lb. units
55 Bear's warning
56 Simile center
58 Flashed sign

86

ACROSS
1 Taps may be heard in them
6 Debra of "The Ten Commandments"
11 Joe Friday's employer, for short
15 "See you later, alligator"
16 National alternative
17 Bogotá bears
18 [I don't care]
19 TROT?
21 HATER?
23 Bursts of energy?
24 Gut reaction?
25 Westerns
27 Teensy
28 __ Harbour, Fla.
29 N.F.L. position: Abbr.
31 "Rough winds do shake the darling buds of __": Shak.
32 Love all, say
34 Broadcasting
36 RIFTS?
39 San Juan native, slangily
40 Cold shower?
41 Sioux Falls-to-St. Paul dir.
42 1040 ID
43 Tattoo, in slang
44 Mother, in British dialect
47 Z producer
50 Tallahassee sch.
51 Tent event
52 GATES?
56 HOSE?
57 Walks
58 World's largest particle physics lab
59 Two-time Banderas role
60 Stern, for one
61 Beliefs
62 Some blades
63 Attempt some Internet fraud

DOWN
1 Snack item whose name suggests a 42-Down?
2 Stick
3 Las Vegas attraction, with "The"
4 Serves, say
5 Army NCO
6 Cruisers
7 "Half __ is better . . ."
8 First senator in space
9 CPR experts
10 Lethargy
11 Lite
12 In unison
13 Many a White House artwork
14 Mil. honor
20 She, in Brasília
22 Clink preceder
26 Neighbor of Turk.
28 Cap'n's underling
29 Street __
30 Racket makers?
32 Colt fans, for short?
33 Augury
34 Stop on the Trans-Siberian Railway
35 Originally
36 Paint and shellac, for example
37 Power outage cause
38 Coffee mate?
39 Rapper MC __
42 Cold response?
44 Drink at Trader Vic's
45 Hello and goodbye
46 Good guy
48 Composer Camille Saint-__
49 U.S.D.A. part: Abbr.
50 Renaissance __
51 Store that's hard to find
53 Each
54 Truth alternative
55 "You're __, ya know that?": Archie Bunker
56 58-Across subj.

by Ashish Vengsarkar

87

ACROSS

1 Not stay fully upright
5 Flower in Chinese embroidery
10 Year the Chinese poet Li Po was born
14 People conquered by the Spanish
15 Fuse
16 10 to 1, e.g.
17 Cabinet dept.
18 Tangy teatime treats
20 Pittsburgh-born poet who was the subject of a Picasso portrait
22 Like some coincidences
23 Virgil hero
26 Surveillance device
28 Denture maker's need
30 Raw materials for shipbuilding
31 Spoil
33 Payola, e.g.
34 Famous quote by 20-Across

38 Spinners?
39 He wrote "Can one be a saint if God does not exist?"
40 Let fly
41 "Spring ahead" hrs.
42 Baked comfort food
47 "Likewise"
49 "___ will ever guess!"
50 Colorful decoration hinted at by 34-Across
55 Carrie Bradshaw had one in "Sex and the City"
57 Kind of poker
58 Mine, to Manet
59 "___ X" (2003 Lisa Kudrow film)
60 Province of Saudi Arabia
61 German cathedral city
62 That is
63 "America" pronoun

DOWN

1 Subjects studied by medieval scholars?
2 Seriously committed
3 Rush
4 Part of a war plan
5 Berg opera
6 Linear
7 It may be on your side
8 They're involved in some reported abductions
9 Twisted this clue's is
10 Sink accessories
11 Wife of Julius Caesar
12 Rib or short loin
13 "___ alive!"
19 Informal top
21 Subject of the 1999 best seller "Dutch"
24 Writer Bierce
25 157.5° from N
27 Gloomy
28 Attended

29 Smith of note
32 Inexpensive pens
33 Buffalo's Triple-A baseball team
34 Snow White's sister
35 "Don't play me for a dummy"
36 Get comfy
37 Was revolting
38 Wave function symbol in physics
41 Cabbage
43 Tails partner
44 Like Chopin
45 Embarrassing way to be caught
46 Character in "Piglet's Big Movie," 2003
48 Response to a stomach punch
51 Slightly
52 Money replaced by the euro

by Elizabeth C. Gorski

53 Mil. awards
54 "___ the jackpot!"
55 Bag, in brand names
56 Med. group

88

ACROSS

1 Formal club: Abbr.
6 Places to press the flesh?
10 Spirited cries
13 Some arts and crafts
16 Red remover, maybe
17 Bonuses
18 It's just a formality
19 "Follow me"
21 Motel extra
22 Diminutive endings
24 Apple pie companion?
25 States
27 Sp. title
29 Psychos
31 Leave in the dust, say
33 Long introduction?
34 English town near Windsor Bridge
37 General on a Chinese menu
38 Hinged pair of pictures
41 ___-Foy, Que.
42 Kind of blocker
44 Start of a Chinese game
45 Either of two emcees
47 Where "wikiwiki" means "to hurry"
49 "The Shelters of Stone" author
50 Clip
52 Anchorage-to-Fairbanks dir.
54 Signs on for another tour
57 Result of an emergency call, maybe
58 Get too big for
61 Prefix with -logy
62 Philemon, e.g.
64 Like the Trojan horse
66 Oil source
67 Starting instruction
68 What circles lack
69 Garden hose problems

DOWN

1 Craggy crest
2 "Tell me!"
3 ← Plastered
4 JFK : New York :: ___ : Chicago
5 ← Gambling game
6 RR building
7 ← Sherlock Holmes novel, with "The"
8 Heat
9 Methods: Abbr.
11 Part of a sob
12 Rarely read letters
13 Race before a race
14 20-vol. work
15 Wee hour
20 ← One starting a career, perhaps
23 Drop the ball
26 Migration formation?
28 Inner self
30 Record label of Bill Haley and His Comets
31 Gambling site: Abbr.
32 Milk
35 What buzzer beaters may lead to, briefly
36 What you keep
39 ___ Desert
40 ← Work period
43 Like some baseball teams
46 Tee follower
48 Penned
50 Archaeological find
51 Cabbie's line
53 Parts of a joule
55 Call that may result in an abrupt hang-up
56 Math figures
59 Diminutive ending
60 Crumb
63 Snake's warning
65 Cost-of-living meas.

by Bill Zais

89

ACROSS

1 Examines a passage
6 Low islands
10 Some Morgan Stanley announcements, for short
14 Maker of Gauntlet and Area 51
15 Cousin of a heckelphone
16 Oscar winner Sorvino
17 Hospital employee's role as an opera girl?
19 Lord, e.g.
20 Swear words?
21 Mattress brand
22 Tiramisu topper
23 Locales for some orators
25 Attorney general before Reno
26 What Starkist decided to do for "Charlie"?
31 Circles overhead?
34 Carbonium and others
35 Boom preceder
36 Grace period?
37 Hard-to-refute evidence in court
39 Boarding zones: Abbr.
40 Veto
41 Does some floor work
42 In turmoil
43 A girl, born 8:48 a.m., weighing 6 pounds 13 ounces, e.g.?
47 You might be safe with them
48 Came out
52 Trajectories
54 Where some dye for a living
56 Band from Japan
57 Hollow response
58 Where a Hungarian toy inventor vacations in the Caribbean?
60 McAn of footwear
61 Valuable deposits
62 Goof-off
63 Orphan of literature
64 1976 top 10 hit for Kiss
65 Talk radio's G. Gordon ___

DOWN

1 Indian royalty
2 Exercise performed on a bench
3 Singer Neville
4 Vets, e.g.: Abbr.
5 Shop-closing occasions
6 Not cultured
7 Slightly
8 His planet of exile is Dagobah
9 Last word of "America the Beautiful"
10 BMW, e.g.
11 Cobbler bottoms
12 Three-layer snack
13 Title sister played by Shirley MacLaine, 1970
18 ". . . bad as they ___"
22 Burmese and others
24 Not long from now
25 Most of the Ten Commandments, basically
27 A little stiff?
28 Furrow maker
29 Almost perfect?
30 Number two: Abbr.
31 Full house, e.g.
32 Gérard's girlfriend
33 Villain from DC
37 Pirouette points
38 Shower time: Abbr.
39 Train in a ring
41 Court stars, maybe, in brief
42 Knife, e.g.
44 Returnee's "hello!"
45 "Yum!"
46 Every which way
49 Creator of "Dick Tracy"
50 Fell back
51 Holder of secrets, often

by Patrick Blindauer

52 Black ___, archnemesis of Mickey Mouse

53 Sore

54 "You betcha!"

55 Support when one shouldn't

58 Take the wrong way?

59 Year Saint Innocent I became pope

90

Note: After finishing this puzzle, color the circled squares blue, and color all the Across answers containing an "R" red, to reveal an image related to the puzzle's theme.

ACROSS

1 Bikini blast
6 Car wash aid
9 Bugs
13 Track branch
17 Film character played by a full-blooded Cherokee
18 Ear: Prefix
19 Cry
20 Name, in a way
21 Ferrari competitor
22 Dorm V.I.P.'s
23 Suburb south of Paris
24 Give a star, say
25 Japanese dog
26 Trendy prefix
27 Cultural org.
28 iPod contents
29 Spruce
30 "Heads for the hills" locale?
33 It may be fired
34 Poker champ Ungar
35 Actress Mendes
36 Whence "Thine alabaster cities gleam" lyric
46 Baseballer with a "W" on his cap
47 Kilmer of "Batman Forever"
48 Mideast capital
49 1775 flag motto
56 Actress Moran and others
57 Stock
58 Lucy of "Kill Bill"
59 Drunk's woe, with "the"
60 Bikers may have them
61 Some RCA products
62 Take on
63 Knack
64 ___ area
65 The right point?
66 Kind of salad
67 "Holy smokes!"
68 Pupil, in Picardie
69 Three-point shot, in slang
70 ". . . ___ he said"
71 Chariot attachment?
72 Pony farm sign

DOWN

1 Hawk's home
2 Lined up the cross hairs
3 Name
4 Possible result of anxiety
5 ". . . ___ the least"
6 "Air Music" composer
7 Not free
8 Turn bad
9 "Forget it!"
10 Pinker, perhaps
11 Hawaiian tourist attraction
12 Hugger-mugger
13 Rugby scuffle
14 Softly
15 Total
16 "The Terminator" man Kyle ___
28 "___ so?!"
31 ___ León (Mexican state bordering Texas)
32 "Law & Order" spinoff, informally
37 U.N.-like
38 Wheels
39 Oil production site?
40 Operator's need
41 Stately thing in Browning's "Oh, to be in England . . ."
42 Like Bar-Ilan University
43 Blacked out
44 Rattle
45 Rodeo rings?
49 Bed cover
50 Jazz's Peterson
51 Sip
52 Delectable
53 Buenos ___
54 As a result of
55 Aromatic compound
56 Whom Bugs bugs
62 "The Wire" shower

by Alex Boisvert

91

ACROSS

1 Source of the line "Frailty, thy name is woman!"

7 Some believers

13 Poor thing about a slouch

14 Vacation destinations

16 Dressed for a white-tie affair

17 Order in the court

18 Some urban digs

19 Shooter on the playground

21 Old Al Capp strip "___ an' Slats"

22 He preceded Joan at Woodstock

23 Former org. protecting depositors

25 Water collector

26 Mens ___ (criminal intent)

27 One who is no longer entitled

29 Golf club part

30 Set off, in a big way

32 Bigger-than-life persona

34 & 35 One who has done the circled things, combined, more often than any other major-league player

36 Attempts to strike

39 Georgia birthplace of Erskine Caldwell

43 Want ad abbr.

44 Cheese dish

46 Hotel addition?

47 U.S.N. brass: Abbr.

49 Photographic flash gas

50 Latin wings

51 Lab tube

53 Action stopper

54 "Can ___ Witness" (Marvin Gaye hit)

55 ___ Sánchez, co-director of "The Blair Witch Project"

57 Turned a blind eye toward

59 Last of the French?

60 Lemonlike fruit

61 Spoke rudely to

62 Classic brand of liniment

DOWN

1 Mother, on the second Sunday in May

2 Whence Elaine, in Arthurian lore

3 Highest peak in the Philippines: Abbr.

4 Baseball All-Star Tiant

5 Goethe's "The ___-King"

6 Where to take an exam

7 Attract

8 Fish that may be caught in a cage

9 Puerto Rico, por ejemplo

10 Gathers on a surface, chemically

11 Reason for a medley, perhaps

12 Apostle called "the Zealot"

13 Enterprise-D captain

15 Permeated, with "into"

20 On the safe side

23 Political proposal from some conservatives

24 Fill, as with a crayon

27 Lend ___

28 Kind of button

31 Special ___

33 Breast enlargement material

35 Branch of technology

36 Like some spoonfuls

37 Salt add-ins

38 Japanese restaurant offering

39 Restaurant offering

40 Bank controller

41 Tidies

42 Rastafarian's do, for short

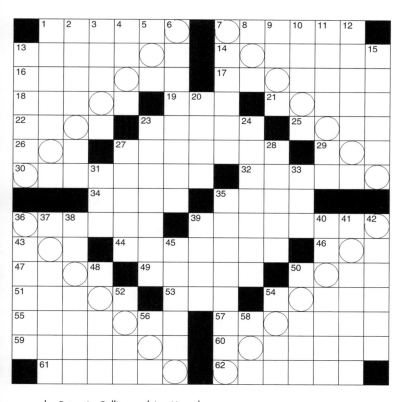

by Peter A. Collins and Joe Krozel

45 34 &
35-Across's
4,256 career
hits, e.g.

48 Penn and
others

50 Pythagoras'
square

52 Speaker
of the
diamond

54 Digging

56 Near
failure

58 Apt
name
for an
ichthyologist?

92

ACROSS

1 Not having big waves
5 Bandmaster from 1880 to 1931
10 The animals for Noah's Ark came in these
14 "Hard ___!" (captain's order)
15 Match
16 Stuck, after "in"
17 Something that's hard to close?
19 Relative of a hawk
20 Mirror
21 Editor's resource
23 Three times, in prescriptions
24 Nothing ___
26 George Knightley, to Emma Woodhouse
28 Prizes
30 Small amphibians
32 ___ Broad College of Business
33 What road hogs hog
34 City in Orange County, Calif.
35 Force felt on earth
36 Advice for the brokenhearted . . . or one of four arrangements found literally in this puzzle
39 Wedding rental
42 Like many a garden
43 Vintner Martini's associate
47 Mozart's "L'___ del Cairo"
48 It may start with "Starters"
49 Dweller on the Bay of Biscay
50 Fathers
52 Skin
54 Diggers' org.
55 Certain computer image format
57 Herbal beverage
59 Hungarian Communist leader ___ Kun
60 One in search of heretics
62 Go weak at the knees
63 Verges on
64 Split
65 Personal reserve funds, for short
66 Eliza Doolittle in "Pygmalion," e.g.
67 "___ Tu" (1974 hit)

DOWN

1 Financing
2 Tree-lined avenue
3 Houdini escape device
4 Where races are run
5 Browns
6 Giants of folklore
7 Ossuary, maybe
8 Samuel, e.g., in the Bible
9 Ford's first minivan
10 George of "Star Trek"
11 Set down
12 Shoe part that touches the floor
13 Marthe or Marie: Abbr.
18 "The Kingdom and the Power" author, 1969
22 Director Van Sant
25 Produce and present
27 Teamster's transport
29 ___ Park, N.Y.
31 Barn sackful
34 Blessing
35 Tribe met by Lewis and Clark
37 1960s Roger Moore TV series
38 Discount store offerings, for short
39 High pitch
40 Brew introduced in the 1990s
41 ___ Gorilla, 1960s cartoon title character
44 Sound before "That's all, folks!"
45 Gershwin's "___ to Watch Over Me"

by Gary Cee

46 Toward the center
48 '70s TV production co.
49 Cook, in a way, as beef
51 Les ___-Unis
53 "It's ___ bet!"
56 French tire
58 The Chieftains' home
59 Songwriters' grp.
61 African plant whose leaves are chewed as a stimulant

93

ACROSS

1 1970 hit for the Jackson 5
4 "Deal!"
10 What a loose thread might be
14 Friendly term of address
15 Río crosser
16 Nest egg protectors
17 Name of Lord Rubble's feudal estate?
19 Slurs, in music
20 English princess
21 Sender of monthly checks: Abbr.
22 Fix, as a pump
24 Present addition
26 Air in a sooty shaft?
28 Removed roughly
32 Big Apple sch.
33 Sly little dog?
35 One stuck in the can
40 Third in a Latin series
41 Carefully search
43 Short evening?

44 Charles ___, "Brideshead Revisited" protagonist
46 Celebration for a Disney dwarf?
48 "The Mikado" wardrobe item
50 Like words?
51 Bamboozle a "Fargo" director?
56 Do sum work
57 Picasso/Braque movement
58 ___ Lingus
61 Title heroine described in the first sentence of her novel as "handsome, clever and rich"
64 It's shrinking in Asia
65 Property claim along the Rio Grande?
68 Realty ad abbr.
69 Alchemic knowledge

70 Mungojerrie or Skimbleshanks, in a musical
71 Wet septet
72 Toadies
73 P.G.A. Tour Rookie of the Year after Singh

DOWN

1 "Money, Money, Money" band
2 Muffin composition, maybe
3 Hot dog coating at a county fair
4 Mirror
5 "___ and Dolls"
6 Judges
7 Pioneer computer
8 Beach time in Bordeaux
9 Offset, as expenses
10 Gorge
11 Choisy-___ (Paris suburb)
12 Pawnbroker, in slang
13 Ruhr industrial hub
18 Recent arrival

23 Month before Tishri
25 Convex cooker
27 Betters
28 Romanov ruler
29 "___ Own" (song from "Les Miz")
30 DHL competitor
31 Sysop, for one
34 Place to overnight in an R.V.
36 Unbeliever
37 Meadow voles
38 Major conclusion?
39 Roger of "Cheers"
42 Sch. that's about 150 mi. north of 32-Across
45 Enormous birds of myth
47 Sumac from Peru
49 City visited in "Around the World in 80 Days"
51 Union foes
52 White-cap wearer

by Patrick Blindauer

53 "The Audacity of Hope" author
54 Slumps
55 Pusher pursuers
59 Cheese choice
60 ___ Dubos, Pulitzer winner for "So Human an Animal"
62 Seder, e.g.
63 Creatures with tunnel vision?
66 Prospector's prize
67 Fled

94

ACROSS

1 Shindigs
8 Elf costume addons, maybe
15 Overwhelmingly
16 Property receiver
17 Vitamin A
18 Game with four jokers
19 Qty.
20 Like loot, often
22 Caste member
23 Spilled the beans
25 Abbr. often repeated redundantly
26 Detection device
28 Monterrey month
30 Big truck
33 Big truck
34 Asian goatlike animal
35 Official gemstone of Alaska
36 ___ school
37 See 21-Down

40 Latin lesson word
43 "___ Gold," 1992 album that has sold 28 million copies worldwide
44 Preceded, with "to"
48 Apple, e.g.
49 Set
50 Loy of old Hollywood
51 Weak ones
53 Self-esteem
56 End of many company names
57 Cork's home: Abbr.
58 Unchanged
62 Boxer's handler?
63 Made safe
65 Composer Antonio
67 Sequestering, legally speaking
68 Cowardly
69 Trudge
70 Foreign currency unit

DOWN

1 1979 World Series champs
2 Literally, "daughter of the wind"
3 Mojave Desert sight
4 Prefix on many chemical compound names
5 + and − items
6 Make a big scene?
7 Comic book sound
8 A pop
9 Wings, zoologically
10 Orange coats
11 Leaves with a caddy?
12 More cracked
13 Sweets, e.g.
14 Cruise, say
21 What all the answers on this puzzle's 37-Across are to each other
24 Weight training unit

27 Fish-eating raptors
29 "You ___ me!"
31 Head light?
32 Pick up
35 Be in sync
38 Not the most authoritative journalism source
39 Slippery ___
40 "The one-l lama," to Ogden Nash
41 Funeral attendee
42 Result of butting heads?
45 Intended to convey
46 Upset
47 More sallow
52 Word with club or mine
54 Fill the tank
55 Rial spender
59 Layers
60 Sharpness
61 Island in the Arcipelago Toscano
64 Weapon first designed in 1950
66 Destination of many filings, for short

by David J. Kahn

95

ACROSS
1 B-ball player
6 Like the Grand Canyon or Fourth of July fireworks
15 "Casablanca" co-star
16 Phobic sort
17 Prayer leaders
18 Rush job?
19 Broadway Joe
21 "American Pie" actress Tara
22 "Burma Looks Ahead" author
23 Head of steam?
24 Give ___ (care)
26 Picasso's muse Dora ___
27 De ___ (by right)
29 Jocund
31 Cigar distributor, perhaps
36 Fictional hero on a quest to Mount Doom

40 Gets past a last difficulty . . . or a hint to this puzzle's theme
42 Creepy
43 Unisex
44 "Show pity, ___ die": "The Taming of the Shrew"
46 Heading in a Keats volume
47 "Notch" on Orion's belt
50 Diaper, in Devon
53 Mandela's org.
56 Agcy. with agents
57 Stuff the piggy bank
58 Take, as an exam
61 Means of some W.W. I raids
64 Complete, quickly
65 Ousters
66 Crunching sound
67 Welcome January 1, say
68 1950s fad item

DOWN
1 New York City tour provider
2 Bodies of organisms
3 Suspended air travel?
4 Humorist Bombeck
5 Kick back
6 Hill denizen
7 ___ smile (grin)
8 Calculus pioneer
9 Teeing off
10 Sud's opposite
11 Where you may get steamed
12 "The Taming of the Shrew" setting
13 1986 Turner autobiography
14 Showtime, at NASA
20 Strings pulled in heaven?
25 The end
26 Some aromatic resins
27 Sonny
28 Milk dispenser

30 Prior to, poetically
31 Paid intro?
32 Beluga delicacy
33 Joint possession word
34 ___ Beta Kappa
35 Classical storyteller
37 Series opener
38 Part of many Dutch surnames
39 Hosp. areas
41 Buffalo Bill ___ Wild West Show
45 Bad way to be caught
47 Teeny dress measurement
48 ___ Fountain
49 Clinton's first defense secretary
51 Par ___
52 Pasta variety
53 Run ___ of
54 Bellini opera
55 Mysterious art visible from the sky

by Elizabeth C. Gorski

96

ACROSS

1 Discombobu-late
6 Reasons some games run long: Abbr.
9 You can get one on the house: Abbr.
13 Lines
15 *Final resting place for old autos?
17 Congo tributary
18 Cow or goat
19 Preceder of bravo in a radio alphabet
20 Showed joy, in a way
22 Canine command
23 Person on the left?: Abbr.
24 *Father of the Ziploc?
29 Extreme Atkins diet credo
32 "Ta-ta!"
33 Author Fallaci
35 Repel, with "off"

36 Pun-crimes committed by the answers to the six starred clues?
41 Like some primaries
42 Team esteem
43 Island attire
46 Like Gamal Abdel Nasser's movement
49 *Wide shoe specification?
51 Work, as a battle station
52 Wm. H. Taft was the only U.S. president born in this month
54 Show unease, maybe
56 ___-Pacific
57 Long key
61 Natural
63 *Recently opened sandwich shop?
64 It's white and fleecy
65 Parts of codes
66 Thataway
67 Crackers

DOWN

1 Pool shades
2 *Multiplyin' by 2?
3 Not heeding
4 ___ moth
5 REM researcher's tool
6 Food whose name comes from a language of West Africa
7 Big print maker
8 Interchange-able with, with "the"
9 Atlas abbr.
10 ___ degree
11 Rev
12 R.N.'s colleague
14 Home of the 2,700-mile-long Lena River
16 First secretary of homeland security
21 Mummify
23 It has feathers and flies
25 Original "Playboy"

26 Reddens, maybe
27 Tiptop
28 Bombs
30 Pinball machine, e.g.
31 Listen in (on)
34 Simple building
36 Outlay
37 On ___ with
38 Actress Gilpin of "Frasier"
39 Extremist
40 Personal flair
44 Like many checking accounts
45 With a silver tongue
47 Categorize
48 *Base of a fragrant tree?
50 Home of the Sawtooth Range
53 Violet variety
55 Sign of sheepishness
56 Start of a magic incantation
57 ___ Digital Short

by Greg Kaiser and Steven Ginzburg

58 Bit of
a stew
59 "How cute!"
60 Bank
offerings,
in brief
62 Penpoint

97

ACROSS

1 Starring role
5 Way to go
9 Certain sultan's subject
14 "There was a time . . ."
15 It's headed by a deputy asst. secy. of labor
16 They need their bearings
17 See 71-Across
20 Romance fiction or horror films, e.g.
21 Midcentury year
22 European tongue
23 Small change
25 Letters at sea
27 See 71-Across
35 Basic education, familiarly
36 House support?
37 Language that contains no adjectives

38 Redolence
41 Do colorful work
43 Coffee break time, maybe
44 Generic
46 "I'll take that as ___"
48 E.T.S. offering
49 See 71-Across
53 "Yes, ___!"
54 Alternative to "roll the dice"
55 Band lineup
59 Microwave
61 Available
65 See 71-Across
68 Drill
69 Def Leppard hit "Pour Some Sugar ___"
70 Approved
71 Shade that defines 17-, 27-, 49- and 65-Across
72 Title grp. in an ABC drama
73 Barbecue order

DOWN

1 High-priced ticket option
2 Great-great-great-grandfather of Methuselah
3 Electrical letters
4 Scrawl graffiti on, e.g.
5 Strength
6 Word with mountain or fly
7 Not us
8 Indigent
9 Klutz
10 Inspiration
11 Decor finish?
12 Us, abroad
13 Bikini, e.g.
18 Culminating point
19 Merlin of football and TV
24 Pointy-___
26 Rebounds, e.g.
27 Swiss capital
28 Documentarian Morris
29 Queen's attendant
30 Like some pyramids
31 "___ got you"
32 Having a bite

33 Almost 80 million people visit it yearly
34 Former Colorado governor Roy
39 Dallas hoopster, briefly
40 Where the Iowa Straw Poll is done
42 Goals
45 "My Fair Lady" lady
47 Fought against
50 One of Isabella I's kingdoms
51 "The Mod Squad" role
52 Mainstay
55 1970s–'80s singer Andy
56 Songwriter Novello
57 Urban sidewalk vendor's offering
58 Boatload
60 Pint-size
62 Golfer Isao ___
63 Financial writer Marshall

by Steve Dobis

64 Attorneys'
degs.
66 Coastal
flier
67 Great Brit.,
e.g., in years
past

98

ACROSS

1 Cry of anticipation
5 Low part
9 Synthetic fabric
14 Game with many balls
15 Carve
16 Cry of accomplishment
17 Revealed when seeking medical help?
20 1979 Fleetwood Mac hit
21 __ Barry, with the 1965 hit "1-2-3"
22 Density symbol
23 "I've had it!"
26 Wing
27 Trixie's mom, in the comics
28 Santa __
29 Instrument in the E Street Band
31 Focus of a hospital center
33 Water passages that don't turn?
37 Exhibitor of dorsiflexion
38 It's low for aces: Abbr.
39 Modern sales
42 One-named R&B singer makes her choice?
45 Locations of some secret meetings
47 Pink-slip
48 "Patience __ virtue"
49 "__ you one!"
50 Drunk
52 Accomplished in
55 Old Vietnamese strongman __ Dinh Diem
56 Slangy conjunction
57 A lot of a Maine forest
58 Continental salve?
64 __ ceremony
65 Ending with flat or spy
66 Prefix with -plasm
67 Staffers: Abbr.
68 "__ View" (1999 Broadway play)
69 Flat, for short

DOWN

1 Approvals
2 Schemer's utterance
3 Sean __ Lennon
4 Question that demands an explanation
5 Recuperation requirement
6 Boy lead-in
7 K.S.U., L.S.U. or M.S.U.
8 Bermuda memento, perhaps
9 Massachusetts town named for a river in England
10 Menace for Sinbad the sailor
11 HNO_2
12 God, in the Old Testament
13 Singer Julius who was famously fired on the air by Arthur Godfrey
18 Place for a headphone
19 American alternative
23 Zilch
24 "Come __!"
25 "Just you wait!"
26 Derive (from) . . . or a two-part hint for understanding 17-, 33-, 42- and 58-Across
27 Drink that may be vanilla-flavored
30 "Just __"
32 Cambodian currency
34 Advice for lovers whose parents disapprove
35 Copper
36 Tabula __
40 "__ deal!"
41 Future atty.'s hurdle
43 Newsstand offering
44 They're under hoods
45 Hollywood business
46 Reprobates
51 Conductor noted for wearing white turtlenecks

by Oliver Hill

99

ACROSS

1 Garland native to Minnesota
5 Not in the buff
9 With 46-Down, site of Cape Breton Island
13 English artist John who's buried at St. Paul's Cathedral
14 Potential sucker
15 The brother in "Am I my brother's keeper?"
16 Lawyers: Abbr.
17 Nickname for a dwarfish piano prodigy?
19 Sleeping cave denizen?
21 "First Blood" hero John
22 Musical sound before and after "da"
23 Comic Dunn and others
24 Bank
27 Collected
30 Adaptable truck, for short
31 Pickled pub quiz winner?
36 Musical Mitchell
38 Said with a sneer
39 Icicle site
40 Ships carrying a smelly gas?
43 Domingo, for one
44 Deli machine
45 One begins "By the rivers of Babylon, there we sat down"
47 Toast
49 Parenthesis, essentially
50 It may be organized
51 Comfy kids?
57 Pride of 12?
59 Bring (out)
60 Part of ABM
61 Move like molasses
62 Combative retort
63 ___ Verde National Park
64 1974 Sutherland/ Gould spoof
65 Contented sighs (and a homophonic hint to this puzzle's theme)

DOWN

1 Bruce Springsteen album "The Ghost of Tom ___"
2 ___ no good
3 Scatterbrain
4 Positive affirmation
5 Mobile home?
6 Counterpart of Apollo
7 Partially
8 Like 10-Down: Abbr.
9 Early Christian convert
10 Only president born in Hawaii
11 Shake, rattle and roll
12 High in the Sierra Madre?
17 "2001" studio
18 Maine university town
20 Unfeeling
23 Comparatively recent
24 1981 Stephen King novel
25 Complete
26 Ashcroft's predecessor
27 Like some waves
28 Online weekly, e.g.
29 Golf's ___ Cup
32 K. T. of country music
33 Early baby talk
34 Devilish
35 Chew (out)
37 People with this don't go out for very long
41 Actor Cary of "Twister"
42 Not at all stiff
46 See 9-Across
47 It can cure many things
48 Laugh-a-minute folks
49 Writer Rand
50 Chowder morsel
51 Prison, slangily

by Patrick Blindauer and Tony Orbach

52 Black Sabbath singer, to fans
53 Pieces of pizza?
54 Celestial bear
55 Bite
56 Pontiacs of old
58 How many it takes to tango in Spain?

100

ACROSS

1 Yeshiva student
4 Happy sound
9 Crazy excited
14 The Cavaliers of the N.C.A.A.
15 Railroad between Illinois and Atlantic avenues
16 Bag
17 Co-creator of Dungeons & Dragons
19 N.B.A. star point guard Kidd
20 Award since 1956
21 Holiday servings
22 Sly
25 Is off guard
28 Fish whose skin is sometimes used for leather
29 Spread selection
30 French auto race
33 Its gatherings are smart things to attend
35 Beginner: Var.
36 N.L. team, on scoreboards
38 Squeeze (out)
39 Trademarked brand of waterproof fabric
42 Grp. with the 1979 hit "Don't Bring Me Down"
43 Rx specification
44 Indigo dye source
45 "Revolutionary Road" novelist Richard
47 Palate-raising response
51 Scourge
52 Sawbuck
53 Snake's bioweapon
54 Splitsville parties
55 Walk, e.g.
57 Raw material?
59 Weird Al Yankovic's "___ on Jeopardy"
61 Vaudeville brother born Milton
66 Starbucks size
67 Eddie Murphy's role in "Coming to America"
68 Fotos

69 BP competitor
70 Ex-lax?
71 Cuff

DOWN

1 Water holder
2 Actress Mendes
3 Drug ___
4 Old N.Y.C. club said to be the birthplace of punk
5 Harvesting for fodder
6 Ready to roll
7 Vitamin abbr.
8 Chicken ___
9 Financial daily, in brief
10 More ridiculous
11 Levy at a BP or 69-Across station
12 Part of an old Royal Navy ration
13 Urges
18 Dingbats
22 Streaker seen at night
23 Pub container
24 Thirtysomethings
26 Femur neighbor
27 Lather
28 Sticker?

31 "Forgot About ___" (2000 Grammy-winning rap song)
32 Compound used in aviation fuel
34 "F Troop" corporal
37 Michelangelo sculpture on a biblical subject
40 Billy Martin, for the Yankees
41 Musical phrase
46 Crosswise to a ship's keel
48 Irritates
49 Minstrel show figures
50 Annual event that includes motocross
55 Say "Uncle!"
56 "I'll take 'The New York Times Crossword Puzzle' for $200, ___"
58 It may need a big jacket
60 Word before ear or horn
61 Bit of "hardware"
62 Hi-strung instrument?

by Brendan Emmett Quigley

63 Police radio message: Abbr.
64 "Road to ___" (1947 flick)
65 Turkey, to a bowler

101

ACROSS

1 What you might push a pushpin in
5 Dimwit, in Yiddish slang
10 International company with the slogan "Home away from home"
14 North African city captured by the Allies in 1942
15 In unison
16 1899 gold rush locale
17 A la ___ (nearby: Sp.)
18 David ___ George, British P.M., 1916–22
19 New growth
20 Start of a poem by Emily Dickinson that continues "But God be with the Clown, / Who ponders this tremendous scene"
23 Levels
24 Barker of the Cleveland Indians who pitched a perfect game in 1981
25 Increases
28 Refuge for David, in the Bible
32 Eur. monarchy
33 Poem, part 2
36 Christmas verse starter
38 Radio geek
39 Former Nebraska senator James
40 Poem, part 3
45 ". . . ___ he drove out of sight"
46 Chinese porcelain with a pale green glaze
47 Sleep disturbers
49 Sedona maker
50 Puts in a snug spot
52 Poem, part 4
58 Warren who founded a rental car company
59 Chew the scenery
60 Spray target
61 Pull-down list

62 Fix
63 It runs parallel to the radius
64 Teacher's before-class work
65 Volume unit
66 Overbrim (with)

DOWN

1 1977 best seller set at Boston Memorial Hospital
2 ___ contraceptive
3 Queen of Bollywood
4 Funnyman Don
5 Shipping mainstay of the 1600s
6 Physician William
7 Appears imminent
8 Singer with the 2008 gold record "And Winter Came . . ."
9 Acts the yenta
10 Double ___
11 The worst of times
12 "Lucky Jim" novelist, 1954

13 Relay division
21 South American monkey
22 ___ tide
25 Monkeyshine
26 Divine water
27 Say with two syllables where one would do, say
28 Promotional item
29 Philly hoopster
30 Extremely large, old-style
31 1985 Meg Tilly title role
34 In the past
35 Is afflicted by
37 Reorganizes drastically
41 Figure in the Edda
42 They have no ties
43 Rain forest implement
44 Sommer of Hollywood
48 Try to see
50 Antique dealer's happy discovery
51 Articulate
52 Anytime
53 Melon's site
54 Drop
55 Fallow

by Edward Safran

56 "___ But the Brave" (1965 Sinatra film)
57 Elderly relative, informally
58 Crank (up)

102

ACROSS

1 Two drinks, for some
6 Reserved to a greater degree
11 1099-___ (tax form sent by a bank)
14 Japanese mushroom
15 Holmes of "Batman Begins"
16 Conjunction that usually has a partner
17 Eco-friendly in Las Vegas?
19 Rapping "Dr."
20 Tai chi instructor
21 Kind of account not used much anymore
23 Food glaze
25 Down Under springers
26 Omaha's waterfront during downpours?
32 Tax-free transaction, usually
33 Position on the Enterprise: Abbr.
34 Reception vessel
35 Cause ___
37 Actress Milano and namesakes
41 Charles I, II, III . . . or X
42 Had something
43 The Bobcats of the Mid-American Conference
44 First-place finishers in Bangor?
48 Planted
49 Feature of an essential oil
50 "Oh yes, I love that dress," maybe
53 Team in College Station, Tex.
58 ___ Thorpe, 2000 and 2004 Olympic swimming sensation
59 Jogging atop Great Falls?
61 Neatnik's opposite
62 Environs for Galatea, in myth
63 Banks in Chicago

64 Places with defibrillators, for short
65 Move along a buffet line, perhaps
66 They're found on staffs

DOWN

1 Stamina
2 Preceder of a case name
3 Plumbing fixture manufacturer
4 General store on "The Waltons"
5 Musician's weakness
6 Biathlon need
7 Milliners' securers
8 Home of Odysseus
9 ___, zwei, drei
10 Guns
11 Like fireworks, infrequently
12 "We can't squeeze any more in"
13 Some migrations
18 Woody vine with violet blossoms
22 Charles of "Death Wish"

24 Yearn (for)
26 Foreign policy advisory grp.
27 ___-necked
28 Shadow, so to speak
29 Having an effect
30 Ottoman sultan known as "the Magnificent"
31 Taste
36 Gift-wrapping aid
37 Part of Lawrence Welk's intro
38 "___ Hates Me," 2002 hit by Puddle of Mudd
39 Melody
40 Pad name
42 Kind of gland
44 High-luster fabric
45 "Dallas" kinfolk
46 Sprinkled
47 Unpleasant reminder?
48 Credit card action
51 Asteroid on which a NASA probe landed in 2001

by Laura Sternberg

103

ACROSS

1 Result of some oil deposits
5 X
11 Drain
14 Certain cable, informally
15 Provincial capital in NW Spain
16 Pres. initials
17 Classic Cadillacs
19 Cry when seeing something for the first time
20 Positive aspects
21 Total
23 Hard fats
24 Ones making snap decisions?
25 Passed quickly
27 Item of sports equipment approximately 43" long
28 The Sun Devils, for short
30 "Mr." whose first name is Quincy
31 Chili accompaniment, often
35 Slip
36 Bygone flier, for short
39 Street sign . . . or a hint to this puzzle's theme
40 ___-eyed
41 "Por ___ Cabeza" (tango song)
42 Incendiary
44 Like humans and ostriches
46 Ohio governor Strickland
47 One-eyed god of myth
51 Fruit waste
52 Paris's Rue ___ Croix de la Bretonnerie: Abbr.
54 ___-Roman
55 Cold and damp
57 Mountain climbing hazard
59 Doo-wop syllable
60 Batman, with "The"
62 Essential
63 Earthen pots for liquids
64 Big name in '50s TV
65 Fingers
66 Naughty
67 Scraps

DOWN

1 Point a finger at, say
2 Confine
3 Sartre novel, with "La"
4 Hastens
5 Quiet fishing spot
6 Company started in 1946 at the Detroit and Miami airports
7 Scratch
8 Red carpet walker
9 Shangri-las
10 Out the window
11 Like a saber
12 North Carolina county seat
13 Educ. group
18 Mad workers, for short
22 1992 top 10 hit "Life ___ Highway"
24 Companion of Panza
26 Knight time?
28 Tiger or Twin, briefly
29 Censors have them: Abbr.
30 E-mails: Abbr.
32 "Be ___!"
33 Last digit in a price, often
34 British author Bagnold
36 Benchwarmers
37 Sang
38 Features of many Olympic broadcasts
43 British fighter plane
45 G.P.'s grp.
48 More like a doornail?
49 Superlatively slippery
50 Frank who wrote "The Pit," 1903
52 Ingratiating behavior
53 Prepared, as a report
54 Dogfaces
56 Turn-of-the-century year in King John's reign
57 ___ chic
58 "That's enough out of you!"
59 What people who head for the hills do?
61 Popular TV drama set in Las Vegas

by David Chapus

104

ACROSS

1 Great Bear Lake locale
7 Blacken
13 Basic pool exercise
14 Lover of Aida
15 Word of warning
16 Potent pitcherfuls
17 Out of action
19 Cold weather wear
22 ___-majesté
23 3-D camera maker
27 Coconut yield?
28 Suckling site
29 Sensitive
30 Put out
32 Rocket first tested in 1957
33 With 16-Down, annual March event
36 Title woman in a Jim Carrey movie
37 Gracious introduction?
39 Schlep
40 Ridged material
42 Certain domino number
43 "What ___?"
44 Learn a lot quickly
45 Fishing tool
46 Big job for a driller
49 It may be revealed by a tree
52 Bingeing
56 Jim Palmer and teammates
57 Fall away
58 Squinted (at)
59 Childish answer

DOWN

1 Ear part
2 Hydrocarbon suffix
3 Unheard of
4 Setting for much of the 33-Across 16-Down
5 "Beavis and Butt-head" spinoff
6 Made like
7 Tony- and Emmy-winning actress Blythe
8 Beat by a point or two
9 What the Athabaskan word for the beginning of 33-Across means
10 Friend of 24-Down
11 Start of an apology
12 Cousin of -enne
14 Cultivate
16 See 33-Across
18 Like some statesmen
19 Representation of a budget, often
20 Fleet person
21 Circulation concern
24 "The School for Wives" playwright
25 Part of the Uzbekistan border
26 Choice marks?
28 Actress Hagen
31 Got down
32 Dull finish?
34 Sermon subject
35 It may provide one's sole support
36 Knock off
38 Six-Day War participant: Abbr.
40 Picked up a point or two
41 Some lithographs
45 More moderate
47 Eye
48 Bayes who sang and co-wrote "Shine On, Harvest Moon"
49 Jump off the page
50 "___ I let fall the windows of mine eyes": Shak.
51 Bite the dust
53 A.F.C. East player
54 Bother
55 ___ Metro (bygone car)

by David J. Kahn

105

ACROSS

1 Toastmaster's offering
5 Worked regularly at
10 Home of Ensenada, informally
14 "The ___ of Frankenstein" (Peter Cushing film)
15 Poet Federico García ___
16 Acct. ___
17 Delft, e.g.
18 "Conversation is ___ in which a man has all mankind for his competitors": Ralph Waldo Emerson
19 "Hard ___!" (captain's order)
20 Residence
23 Some music on the Warped Tour
24 "___ see!"
25 It has to be asked
34 Troubled
35 Like Petruchio's wench in "The Taming of the Shrew"
36 Middle year of Nero's reign
37 Santa's reindeer, e.g.
38 Common origami figures
39 Ask for
40 ___ de coeur
41 Clean, in a way
42 Consumer electronics giant
43 Alumni weekend V.I.P.
46 1961 Top 10 hit "Hello Mary ___"
47 Texans' grp.
48 Many Haydn compositions
56 It comes from Mars
57 Casts
58 Firm honcho
60 Centers of activity
61 Finnish architect Alvar ___
62 Ambiance
63 Something in the air
64 Words repeated after "O Absalom" in the Bible
65 Occurrence in the moon's first quarter

DOWN

1 Wandering
2 Eyeglass lens shape
3 ___ Davis, "A Girl Like Me" documentarian
4 Matinee showing time, maybe
5 Have in mind
6 Pants spec
7 Modern home of the ancient Akkadian empire
8 It's similar to cream
9 Records for computer processing
10 "Vamoose!"
11 Part of a wheelset
12 Raspberry
13 Reno's AAA baseball team
21 "You're looking at your guy!"
22 Upbeat
25 Bake sale display
26 "In ___" (1993 #1 album)
27 Adjust, as a satellite dish
28 Twilight, old-style
29 Somewhat
30 Old hwy. from Detroit to Seattle
31 "The L Word" creator/producer Chaiken
32 False sunflower
33 Coolpix camera maker
38 Closed carriage with the driver outside in front
39 Its home is on the range
41 Capital subj.
42 Carpet meas.
44 Alchemist's concoction
45 She played Mrs. Miniver in "Mrs. Miniver"

by Brendan Emmett Quigley

106

ACROSS

1 One of the Untouchables
5 Disney's "___ and the Detectives"
9 "That's great . . . not!"
14 Ryan of "Star Trek: Voyager"
15 Film character who says "Named must your fear be before banish it you can"
16 It's good for Juan
17 School ___
18 What might have the heading "Collectibles" or "Toys & Hobbies"?
20 Words with innocence or consent
22 Confused responses
23 Optimistic scan at the dentist's?
26 Not recorded
30 Boomer's kid
31 Org. in the Bourne series
32 Conjured up
34 Story of Ali Baba?
37 Many truckers
40 One may be caught in it
41 Sycophant
42 Transmits a message to Pancho and pals?
45 Pressing
46 Naut. heading
47 Letters on some churches
50 Scrabble 10-pointers
51 Amazes a horror film director?
55 Bond villain in "Moonraker"
56 Starters and more
57 Old street cry, or what's in 18-, 23-, 34-, 42- and 51-Across?
63 Bone meaning "elbow" in Latin
64 "Sorry, I did it"
65 A seeming eternity
66 Sale caveat
67 Conductor noted for wearing turtlenecks
68 Unfortunate date ending
69 Dickens's Mr. Pecksniff

DOWN

1 Marshalls competitor
2 Thin, overseas
3 Amount of debt, old-style
4 "I Am Spock" autobiographer
5 Socket filler
6 Kind of scene
7 Home of the City of Rocks National Reserve
8 Easy two points
9 They have bows
10 Ancient pillager
11 President Bartlet on "The West Wing"
12 "Wedding Album" recording artist
13 "That hurt!"
19 Prop on "The Price Is Right"
21 Pay strict attention to
24 Center of holiday decorations
25 Speak in Spanish
26 Racecar adornments
27 Furniture chain
28 Deal in
29 Swirl
33 Nay sayers
34 Essays
35 Second part of a three-part command
36 Dortmund denials
37 "Volver" actress, 2006
38 Not decent
39 Advantage
43 Unsettling look
44 Health supplement store
47 Tear off forcefully
48 Be serious
49 Long hyphen
52 Becomes fuller

by Kevin G. Der

107

ACROSS

1 "Slumdog Millionaire" locale
5 Find fault
9 Old auto control
14 Move to solid food
15 Scene of classic flooding
16 The Four Seasons, e.g.
17 Influential work by 28-Across, familiarly
20 Bygone leader with a goatee
21 Bit
22 Health __
23 Dastard
26 Where to see 20th Century Fox studios
28 Notable born 2/12/1809
33 Grp. founded in Jerusalem
34 Part of a knave's loot, in a rhyme
35 1970s Big Apple mayor
36 Sony brand
38 Cheese and crackers, maybe
41 Some
42 Great Lakes fish
44 Tills, in a way
46 Excess
47 Notable born 2/12/1809
51 Role played by 52-Across in "The Story of Mankind"
52 See 51-Across
53 Signs off on
56 Lake Thun's river
58 Absinthe flavor
61 47-Across led it
65 What almost always goes for a buck?
66 2004 Brad Pitt film
67 Tinware art
68 Tour stops
69 End of a phonetic alphabet
70 Genesis grandson

DOWN

1 Object of a hunt, maybe
2 "Runaway Bride" co-star, 1999
3 Drought easer
4 Chest pain
5 Atlanta's __ Center
6 "A Rainy Night in __" (1946 hit)
7 European sports car, informally
8 Rouse
9 Beaker site, for short
10 Ad __
11 Bluesman Rush
12 Not go bad
13 Old-time gossip queen Maxwell
18 Like neon
19 Place for a lily
24 "__ the day!" (Shakespearean exclamation)
25 "Can't Help Lovin' Dat Man" composer
27 Quarter
28 Scale
29 "60 Minutes" correspondent starting in 1991
30 Kitchen appliance
31 "Er . . . uh . . ."
32 Slender amphibian
33 "Qué __?"
37 Singer Jackson with more than 20 #1 country hits
39 Stamp purchase
40 Numbers game
43 Kindergarten learning
45 Go at it
48 Salty inland __ Sea
49 St. __, Switzerland
50 Flowery
53 Christmas tree ornaments, typically
54 R&B singer Hilson
55 Descry

by Gary and Stephen Kennedy

57 Literally, "raw"
59 1944 battle site
60 Checks out
62 "___ Saison en Enfer"
63 Comcast alternative
64 Home of the Stern School of Business: Abbr.

108

ACROSS

1 Rallying cry supported by some monks
10 When Antony says "I am dying, Egypt, dying"
15 Company with a maple leaf logo
16 Part of a college cheer
17 2004 horror film about a passed-on curse
18 Major processing center
19 Memorable 1968 movie villain
20 Geophysics topic
21 Chaffed
22 Book of Mormon book
24 Chilled
26 A year abroad
28 Jazz-loving TV sleuth of the 1950s–'60s
29 Second indicator?
30 He sighted and named Natal on Christmas Day of 1497
32 Airport waiter?
34 Wish unmade
35 Cans
37 Hawthorne novel stigma
39 Recruiting org.
42 Recruiting org.
44 Literally, "already seen"
48 Words teachers like to hear
50 Princess Fiona's voicer in "Shrek"
52 Pops
53 A bug may cause it
56 All of them may be off
57 Leaves out
58 That's a wrap
60 Hunting req.
61 Lethal compound
62 Congenial
64 High-tech subscription aid
65 Construction with many locks
66 Brand for hobbyists
67 Where "all the people that come and go stop and say hello"

DOWN

1 Dolt
2 One-named Grammy winner of 2007
3 By and by
4 Beat recorder: Abbr.
5 Napoleon's cousin
6 Kayak propeller
7 Rebuke to Bowser
8 Barely best
9 Inventor's inits.
10 Superior title?
11 One with staying power?
12 Right in every detail
13 Two-time president of Romania
14 Facial feature with a point
21 Under a whammy
23 Bottom
25 Wood blemish
27 Kaffiyeh-clad commander
31 Some poles
33 10/15, e.g.
36 The cooler
38 Do __ on
39 Transmission blocker?
40 Title syllables in a hit 1964 song
41 Swiftly done?
43 Shoulder inflammation?
45 Legendary soprano __ Patti
46 Swiss Guards' setting
47 Destroyer in 2000 headlines
49 Happily humiliating type
51 Get close, maybe

by David Quarfoot

109

ACROSS

1 Feature of Psalm 119
9 People work for them
14 "How rude!"
15 Call on the carpet
16 1997 Jim Carrey film
17 Cuban-born jazz great Sandoval
18 Isolated
19 Tracked vehicle
20 City where French kings were crowned
21 Spur-of-the-moment
23 Virus's need
24 Swimmer's sound
25 Onetime popular musician . . . or a radio station where he might be heard?
26 "Ella and ___!" (1963 jazz album)
27 Suffix with absorb
28 Sweet loaf
30 Separate
31 Lowdown
32 First athlete to appear on the cover of Time magazine
36 Amigo
39 Ungentle giants
40 As bad luck would have it
41 Blubber
42 Caspian Sea feeder
43 Hitch
44 It may get you out of a trap
45 Excise via an operation
47 Switch hitter?
49 Coffee-mate producer
50 It's unbelievable
51 Went on a dinner date, e.g.
52 Shows the ropes
53 TV producer Michaels
54 Least accessible

DOWN

1 Loose
2 Poet Pablo Neruda, for one
3 Dreamer's opposite
4 It's designed for quick entrances
5 Plugs
6 Chad Mitchell ___ (1960s folk band)
7 Director of "Meatballs" and "Stripes"
8 Post boxes' contents
9 Premonish
10 Zither with buttons
11 What insulin regulates the metabolism of
12 "1984" superstate dominated by Neo-Bolshevism
13 Like pinto beans
15 Jumble
22 Goes from first to third, say
25 Pottery
26 Rap devotee, in slang
28 Some retinal cells
29 Disappointing R.S.V.P.'s
30 One hanging around med school?
32 Personal writings
33 Accept, as conditions
34 More boorish
35 Part of a caterer's display
36 One who's on the other side?
37 Entertains
38 Most accessible
41 Attacked
43 Unmake changes
44 "Consider it done"
46 Mystery novel element
48 Chemical used to cure animal skins

1	2	3	4	5	6	7	8			9	10	11	12	13
14									15					
16									17					
18									19					
20						21		22			23			
24					25					26				
27				28					29					
			30				31							
32	33	34				35						36	37	38
39					40						41			
42				43					44					
45			46			47		48						
49						50								
51						52								
53						54								

by Patrick Berry

110

ACROSS

1 Alternative to newspaper classifieds
11 Loses intensity
15 Constitution precursor
16 Short
17 Curaçao ingredient
18 Top status
19 Member of the Julio-Claudian dynasty
20 "Stillmatic" rapper
21 Stuff
23 19th Amendment champion
25 Editor's job, often
26 Dessert, in Dover
29 Time before TV
30 Had a spirited session?
31 Rate
32 "Les ___"
33 E.U. mem. since 1995
34 Like the scriptures on which Hare Krishna is based
35 Thing caught near the shore
36 Sch. in the New England Football Conference
37 School area with mice
38 A light may be set on one
39 Restaurant staffers
41 They're reflective
42 Groups
43 "The Human Stain" novelist
44 Storied shrine
45 Something to shoot for
46 Bodice fastener
50 Lumber
51 A bout to remember?
54 Golden Triangle land
55 Have some humble pie
56 Possible result of pulling the plug
57 "The Wrecking Crew" actress, 1969

DOWN

1 "Don't be shy!"
2 Like some gases
3 Food stabilizer
4 Papal name last used in 1724
5 Shut up
6 Dogs often pick them up
7 Splash gently against
8 Burns up
9 Ursule, e.g.: Abbr.
10 Like yeshiva studies
11 Her 1965 Met debut was as Cio-Cio-San in "Madama Butterfly"
12 Play for which Peggy Cass won a Tony in 1957
13 Largest tributary of the Colorado
14 Night watchmen?
22 In a row
24 Major ancient construction project
25 Native Trinidadian
26 It goes up and down at dinner
27 Picnic staple
28 "Mmm!"
29 ". . . thy cheeks look ___ Titan's face": Shak.
31 Unites
34 Maxell products
35 It has things you want
37 Ponderosa pal
38 Subject of a 1976–79 Met exhibit
40 Like the smell of fresh pine
41 Puerto Rican-born Oscar winner of 1961
43 Trimming aid
45 Bun alternative
47 Muslim honorific
48 Many people do it online

by Barry C. Silk

49 Couch extension?
52 Motivation exclamation
53 Setting for sedges

111

ACROSS
1 "The loneliest guy in town"
16 "Hold on"
17 Handles things evenhandedly
18 Important part for a jig
19 Cracker shapes
20 Substitute acquired by about half a million people a year: Abbr.
21 Representative
23 Scale start
24 ___ Fein
25 "The Bridge on the River Kwai" setting
26 City where Einstein developed his special theory of relativity
27 Vinegar: Prefix
28 More fashionable
30 Sudden light seen through the clouds
32 Catch-22

34 1970s–'80s sitcom setting
35 Using high-flown language
39 "Mother of the believers"
43 "Bonne ___!" (French cry on January 1)
44 Undershirt, in Britain
46 "You're putting ___!"
47 Office stamp
48 "Say ___" (1940 Glenn Miller hit)
49 Ones in control of their faculties?
50 "___ Girl Like You Loved a Boy Like Me"
51 Mount from which people can see far away
53 Company that makes Styrofoam
54 Viking stories, e.g.

57 Took flak for something one said, say
58 Bedazzlement

DOWN
1 Maximum, slangily
2 For whose benefit "the quality of mercy is not strain'd" in Shakespeare
3 Capital of Armenia
4 1979 nuclear accident site: Abbr.
5 Hunky-dory
6 Some raiders, informally
7 Lodge
8 Charms
9 Businessman-entertainer who was once mayor of Bridgeport, Conn.
10 "Behold ___ Horse" (William Cooper book)
11 Targets of remedies

12 Stephen of "Stuck," 2007
13 More itchy, maybe
14 Balloonists' doings
15 Is unobliged to
22 Missing
24 "Beg pardon," in casual talk
26 Bric-a-___
27 Well
29 Iroquoian language
31 All lined up
33 Fair place
35 Cut rinds, e.g.
36 30.48 centimeters
37 Something once bundled with Microsoft products
38 Basutoland, today
40 Navy service
41 Center of a roast
42 "Jeopardy!" fodder
45 Dinah's avenger in the Bible

by Manny Nosowsky

112

ACROSS

1 "___ better be!"
6 Factory staple
9 Abbr. in a "works cited" list
13 "I'm not done yet!"
16 It's passed on
17 Oscar-nominated portrayer of Frida Kahlo
18 Discipline
19 Financial statement abbr.
20 Reason to make a prank call, maybe
21 What a player may mean by knocking on the table
22 Relatively close
26 Subject of the 1955 film "The Last Command"
28 Baby shower gift
29 Band members with long necks?

31 Many students on "Gilmore Girls"
32 It's 11 miles NNW of J.F.K.
35 Something not on the menu
37 Roll top?
39 Certain correlative
40 Really appeal to
42 Early TV news commentator famous for doing Timex ads
43 Heads up
45 Makes scarce
46 Where a fouled player might go
50 Crystallizes
51 Passage blockers
52 Stars participate in it: Abbr.
55 Pendant option
56 Comics character with a "gang"
59 Not be a nobody

60 Passage enabler
61 Not natural
62 Bond
63 City in 1917 headlines

DOWN

1 Minute, informally
2 "Not ___!"
3 Wasn't full of holes
4 The Adriatic vis-à-vis the Mediterranean
5 Red-handed
6 Helen Thomas in the White House press corps, e.g.
7 Boiling point?
8 Cry of surprise
9 March on
10 It contains 613 mitzvot
11 ". . . love's shadows ___ rich in joy!": Romeo
12 ___ of all
14 Onetime C.I.A.-backed foreign leader
15 Plumber seen in an arcade
21 Mayo sauce?

23 Computer debut of 1998
24 They might store electric charges
25 Nike rival
26 Part of M.P.A.A.: Abbr.
27 Slimming option, for short
30 Fast Eddie's girlfriend in "The Hustler"
32 It might store an electric charge
33 It's often piercing
34 Vultures were sacred to him
36 Refuge
38 Cardinal
41 Like many beachgoers
43 Single-___
44 Become rapturous
46 Product of glacial erosion
47 Square things
48 Make rapturous
49 Independent, noble types, it's said

by Mike Nothnagel

113

ACROSS

1 It doesn't exist
12 Find fault with
14 A soldier's gear, for example
16 Bloomer after whom bloomers are named
17 Raison ___
18 Rent to another
19 Toy from China
23 "Young ___ Boone" (short-lived 1970s TV series)
24 You might grind it out
25 Fast hits
27 With 5-Down, snooping aid
28 Discussed at length
29 Musical direction that means "lyrical" in Italian
30 Actor who debuted in "Kung Fu: The Movie"
32 Snooping aid
35 Activities at punk rock concerts
36 "Gotta run!"
37 High bark
38 End ___
39 Foolish, in British slang
40 Fruit salad ingredient
42 Folk singer Tom with a Grammy Lifetime Achievement Award
43 It gets you up and around
48 Words from one who won't settle
49 People in a line

DOWN

1 Whim-wham
2 It might contain a filling
3 Diagonally set spar
4 Bone involved in pronation
5 See 27-Across
6 Move quickly
7 Spike's former name
8 Ring contents, maybe
9 Bibliog. equivalent of "ditto"
10 Calamitous decline
11 French painter Courbet
12 Arise
13 Pulitzer-winning historian Frederick Jackson ___
14 Outfits
15 Fish that can move equally well forward and backward
19 Team whose home arena is the Palace of Auburn Hills
20 Better
21 Company with a tree in its logo
22 Fluid dynamics phenomena
25 Convertible carriage
26 It's assumed
28 Bit of assistance
29 Local or regional Boy Scout gathering
30 Nullifies, as an oath?
31 Made a comeback
32 Medieval conquerors
33 Maximally
34 Max of video game fame
35 "___ by Sinatra" (1982 collaborative jazz album)
36 Reaganomics recommendation
39 One addressed as "lord"
41 Parliamentary faction
42 ⅙ of an inch
44 Ad ___ (at the place: Abbr.)
45 Good name for a trial lawyer
46 Ingredient in Delftware glazing
47 "What next?"

by Patrick Berry

114

ACROSS
1 Reasonable treatment
10 Striking ends
15 63-Across?
16 Moon of Uranus
17 Having a lot to lose?
18 CD player part
19 Supply for driving
20 Most night owls
22 Pietà figure, literarily
23 Turned up
24 With 54-Down, approach with a line
27 Tawny
29 Factory
31 Kind of door or window
33 Draft sources
35 Have yet to settle
36 Highway caution
39 Rich or famous: Abbr.
40 Particular
41 Michael of the G.O.P.

42 Word accompanying finger-pointing
44 People of the Platte, once
46 Lump in cloth
47 "If I Had ___" (Lyle Lovett song)
49 Symbol of innocence and purity
51 Lucy and Ricky Ricardo's residence, e.g.
53 Eschewer of convention, in slang
57 One way to be taken
58 Comment from the beat
60 Big maker of communications satellites
61 One singing in the kitchen
62 Artist with the 1999 6× platinum album "2001"
63 Opposite of avant-garde

DOWN
1 It's not fancy
2 Tropical flower
3 Hungarian writer Madách
4 62-Across offerings
5 Big D campus
6 Berry with juicy parts?
7 Chilling, so to speak
8 Honorary title bestowed on Bill Clinton, Muhammad Ali and Mae West
9 "Manhattan Mary V" artist
10 Woman on a 2008 ticket
11 Takes back one's words?
12 He said "A people that values its privileges above its principles soon loses both"
13 Bum

14 Pentax Spotmatic and Nikon F2, for short
21 Sketches (out)
22 Some Cherokees
24 Site of Robert E. Lee's last victory
25 Means of getting some answers
26 Shooting star, briefly?
28 Opposite of FF
30 Rose with a hit record
31 180 is its max. score
32 Does a nursery job
34 Put aside
37 Emeritus: Abbr.
38 Modern, to Beethoven
43 Crash site sight
45 "Hoffman" co-star Cusack
48 ___-high
50 Amaryllis family members
51 Completely smooth

by Doug Peterson and Barry C. Silk

52 Outfielder Francona

53 Some like it hot

54 See 24-Across

55 Solar or lunar phenomenon

56 2009 G.M. spinoff

59 Part of the fourth qtr.

115

ACROSS

1 Fiscal exec
4 Form check box option
7 & 9 Missouri city whose name means "broken heart"
11 Composition of some old crowns
13 1941 #1 hit for Tommy Dorsey
15 They're irregular
17 The Monkeemobile, e.g.
18 Former British mandate
19 Greeting with a salute
20 Puts (on) thickly
21 Mainstay
23 W.W. II factory wear
24 Bring back on board
25 Bill word
26 Frequently exhibiting, by nature
28 Block
30 Like some relations
33 It may not have been intended
34 Connect
35 Chemical ending
36 Radio figure who co-wrote "Two Guys Four Corners"
38 Like bellwethers
39 Records
40 Floria ___, Puccini title role
42 Intl. trade letters
43 Bar
44 Story-filled magazine since 1922
47 Flowing forth
48 Argentine port on the Paraná
49 Strikes
50 Housekeeper player on "Benson"

DOWN

1 Torturous, perhaps
2 Dig up
3 Rubber
4 Compound fractions: Abbr.
5 Old bus maker
6 They may avert computer damage
7 Intriguing bands
8 High
9 Side opposite 30-Down
10 Fix, as a shower stall
11 Pool regimen
12 Kindle
13 Fawning type
14 Print maker
16 Connections
19 It has departments named Nord, Sud and Ouest
21 A house divided?
22 "All done!"
24 Beaus
26 Checks
27 What some maps show
28 Stuck at a roast
29 "C'mon, at least consider it!"
30 Side opposite 9-Down
31 The merchant of Venice
32 Seizes, as an opportunity
37 Happening spot
39 ___ Games (quadrennial event)
41 See 45-Down
43 Forum infinitive
45 With 41-Down, quaint sandlot game
46 Broadcast

by Joe Krozel

116

ACROSS

1 "In one era and out the other" phenomenon?
9 Pianist Jarrett and others
15 Basis of Tony Martin's "There's No Tomorrow"
16 Decline
17 Cutter, e.g.
18 Smoke and mirrors
19 Show of affection
20 Subject of therapy
22 First name among U.N. secretaries-general
23 One who has a quick point to make?
24 Where Duff Beer is sold, on TV
25 Outfielder Guillén
26 Off course, in a way
29 Hornswoggles
30 Office bldg. division
33 Hot stuff
34 Half a 1980s TV duo
35 One might stand in a chamber of horrors
37 Calligraphy, some say
39 "Joy to the World" penner Hoyt ___
40 Army of the Potomac commander
42 They may get waived: Abbr.
43 What you may experience when going around the world?
44 Muhammad Ali cornerman Dundee
46 "The Unanswered Question" composer, 1908
47 Alternative to Genuine Draft
48 ___ Québécois (political party)
52 Beat it

53 Its logo is four interlocking rings
54 Historical figure on whom a Verdi opera is based
56 Cheerios, abroad
58 Certain fricassee
60 Rub the wrong way
61 Hollandaise, e.g.
62 Tree dwellers
63 Like duck soup

DOWN

1 Opera singer in an opera
2 Half brother of Midian, in the Bible
3 Waves on garments
4 Queen who wrote popular novels
5 ABC, Fox, etc., in Variety
6 Half a 1950s TV duo
7 Coastal feature

8 Hogwarts class taught by Severus Snape
9 Target competitor
10 Apollonius of Rhodes' "Argonautica," e.g.
11 First woman to land a triple axel in a major competition
12 An exorbitant amount
13 Grassy bottom
14 Things to get a grip on?
21 21, maybe
24 Girl with considerable pull?
25 Dump without warning
27 "___ for You" (1975 Temptations album)
28 Campaign setting
29 City where Erasmus taught
30 Its flag includes a shield and two spears

by Kevin G. Der

31 One cooking a return

32 Arm or leg

36 Tries to get

38 Lines that lift up

41 Decoy

45 Not sharp

47 Meter-candles

49 Octavian's wife

50 Gallimaufries

51 Sharp

53 Holiday tune title starter

54 Shade close to beryl

55 Like Magic?

57 Flight projection, briefly

59 "___! What fray was here?": Romeo

117

ACROSS

1 What a 17-Across might get assistance with
5 Lower Slobbovia creator
9 Bygone magistrates
14 Was perpetually dishonest
16 Calendar listing
17 One calling about a tower, maybe
18 1998 Grammy winner for narrating his book "Still Me"
19 To the extreme
20 Ellen of "Ocean's Thirteen"
21 Fine, in a sense
22 Made a claim
23 Nickelodeon title character
24 Formal discussion
26 "All the world's a stage" monologue setting
29 Cattle drivers
30 Grp. of major supporters?
31 Give up for a while
32 Like drag shows
33 Resist
34 Recalling org.
35 Be indifferent
36 Make even brighter, say
37 Softens
39 Dog holder
40 Kangaroo carrier?
41 Rumble
45 More vaporous
46 Cry of reproof
47 Concentration problem
48 Occasions that begin with misses?
49 Knitwear material
50 Walled-off enclave in Iraq
51 Tool parts for bending and shaping
52 Make sound
53 Franklin in Phila., e.g.

DOWN

1 Beat
2 Tropical climber
3 Check from a deck?
4 Like some steel
5 New Jersey city that was home to Walt Whitman
6 Winner of three Pulitzer Prizes for Drama
7 Quiches, e.g.
8 Minute or hour lead-in
9 Thwarts
10 Exaggerate
11 Techies affiliated with a major electronics chain
12 Way to watch someone win the lottery?
13 Antique gun
15 Pierce the ears of
20 Guy who needs no 24-Down
22 Ivory-covered?
24 Dopp kit items
25 It can hold a team together
26 Romeo might go after it
27 Military parade site
28 Bit of forensic evidence
29 Mountain passes
32 It usually has a band around it
33 Libya's second-largest city
35 Sheet materials
36 Arrests
38 People often sing in it
39 Forbidden
41 Bridge guru
42 Family car, informally
43 Famous last words
44 Back to zero, say

by Lynn Lempel

45 Lay an
egg
46 It's taken
for a ride
48 Letters
associated
with a lion

118

ACROSS

1 South-of-the-border sign-off
12 Consumption meas.
15 "Babette's Feast" author, 1950
16 Cause an interception, e.g.
17 Carry on
18 Where the wild things are?
19 Round number, maybe: Abbr.
20 Piddling
21 Market surpluses
23 Cassette components
25 Speaks about gravely?
28 "Miss Pym Disposes" mystery novelist
29 Husband of a sorceress, in myth
30 Calendar unit
31 Big name in radio
33 They may go forward or backward
35 Present day demand?
38 Origin
39 Reached the age of
41 See 56-Across
42 Horse-pulled vehicle
43 Sigourney's role in "Alien"
45 Mil. authority
48 Actor who said "Only the gentle are ever really strong"
50 Get around
52 Direct deposits, e.g.
53 Earthy deposit
55 Fed. agency with an annual almanac
56 With 41-Across, it makes short hops
57 1950 movie on which the musical "Applause" is based
61 Verdi's "___ giardin del bello"
62 Setting of many New Yorker cartoons
63 Jacksonville-to-Daytona Beach dir.
64 Something to pass in

DOWN

1 Engaging sort
2 How dishes are often sold
3 South Carolina river to the Atlantic
4 Conductor's request: Abbr.
5 ___ apple
6 Elevator locale
7 Two-time Greek P.M. Papandreou
8 Mythical Aegean Sea dweller
9 Civil-rights leader ___ Philip Randolph
10 Home of the Black Rock Desert: Abbr.
11 Lay ___
12 Jewish parchment scrolls put on doorposts
13 She has a personal trainer
14 Least refined
22 Contents of a cylindrical case
24 What "you can't hide" per a 1975 Eagles hit
26 L.A.P.D. division?
27 Out, in a way
29 Stuck (out)
32 Morning or night lead-in
34 Dumas's "La Dame ___ Camélias"
35 They may be patched
36 Crimes on the high seas
37 Saint of acting
40 Shout to someone in danger of getting stuck
41 Sound
44 Strange woman player in "The Strange Woman," 1946
46 2001–06 secretary of transportation
47 Motivated
49 Straighten (up)
50 Not-always-taken tokens
51 1995 Bon Jovi album "___ Days"
54 Artist Lichtenstein and others
58 Big Apple ave.
59 Provider of PC support
60 "Qué ___?" (José's "How's it going?")

by David Levinson Wilk

119

ACROSS

1 Served well
5 Without ___ (religiously)
9 It has a facility with animals: Abbr.
14 Nice figure
16 Truffula Tree defender, with "the"
17 Red carpet events
18 Playwright Pirandello
19 One of Darrow's clients
20 Enters via osmosis
22 Hunting companion, maybe
23 Uninteresting voice
24 Main ingredients in hasenpfeffer
25 "Don't give up!"
26 Manufacturer of boxy cars
27 Friend of Harry and Ron
28 Isolated PC key
29 Unilateral decision-makers
30 Excellent, slangily
33 Frequent subject on "Desperate Housewives"
35 Empty bottles
36 Like some jewel cases
37 Bygone players
38 Wasted
39 "Char-r-rge!"
40 Head set?
41 Lousy driver, say
42 Imaginary surface coinciding with the earth's sea level
43 Alopecia sufferer's purchase
46 "Donnie ___" (2001 cult film)
47 Like gazebos, often
48 Pitching staff?
49 Communism battler, with "the"
50 Miss

DOWN

1 Deadly desert denizen
2 They come with belts
3 Potential blackout cause
4 Puts in a bad position?
5 Less reserved
6 Show of superiority
7 Winter coat
8 Central concept of minimalism
9 Quick movements
10 "Come and get it!"
11 1894 adventure novel, with "The"
12 Putting away
13 Giving a pink slip
15 Singer's gift, colloquially
21 Body
22 Mule, e.g.
23 Midgard ___ (monster of Norse myth)
25 Top dog
27 Author of "Something Happened," 1974
29 Bad-mouthed
31 Things getting a lot of buzz about them?
32 Portrayer of TV's Ricky
34 Find objectionable
35 Early phonograph cylinder covering
36 Musical O'Connor
37 Swordsmen's grips
38 One of the Gabor sisters
39 Very well done
41 Conks out
44 Caricature
45 Certain investments, for short

by Patrick Berry

120

ACROSS

1 Important church
8 Like controversial issues
15 Bob Marley classic
16 It lets you see who's calling
17 Something to prove
18 Fictional psychiatrist
19 "___ sow't with nettle-seed": Shak.
20 Gang members
22 Year in Nero's reign
23 Psychoana-lyst Fromm
25 From, in some European names
26 It may be worn on a sneaker
28 Phnom Penh cash
29 Like many an omen
31 Works in the Uffizi
32 Poorhouse bedding

35 Termini
36 Totally benign
42 It's often pinched
43 Act rudely, in a way
44 Foul
45 Street magician ___ Angel
47 Character lineup
48 Proceed (from)
49 Regional setting for almost eight months per yr.
50 It may begin with an exordium
53 Got into a pickle?
54 1912 headline name
56 Got high gradually
58 Like Victor Hugo when he finished "Les Misérables"
59 Pole position or pool position

60 Some like them hot
61 Registered for

DOWN

1 They deliver
2 Be a willing participant?
3 Requiring more support
4 Brief warning
5 What an unrequited lover carries
6 Loving leader?
7 30-Down thoroughly
8 Billy the Kid used one for his nickname
9 Jane Rochester's maiden name
10 Half of a Disney duo, with "the"
11 They often mean "I see"
12 Slaves
13 Up
14 Pooh-poohs
21 One between two cardi-nals?
24 Red choices

27 Part of a backwoods mix-up
29 Lets off
30 See 7-Down
33 Not sanguine
34 ___ Reiss Merin, babysitter player in "Don't Tell Mom the Babysitter's Dead"
36 Like some monks
37 Subway rider during rush hour, metaphori-cally
38 Striking brilliance
39 Post, for one
40 Make a B instead of an A?
41 Like some profanity
46 "Peter and the Wolf" duck
48 Regarding
51 Moon marking
52 North African harbor site

by Martin Ashwood-Smith

55 Bad ___, Mich. (seat of Huron County)

57 Peruvian capital?

121

ACROSS

1 Place holder?
6 "Lost" category
15 Online message
16 Equal, essentially
17 G neighbor
18 Introducer of 45's in '49
19 Memorable
21 What busy people are on
22 Ice cream mix-in
23 Like some opinions
25 "In the Heights" Tony winner ___-Manuel Miranda
26 Middle of the British Isles?
27 Congregational
31 Long while
33 Allied landing site of September 1943
35 Derby dry-goods dealer

36 "Everybody Loves Raymond" Emmy winner Patricia
37 Gets in sync
39 Kennel clamor
40 Action figure?
41 Charcoal wood sources
43 Backwoods pro?
44 Some are blank
45 Oracular
46 Jet
50 Producers of some bold words
52 Charlton Heston's "The Prince and the Pauper" role
54 Columnist Molly
55 Homeostatic
56 Flat piece of paper?
57 From this moment on
58 Where some sunflowers were painted

DOWN

1 Pops
2 Beneath
3 Sir Francis Drake discovery of 1579
4 Ethnic prefix
5 Head of Notre Dame
6 Series kickoff
7 Way up
8 They let people off
9 Torah's beginning?
10 Singer of the #1 country hit "Foolish Pride"
11 Prepare a plate, perhaps
12 With 20-Down, kiddie-lit counterpart of Sherlock Holmes
13 Cause of a bad air day?
14 Finnish pentathlete Lehtonen
20 See 12-Down
24 Cousin of a stickleback

26 Columnist who wrote "Don't Call It Frisco," 1953
27 One that's stalked
28 Like 16-Across
29 From a particular perspective
30 Meetings of delegates
32 Poker variety?
34 Some July arrivals
38 Roof work
39 Comparatively maudlin
42 Picnic cooler
44 Parisian pen
45 Not stick to one's guns
46 Ayatollah, e.g.
47 State-founding Friend
48 "Walk ___" (1964 hit)
49 The Ilek is one of its tributaries
51 Adidas alternative
53 It'll help you make your move

1	2	3	4	5		6	7	8	9	10	11	12	13	14
15						16								
17						18								
19					20					21				
22					23			24						
25				26						27	28	29	30
31		32					33		34				
35								36					
37					38		39						
40				41		42					43		
			44						45				
46	47	48	49			50			51				
52				53				54					
55								56					
57								58					

by Randolph Ross

122

ACROSS
1. Magazine since 1850
8. Enlightens
15. Accepted PayPal payments, e.g.
16. Cry upon reaching an impasse
17. Verne's Fogg
18. Lens-grinding Dutch philosopher
19. Bill sharer
20. Stay up nights, say
21. Acad. goal
22. Within
23. Scandalmonger's love
24. Goal-oriented superstar?
25. Ravel's "Boléro" calls for one
28. Such that one might
30. Assets
32. It may be striking
33. "Not in my experience"
37. Celestial neighbor of Scorpius
38. Private

39. Crack, e.g.
41. "Wait'll you see this!"
45. Its sports teams are called the Phoenix
46. Accolade for a great play
48. Hubbard of science fiction
49. "I didn't need to know all that!," informally
50. Whipped up
51. Real low life?
53. Frequent flier's credit
55. It's heard before many a face-off
56. Sluggard's problem
57. Makes warmer, maybe, as boots
58. Selling point for some lights
59. It might improve your focus

DOWN
1. Old swing digger
2. In familiar territory
3. ___ bread
4. Its teeth were actually a chimpanzee's
5. Home of Parmenides
6. Can
7. Port Huron Statement grp.
8. Music producer: Abbr.
9. Apartment restriction
10. E-mail disclaimer
11. Consistently defeat, in slang
12. It was NE of Bechuanaland
13. Literally, "good luck"
14. Initial part
20. Cardinal that looks the same when viewed upside down
23. Ocean, in Mongolian
24. Of fraternities and sororities collectively

26. Change the price on
27. World's first carrier with a transpolar route
29. "Under Two Flags" novelist, 1867
31. Precipitate
33. Blow-by-blow
34. Where pit stops are made to get fuel?
35. Bedroom furniture
36. Provider or wearer of some hand-me-downs
40. Stand-in for unnamed others
42. It has a twin city in the Midwest
43. Construction machine
44. Distress
47. "___ Cassio!": Othello
50. Paw
51. ___-deucy
52. Like some electrical plugs

by Manny Nosowsky

54 Questionnaire
check
box option

55 100ths
of a krona

123

ACROSS

1 Tower that's typically scaled from the outside
5 Confederate general Early
10 Concern for a checker
14 Confident assertion
15 Harmoniously
16 Cap material?
17 Fun application
20 Before making the cut?
21 Subterranean lines
22 Bare-bones
25 "Ubu Imperator" artist, 1923
26 Boom producer
27 Beach houses, often
31 "Tip-Toe Thru' the Tulips With Me" instrument
32 Pot cover
33 Playback problem
34 Argue (with)

37 Ann of "Rebel Without a Cause"
38 Some dolls
39 Get together (with)
40 The annus in Dryden's "Annus Mirabilis"
42 Response to an e-mailed joke, maybe
43 Giggles
44 Dwindle
47 Stuffy, as air
49 Barely boiling
51 Captain Marvel, to Billy Batson
55 Hit the big leagues
56 Means of secret writing . . . or a description of a 17-Across?
59 Supermodel Sastre
60 Soon to experience
61 Lake bordering four states
62 Three-___

63 Nobles and knights in the Middle Ages, e.g.
64 Start to do well?

DOWN

1 Be content with where one is
2 Annual river thaw
3 Like the worst of excuses
4 High, in a way
5 It holds the mayo
6 ___ Patriot Act (2001 measure)
7 Wimbledon champ, 1976–80
8 "Dragonwyck" author Seton
9 Do-overs
10 Canopus or Polaris
11 Protesting the pro-testers?
12 Kind of cap with a tail
13 Some ballroom dances

18 ___ citato
19 C.I.A. betrayer arrested in 1994
23 Computer instructions heading
24 Secure, in a way
28 Image on a dime
29 Garden shrub
30 Largish animals with black ear tufts
32 Go for it
33 Biathlon need
34 Party dishful
35 Stripped-down story
36 Hopelessly confuddled
41 Winning move?
43 Maryland player, informally
44 Result of many conquests, perhaps
45 Late comedian Mac
46 Stock figure

by Xan Vongsathorn

124

ACROSS

1 Military trials?
10 "From hell's heart I stab at thee; for hate's sake I spit my last breath at thee" speaker
12 Order given before shooting starts
14 Six-footer, maybe
15 ___ toy (pet shop purchase)
16 Magic show reactions
18 Glimmer
19 Allowed
22 Steamed pudding ingredient
23 Creator of the "Microsoft sound" played when Windows 95 starts
24 More inclined
25 Mediterranean port since ancient times
26 Lantz of the 1960s–'70s N.B.A.
27 Coastal features
28 Go to the limit
29 Fruit for a tart
31 Egg maker
32 Untimely cry?
33 Superficial
34 Small bird
35 Get a hand on the road?
36 Brilliant display
37 Naval chart abbr.
38 Settle in
39 Used butter on, maybe
40 Inc., abroad
41 Some proctors, for short
42 Comment from the chattering class?
43 Early TV host Garroway
44 Science class decoration
49 Landmark in Elvis Presley's "It Happened at the World's Fair"
50 Common mica

DOWN

1 Chum, e.g.
2 "Behold, the heavens do ___": Shak.
3 Giant on the cover of Time magazine, 1945
4 "That was Zen, this is ___" (bumper sticker)
5 They're duck soup
6 Pollen bearer in a flower
7 "Real Time" host
8 "They almost got me!"
9 Lander at Arlanda
10 Advice in a bear market, maybe
11 The higher this goes, the more it blows
12 Abrupt change
13 TV drama featuring Dr. Richard Kimble
14 Visionary
17 Magnolia or pecan
19 Class that's not just for kicks
20 Give a piece of one's mind?
21 Steals, e.g.
22 ___-Weimar-Eisenach (duchy until W.W. I)
25 Drew a cross response?
28 It comes in ears
30 In reverie
31 Linen fiber
33 Hard to miss
36 Cremora brand
39 Perennials with cup-shaped flowers
42 Color
43 Some baseball hits: Abbr.
45 Upstate N.Y. school

by John Farmer

46 Old Walt Disney production
47 "___ With Mussolini" (Zeffirelli film)
48 Some spreads

125

ACROSS

1 Take the wheels out from under?
8 Arms on shoulders
15 Opposite of depression
16 Object of many an appraisal
17 Like wingdings
18 Win
19 Add (up)
20 Nombre after six
22 Way to repay
23 They may create a buzz
25 Hidebound
27 Stumper?
28 They're not exactly user-friendly
30 Completely dominate
31 50-Across sight
32 Venezuela is in it
34 Claims
37 Block
40 Polar bears, e.g.
41 Subject of plays by Sophocles, Sartre and O'Neill
42 Turnoff
43 Indication of longing
44 Poule's partner
46 The appendix extends from it
50 Hydrospace
51 Arrangement
54 Mounted
55 Catch
57 Donald of the Major League Baseball Players Association
59 "___ in Love" ("Kismet" song)
60 Guy making passes
62 Picks up
64 Stand against a wall, perhaps
65 One who's registered for work?
66 Doesn't take well
67 Presses

DOWN

1 Unisex wear
2 Small hollow in a surface, in biology
3 Diamond information
4 Protuberate
5 Just like that
6 Relents
7 Government marked by rampant greed and corruption
8 It may contain the whole world
9 Strip of gear
10 Expressionless
11 What a spiked drink has
12 Army outfit
13 Gridiron boo-boo
14 Like ferns
21 Request after breaking down
24 Assail scathingly
26 Biochemical arrangement
29 Stick in the fire
31 Tumble and toss about
33 "Most miserable hour that ___ time saw": Lady Capulet
35 Imperator's law
36 Flock member
37 Big name in steelmaking
38 Put off
39 Meets near the shore?
45 Reaction to a slug
47 Sibling, often
48 Predecessor of Web forums
49 Quaint letter opener: Abbr.
51 Afflicted (with)
52 Left on board
53 Bad thing to get from your boss
56 Be uncontrolled
58 Precipitate
61 Image specification, for short
63 However briefly?

by Joon Pahk

126

ACROSS

1 Now out . . . or "it"
7 Its flag features an image of a stone-carved bird
15 Weightlifting set
16 Like a relatively minor fire
17 Like olde shoppes
18 Running
19 Kings Peak's range
20 Jambalayas
21 Inconclusive result
22 "Regrettably . . ."
23 ___-Car
24 1984 perfect game pitcher Mike
25 Rapper ___-A-Che
26 Texas county named for a Civil War general, with its seat in Longview
27 Millionaire's plaything
28 Carrier of very destructive cargo
30 Cooking vessel
31 One may be held in court
32 Pair of elephants?
36 Aviator's concern: Abbr.
37 "L.A. Law" Golden Globe winner
38 Reducer of pier pressure?
41 U.R.L. opener indicating an additional layer of encryption
42 45, e.g.: Abbr.
43 Mineralogist's sample set
44 Toadlike
45 Vault
46 "Nightly she sings on ___ pomegranate-tree": Juliet
47 Phenomena associated with some dwarfs
48 Way up state?
49 Succeed somehow
51 Studio occupant, say
52 The Anteaters of the Big West Conf.
53 What wisdom outweighs, according to Sophocles
54 Not too long ago
55 Too punctilious

DOWN

1 Drafting aids
2 Hooked, as a nose
3 Residents of dry, open country in South America
4 Ways to go
5 European smoker
6 Reason to do a 2 a.m. shift
7 Alfred Kinsey's field
8 It has top and bottom parts
9 "Join the club"
10 Cross words
11 Yard sale?
12 Like Old Prussian
13 Spirit
14 Daniel Decatur ___, minstrel who wrote "Dixie"
20 Big drink
23 Plant problem
24 Reanimate
26 In a 38-Down way
27 Gym classes
29 Hurdles for future D.A.'s
30 Not solid
32 Home of the World Museum of Mining
33 They're located above the kidneys
34 Does some home maintenance
35 What some cards express
37 Lost soul
38 Transported
39 It was first publicly performed in Vienna in 1805
40 Racketeer's pastime?
41 Plaza de la Revolución locale
44 "Unbelievable!"

by Barry C. Silk

45 ___ City, Hawaii
47 Sub group
48 Physics Nobelist Simon van der ___
50 Richard Gere title role of 2000
51 Local govt. unit

127

ACROSS

1 Apologies, in Apulia
6 Slow-smoked Southern grub
14 Some nest sites
15 "No, no, this one's on me"
16 Many rappers' personas
17 Read rights to, as a perp
18 Work in a gallery
19 One way to turn
21 Parisian possessive
22 Something Mr. Olympia lacks
24 Play ___
25 Rec rm. locale, often
26 French kings' emblem
28 Picnic places
29 Dark times abroad
30 Hot pot spot
31 Where many lines are dropped
32 Appt. book headings
34 It can be cracked
35 Frijoles go-with
36 Like lumber in a mill
37 Information, slangily
42 Side for passage
43 Split up
44 Key of Mahler's Symphony No. 1: Abbr.
45 "Fresh Air" airer
46 Considering, with "of"
48 Letters in some church names
49 Handles
51 Puritan ___
53 Our neighbor's nickname, with "the"
54 Not inadvertent
55 On the lookout
56 Fast results?

DOWN

1 Depart
2 John Wayne title marshal of 1973
3 Anatomical hangers
4 Div.
5 Petrol brand
6 Stars of "90210," e.g.
7 How something might be familiar
8 Event held each summer and winter
9 Crack
10 Not an upgrade: Abbr.
11 Per se
12 Montana State University setting
13 Story lines of Indiana Jones films
15 Near Eastern hospices
20 Depths of despair
23 Podiatrists' concerns
25 Overwhelmed and destroyed
27 Monday morning quarterback, maybe
30 "Lost" character Jin-Soo ___
31 Coca-Cola product
32 The perfect match, for some
33 Loyalty
34 Crack of dawn, old-style
35 Like some classes and books
36 Painter Botticelli
37 Park since 1912
38 How some people shop
39 Warren Buffett, e.g.
40 Kind of ceremony
41 Sends packing
46 Singapore, for one
47 Certain sub

by Corey Rubin

50 Hosp. employee

52 Event at which some people wear gloves

128

ACROSS

1 Laugh-a-minute
8 So-so poker holding
15 In an unoriginal way
16 Circus performer, e.g.
17 Kind of strength
18 Toy trains
19 Swallow
20 Food label for the health-conscious
21 Electric device with terminals
23 News on the bus. page
26 Ingredient in many toothpastes
27 Spit for a kebab
32 Be doomed
36 Obtain service from
37 Felt bitter anguish
38 Maestro Koussevitzky
39 Grows pale
40 Twisted
41 Court figures
44 Like rivals, often
49 Not much, with "a"
53 Tourist guide
54 Vitamin C source
55 Make like new, as a bathtub
56 Nicely tan
57 Kitchen device first patented in 1921
58 Court figures

DOWN

1 Wife in "8 Simple Rules for Dating My Teenage Daughter"
2 Ready to do business
3 Chinese dynasty during which trade with Portugal began
4 Give out
5 Flu symptom
6 Like the pop group the Pussycat Dolls
7 Burning substance
8 Representative of Hollywood
9 Where to wear an armilla
10 Platte River tribe
11 Immobilizes
12 Where gobs go
13 "One day ___ all make sense"
14 Doctor's prescription
20 Be of assistance
22 Popular computer logic/guessing game
23 "Young Frankenstein" woman and others
24 French versifier
25 Burrow : rabbit :: holt : ___
27 Subject of "Toots" by Bob Considine, 1969
28 High in the French Alps
29 Following obediently
30 Scrub
31 Substantial
33 Gray blanket
34 Pitchfork part
35 Occasion to drop one's arms
41 Slinkys or Magic 8 Balls, once
42 ___ gin fizz
43 Surgical tube
44 Trolley
45 Round sandwich
46 Prefix with dose
47 Buds
48 Part of a Latin 101 conjugation
50 Not do one darn thing
51 ___-Neisse Line
52 Dries, as hay
54 ___ Ranch (former Western White House)

by Manny Nosowsky

129

ACROSS

1 Something to be negotiated
9 "___ Be the Tie That Binds" (Christian hymn)
14 Looking for trouble?
15 Visit on an ocean cruise, say
16 Hairstyle popularized by David Beckham
17 Affected to a greater degree
18 With 4-Down, smoker's fee
19 Walpurgis Night vis-à-vis May Day
20 Syllable repeated after "hot"
21 ___ Emblem (2002 Kentucky Derby winner)
22 Own responsibility
25 Refine
27 It has energy in reserve
28 It may be cracked open
29 Emmy award-winning Ward
31 World view?

33 Little ones
35 Aching
36 Lances
37 Having a good vantage point
38 Vantage
40 Peace Nobelist Ralph Bunche's alma mater
41 "Falling Man" novelist Don
43 Métier
45 "I won't ask again"
47 Harvey Wallbanger mixers, briefly
48 "Win a Date With ___ Hamilton!" (2004 film)
49 Moriarty, to Holmes
50 Scuba tank meas.
53 When, colloquially
55 Subjects of some Toulouse-Lautrec paintings
57 Electrolux brand
58 Ringing response?
59 Pomme ___
60 Some yo-yo tricks

DOWN

1 Comic book exclamations
2 Sons of, in Hebrew
3 Like yarn
4 See 18-Across
5 Close behind
6 Attire worn with frock coats
7 Dim
8 Black ___ (Lakota visionary)
9 1961 Anthony Quinn title role
10 Stewed
11 Hollywood star whose memoir was titled "The Good, the Bad, and Me"
12 Caterer's setup for a hot buffet
13 1971 N.L. M.V.P. who was later twice A.L. Manager of the Year
15 Savanna region stretching from Senegal to Chad
20 Leader with Roosevelt and Churchill at the Cairo Conference, 1943

22 Dramatist Brecht
23 Old Spanish swords
24 Head on a plate?
25 Restaurant special
26 Education pioneer Maria
28 "She Wore a Yellow Ribbon" co-star, 1949
30 Something most fish lack
32 Org. that's got your number?
34 Surprise shower?
39 Honor
42 Setting for Martin Scorsese's "Kundun"
44 Wintry stretch
45 ___ K., Kafka's protagonist in "The Trial"
46 Without exception
50 Jim's partner on "Adam 12"
51 Ferment
52 Cult followers?
54 Have left when all is said and done
55 Post-cold war inits.
56 Stock company, for short

by John Farmer

130

ACROSS

1 Detoured to pay a visit along the way
8 Gallimaufry
15 One of the 10 brightest stars
16 Engine line
17 Having superior amenities
18 Cools, in a way
19 Literature Nobelist Andric
20 It may fall flat
22 Critical cluck
23 Hippie happening
25 1971 title role for Donald Sutherland
26 Height of fashion?
27 These, overseas
29 Periodical output: Abbr.
30 Shifting sequence
31 Sully
33 Liberal, informally
34 Certain sex scandal, in slang

37 Their beans were used as currency by the Aztecs
38 Connecticut town attacked by the British in the War of 1812
39 Instrument
40 Wassailing choice
41 Not quite mashed
45 Sitcom character discussed in the 2003 biography "Ball of Fire"
46 Quaint aviation accessory
48 Former Yankee Martinez
49 "Magnificat anima ___ Dominum"
50 It's not really mink, for example
52 Bit of the Bahamas
53 Chef's cry
55 Finger food at a Japanese restaurant

57 Diamond-shaping choice
58 Prodded
59 One way to die
60 Fleet activities

DOWN

1 Worker who sets things down
2 Doesn't take advantage of
3 Game
4 Arôme detector
5 Smooth to a fault
6 Discouraging
7 Grid marking
8 Transforming Tonka toys
9 "The Book of Hours" poet
10 Natural treatment
11 Start of a text-message afterthought
12 Enter like a storm trooper
13 Crawl with
14 Guest at a synagogue
21 "Cool your jets!"
24 One or two

26 Recipient of a honey-do list
28 Cousin of a clog
30 Fizzle (out)
32 Island SSW of Naxos
33 Old track holders
34 Diamond-shaping choice
35 Some permafrost features
36 Tolls, essentially
37 Still the most
40 Needle-shaped
42 Shrill flier
43 Bewitch
44 Ones with seniority
46 Gallic greeting
47 "Oh, phooey!"
50 W-2 inclusion
51 Music that influenced the Beatles' "Norwegian Wood"
54 Elect
56 Cry from a litter

by Paula Gamache

131

ACROSS

1 Bit of back-and-forth
5 "___ Warning" ("Das Rheingold" aria)
10 "Yeah . . . whatever!"
14 Cherry ___
15 It goes a long way before the Olympics
16 ___ Independent Press Awards
17 Their parts are usually unusual
20 Hero, to some
21 Name on a Chinese menu
22 You don't want them to be dashed
23 Took a course?
24 Surreal beginning?
25 Surreal ending?
26 A person who's short might run to it
28 Some Windows systems
29 Comparison component
32 Not merely having wet clothes
39 Later
40 Provide what's missing
41 Faline's mother in "Bambi"
42 Fathers and sons
43 Heat on the street
44 Series standout, briefly
47 Apnea specialist: Abbr.
48 One of a pair of mice in "Cinderella"
50 Oscar nominee for "Stand and Deliver," 1988
52 Abbr. on a residential street sign
53 Very big
56 Just know
59 Can
60 Less formal
61 Dreaded letters for a procrastinator?
62 Reason for parental scolding
63 Basket on a court
64 Coastal bird

DOWN

1 Letters on old Russian maps
2 Chocolaty treat
3 They include amaretto and sloe gin
4 The Emperor, The Empress or The High Priest
5 Condensation indication
6 As bad as can be
7 Get all dapper
8 Very close, in a way
9 Al Green's "___-La-La (Make Me Happy)"
10 Jam ingredients
11 1984 Talking Heads concert film and hit album
12 Dictator's opening
13 Utter guilt, with "up"
18 Assembly call
19 46-Down preceder
26 "___ Place," 1971 Orson Welles movie
27 Gun-___ (like Yosemite Sam)
30 Carol Kane's role on "Taxi"
31 "___ of traitors!": Shak.
33 ___ Nidre (Yom Kippur prayer)
34 Virgin's parent
35 Relaxation location
36 Likud lang.
37 Schubert's "The ___ King"
38 Stopping point: Abbr.
45 Crop-damaging animals
46 19-Down follower
48 Lot
49 German diver
50 Wastes
51 Royal from the planet Alderaan
54 Cauterize

by David Levinson Wilk

55 It shows
many matches
57 Grp. with
East and West
divisions
58 Tabasco title:
Abbr.

132

ACROSS

1 It's shared by Russia and Ukraine
10 Dated will?
15 Flawlessly crafted
16 Less well-looking
17 They're produced in great quantities by supernovas
18 Mosaic work
19 Honorific that's Sanskrit for "majesty"
20 O, say
21 Light haulers
23 8 for O, say
25 "Twenty Love Poems and a Song of Despair" writer
27 "Silent Spring" subject
28 "Like Niobe, all __": Hamlet
30 It may concern arms or contain legs
31 Supportive side
32 Old bombs
34 __-cat
36 Finno-Ugric tongue
38 __ de la Société
39 Isabella's home
42 Piltdown man locale
46 Make fun of
47 100 cents, in East London
49 Dish cooked in seasoned broth
50 Extraction target
51 Wildcats and Cougars play in it
53 Pro __
54 "Sartor Resartus" essayist Thomas
56 Payoff
58 1951 A.L. strikeout leader Raschi
59 Become part of history
60 It's open to debate
63 Start to prepare, as 49-Across
64 Italian meal starter
65 A lot of assessments?
66 Saloonkeeper of note

DOWN

1 Having feeling
2 Brought to bear
3 "Summa Contra Gentiles" theologian
4 Tag cry
5 Tofu specification
6 See 9-Down
7 It may be fired back at someone
8 Chiwere dialect
9 He demonstrated that what Columbus had discovered was not 6-Down
10 Virgo's alpha star
11 Bit of hair
12 Referred
13 March preceder, periodically
14 Couples might set them up
22 They can't get any better
24 Ominous words
26 __ the Destroyer (rabble-rouser in Ralph Ellison's "Invisible Man")
29 Strip on a bed
31 Drill bit?
33 Like some shells
35 Go for another tour
37 Put-down in a restaurant?
39 City due south of San Juan
40 Quick impressions
41 Specialized M.D.
43 Blindly imitative
44 Deplete
45 Hard-to-define influence
46 Sportive
48 He joined Pizarro in the conquest of the Inca Empire

by Joon Pahk

51 Funeral arrangements
52 Tag cry
55 It's featured in two Vivaldi concertos

57 Afterthought #3: Abbr.
61 "Revolution 9" collaborator
62 Intl. group with 35 members

133

ACROSS

1 Tetanus symptom
7 1980s-'90s action/ adventure series
15 Square off against
16 Being borrowed by
17 The world, per the Bard
18 Be in a fix, say
19 It may be glassy
20 Key
21 Low reef
22 Sender of the Calydonian boar
24 Insignificant injury
26 Prefix with -polis
27 "The Great Broxopp" playwright, 1921
29 1989 French Open winner and others
31 Academic area
35 Name tag?
36 "Cómo es ___?" ("How come?" in Cádiz)
38 Follower of drop or shut
39 It includes mayo
40 Doctor who's friends with Matthew Mugg
43 Prize
45 New Jersey setting of "Coneheads"
47 "All You Need ___" (2008 Morrissey song)
48 Dance around a high chair?
49 It doesn't include a bonus
51 Annual stretch of trois mois
53 Physicist Ampère
55 Noted role for Maria Callas
57 With 60-Across, hypocrite's mantra
59 Cry that may forestall a lame excuse
60 See 57-Across

61 Backpedaler's words
62 Forward and back, e.g.
63 "St. Elsewhere" actor David

DOWN

1 Stepping-off points: Abbr.
2 Yellow-green shade
3 Place to receive communion
4 Tackle
5 1966 Tony winner for "Marat/ Sade"
6 Julie, e.g.: Abbr.
7 Philosophies that regard reality as one organic whole
8 Without ___ (daringly)
9 It's next to 10-Down, both in an adage and literally in this puzzle
10 See 9-Down

11 Derisive cry
12 Feature of some shirts
13 See 28-Down
14 Thickly fibrous
20 Using
23 One way around town
25 What few people live for: Abbr.
26 Breakdown cause
28 With 13-Down, here and there, to Henri
30 Start pulling down more?
32 Certain section
33 Barry B. Longyear novella that won Hugo and Nebula awards
34 Certain
37 Brazilian greeting
41 Subject for a W.S.J. article
42 Early developments
44 Upset
46 Sharjah's fed.

by Corey Rubin

48 Ledger with lines
50 As a friend, to Frédéric
51 Mom in "Hairspray"
52 Blow
54 ___ City, Fla.
56 Pro in briefs?: Abbr.
58 Paradise in literature
59 Family member

134

ACROSS

1 Bygone flag
16 Think a certain way about
17 Make a call
18 New York's Bear ___: Abbr.
19 Ballyhooed new product of 1998
20 Name repeated in a nursery rhyme
21 Short dog, for short
22 It's nothing
23 Before the races
25 Kind of depth finder
27 Bit of noise pollution
28 B and O figures: Abbr.
29 Brilliant moves
30 Roll
33 Bubbly name
34 Loosens (up)
35 Big copper exporter
36 Cover girl, e.g.?
37 Laid-back
38 Time being
39 Mammonism
40 "Something to Talk About" singer, 1991
41 Words starting a simple request
44 1960s–'70s touchdown maker
45 Mission statement part
47 First name in conducting
48 Actress Mazar
49 Lab subj.
50 Much of Central America, once
54 "This would be a first for me"
55 Trading posts?

DOWN

1 Beat but good
2 Can't continue
3 A tossup
4 Not hurting for cash
5 Pastes in Mideastern cooking
6 Hardly hearty
7 Relating to wheels
8 You might not get paid while working on it
9 Hurt
10 Dayton-to-Toledo dir.
11 Ladles
12 "Scènes de la Vie de ___" (novel on which a Puccini opera is based)
13 Make ___ of it
14 Actress Blakley
15 Comics dog
23 Downright
24 Emulates Eve
26 With 41-Down, shrunken
27 Yet to be engaged?
28 Early times, for short
29 "The Insect Play" playwright
30 Withdrew quietly
31 It's a little over 65°: Abbr.
32 Deserved
34 Things that open and close yearly?
35 Maui mouthful
37 Coach
38 Home of Walvis Bay
39 1997 Demi Moore flick
40 Co-firing technique used to reduce pollution from electrical power plants
41 See 26-Down
42 Furlough
43 Chambermaid's charge
44 Pennies : dollar :: ___ : drachma
46 Producers of sunbows
48 Skin: Suffix
51 Palindromic girl's name
52 Bill of Rights subj.
53 Kicker

by Joe DiPietro

135

ACROSS
1 Aids in artful deception
12 Knowledge base?: Abbr.
15 Correctly positioned
16 Org. in the 1982 film "Enigma"
17 Babble
18 Where people wear gowns, for short
19 "The Daughter of Time" novelist
20 Big Daddy player on 1950s Broadway
21 Gabfest
23 Hit
24 Sink
25 How Viola is disguised in "Twelfth Night"
28 Crude dwellings
29 ___ of Galadriel (gift to Frodo Baggins)
30 Go for ___
31 "Livin' Thing" group, in brief
32 Like some details
33 Antigen attacker
34 Year of the last known Roman gladiator competition
35 Plot line
36 Street show
37 2003 memoir of a TV executive
38 Back out?
40 One may be backed up
41 Wrote
42 Something fit to be tied?
43 Center of learning
44 Switch
45 Followers of closings: Abbr.
48 Duct opening?
49 1970s–'80s sitcom put-down/catch-phrase
52 Loch ___, on the River Shannon
53 Recyclable
54 Not be on target
55 Components of some alarms

DOWN
1 Bailiff's concern
2 Strauss's "___ Nacht in Venedig"
3 Part of 16-Across: Abbr.
4 "The Tudors" airer, briefly
5 Like straight shooters
6 Square, in 1950s slang, indicated visually by a two-hand gesture
7 High on amphetamines
8 Dedicated compositions
9 TV pooch
10 Decoy accompanier
11 Cave
12 Pet with short legs and a hard coat, informally
13 Big Apple excursion operation
14 Reviews repeatedly
22 Court figure: Abbr.
23 Words after "if" or before "as well"
24 Slate, originally
25 Measure of a newborn's health, named for its developer
26 Extension of the terms of a marine insurance policy
27 American, for one
28 "Nice!"
30 Bitter
33 Wealthy Cayman Islands resident, maybe
34 Juniper product
36 One of Judaism's four matriarchs
37 It can be a stunner
39 Slowing, in mus.
40 Private detective Mike of Brett Halliday novels
42 Round of four

by Paula Gamache

136

ACROSS

1 Activity involving a needle
10 Expression of praise
15 Household help?
16 Flavor of Calvados brandy
17 Wave measurement
18 Unusually high 17-Across
19 Closest to nil
20 Potential sucker
22 Wretched
23 Gallimaufry
24 One getting pinned?
27 Even's counterpart
28 It's hard to penetrate
29 "Desperate Housewives" housewife
30 "Point taken"
31 Out-of-the-way spots
32 Big draw of early Broadway
38 Putters

39 Ray in pictures
40 Dispensary stock, for short
41 Cat's-eye alternative
43 Furry sci-fi figure
47 Self-starter's equipment?
49 Something that's picked up
50 Field of field workers: Abbr.
51 Small dabbler
52 Grinder in an Italian restaurant
53 Indication of a job well done
55 Getting ready to make one's move?
58 Crane, e.g.
59 Command
60 Act unprofessionally
61 Merrie Melodies regular

DOWN

1 Peace
2 Thick-skinned fruit
3 Debilitate
4 "The Simpsons" bully
5 Set down
6 Choosing method
7 19th of 24
8 Locale of Krypton in the Superman saga
9 Feigned
10 Madrid's ___ del Prado
11 Useful piece of code, briefly
12 Series kickoff
13 1955 A.L. batting champ
14 Gratuitous
21 Part of N.Y.C.: Abbr.
24 Boughpot
25 City liberated during the Battle of Kursk
26 Hollow
30 Hypotheticals
31 ___ Worm (1980s light-up toy)

32 Victoria Falls forms part of its border
33 "No smoking" symbol, e.g.
34 Poe poem about a knight's lifelong quest
35 Exploit
36 Disrespectful
37 Expressions of praise
41 Bolted things down
42 Balsamic vinegar source
43 Composition of some chains
44 Ad-lib
45 Thick
46 Big-enough catch
48 Browser setting?
52 Very serious
54 Clinic worker
56 Person in the fourth grade: Abbr.
57 "The Wonder Years" teen who loved Winnie

by Doug Peterson

137

ACROSS

1 2001–08 Yankees pitcher with seven Gold Gloves
8 Headline during the Dreyfus Affair
15 Revealing pieces
17 Some coverage providers
18 Heavy hitters
19 Conjurers
20 City or state lead-in
21 Puts it to
22 Acted out
23 "Keeper of the Keys" was the last novel he was featured in
24 Artichoke heart?
25 Inattentive type
26 Classical lyre holder
27 Particularly prized possession
28 Carpentry machine
29 Credited

32 Appear before
33 Worker in a big house near Big Ben
34 What an antsy person might watch
35 Boot part
36 Cow
37 Hymnbook holder
40 Some farm stock
41 Otto follows it
42 Straw unit
43 Seasoning cristales
44 "Peter and the Wolf" bird
45 "Peter and the Wolf" duck
46 Something shown off on a half-pipe
49 Russia, China and France are in it
50 Greek salad ingredient
51 It can be brutal

DOWN

1 Algonquian language
2 Butterflies, say
3 He wrote of the prodigal son
4 Sash supporters
5 Hell-raisers
6 "Ixnay"
7 Like turbojet fuel
8 Bullying seabird
9 "Nell" director Michael
10 Coast Guard noncoms
11 Field call
12 Bowling ball material
13 Like many leaves
14 "To be, or not to be" soliloquy setting
16 Coat in one's mouth
22 It may be pushed or ridden
23 Figure out
25 Check
26 Awaiting induction

27 Pulitzer-winning cartoonist Feiffer
28 Back up?
29 "Um . . . all right"
30 Creator of the stuff of legends?
31 Hoi polloi
32 "On the Malice of Herodotus" author
34 Old Silk Road destination
36 Studebaker alternative
37 Loses it
38 Summon up
39 Without conviction
41 ___ vaccine
42 Shouldered
44 Clinic supplies
45 Overwhelm
47 Harbor pusher
48 Ending with Sea or Ski

by Doug Peterson

138

ACROSS
1 Spook's break-in
7 Gallery
15 Deafening
16 Co-composer of the "Prophecy Theme" in "Dune"
17 Like some wages and wastelands
18 Fractions of a gourde
19 Muffed on the green
21 Kyle's baby brother on "South Park"
22 They occur when things are all tied up, briefly
23 Quick flights
24 Herd : horse :: knot : ___
26 Asian royal
28 Very unpopular model
30 Very unpopular worker
32 It might get rolled off
33 Assemblée législative

35 Blue Light brewer
37 Olympic gold medalist who was a "Dancing With the Stars" champion
41 One barely living?
42 Reference abbr.
43 Home of the Viking Ship Museum
44 Enthused
46 Kid that has a nap
50 "___ the last time . . . ?"
52 Fresh
54 Physical, e.g.
55 Razor handle?
56 Creed component
58 Italian city with an annual music festival
60 Betters
63 Plumlike fruit
64 Cut short in performing
65 Place for many a piano

66 Was close to failure
67 The Sierra Nevada Minarets, e.g.

DOWN
1 Cause to be stuck
2 In wide circulation
3 Depressions
4 Swingers' get-together?
5 Russian oblast or its capital
6 "By the Waters of Babylon" author, 1937
7 Where Alex Trebek worked as a newscaster
8 Brand of 17-Across food
9 Setting for 37-Across
10 Critic
11 Ristorante suffix
12 One who may get dispossessed?
13 Agent's cut, maybe

14 "Beata Beatrix" painter
20 "I'm all ears!"
25 Mythological hunter
27 Home of the annual Gathering of Nations powwow, the world's largest celebration of Native American culture
29 Response of assent
31 Panama's San ___ Islands
34 New York congress-woman Lowey
36 A long stretch
37 Have the most reliable info
38 Undertake precipitately
39 Yak
40 You can get them on the house: Abbr.
45 It passes through a pollen tube
47 Dramatic order to leave
48 Hit to the wallet

by Karen M. Tracey

49 Doesn't play conservatively
51 From
53 When repeated, Columbia feeder
57 Cutting-edge development?
59 American-born queen
61 Performance piece?
62 Green stuff

139

ACROSS

1 Brig pair
6 ___ Vaishnavism (Hindu sect)
9 Org. that trademarked "Pony Express" in 2006
13 Like some leaves
15 Mad
17 They appeared on "The Ed Sullivan Show" 36 times
19 Scathing review attributed to Ambrose Bierce, part 1
20 De, across the Rhine
21 Sources of some leather
22 Grade school comeback
23 Holdup accessory?
24 Hosp. units
25 Reaction dreaded by a performer
26 Minstrel percussionist
28 Pursue, in a way
30 Wear that's worn
31 Review, part 2
34 Some batteries
35 Big productions
36 They're often stuffed
39 16th letter of the Spanish alphabet
40 Old TV ministry inits.
43 Agcy. concerned with ergonomics
44 Prayer start
46 Last thing
47 Onetime foe of the Navajo
48 Review, part 3
50 "Hot" political topic
52 Where sledders start
53 Strikingly original
54 Cause for a kid getting grounded
55 Sweet ending?
56 Half a leaf

DOWN

1 Summon
2 It's often played before the first play
3 Hucksters' deliveries
4 Baby showers?
5 Titan's home
6 Whiplike?
7 Free, but not for free
8 Like much plumbing
9 OPEC member: Abbr.
10 Be a garbage collector
11 Releases from a spring board?
12 They're not on the level
14 Not on the level
16 Global lending org.
18 Break down and assimilate
23 Sources of some leather
25 Snake feeder
27 Pair
28 Grammy winner Khan
29 46-Across part
31 Cape Fear natives
32 They're seen at Venice's La Fenice
33 Like-minded
34 Wienerwald's whereabouts
36 Ruffians
37 "Hello-o-o!"
38 Cousins of cutters
40 Occurring in stages
41 Letter's sign
42 Chooses to 46-Down
45 Valuable
46 Show clemency
48 Cause of a major downfall?
49 Bacteriologist's base
51 Lines up?

by Matt Ginsberg

140

ACROSS

1 Crack squad
6 Club for bulking up?
10 Wound, in a way, as a fellow G.I.
14 Patterson who played the title role on TV's "Private Benjamin"
15 One of Laban's daughters
16 Four-time Grammy winner Schifrin
17 He said "You are free and that is why you are lost"
19 Spanish seers?
20 Offensive action
21 Pitcher Orlando Hernández's nickname
23 Author ___ Easton Ellis
24 Capital of the Buryat Republic
25 Little auk
28 Cousin of an Omaha
29 Home of the Knockmealdown Mountains
30 Did course work?

33 Inspirational delivery: Abbr.
34 1989 Broadway monodrama
35 Like some eye surgery
40 Test control
44 See 57-Across
45 Moves in a tired way?
46 "The Great Gatsby" setting
48 Figures at a pileup
49 Stumps
50 2003 Anthony Swofford Gulf war memoir made into a 2005 film
54 Even around the Seine?
55 "Close . . ."
57 With 44-Across, Champion rider
58 Old royal residence in 29-Across
59 Pianist with 15 Grammys
60 Cramped urban dwellings, briefly
61 Easy to get into
62 One who was recently a child

DOWN

1 Starting code word
2 Places for some aeries
3 Succession of history
4 Title girl of a 1906 L. Frank Baum novel
5 One of 58 Chopin compositions
6 Like fruit crates
7 W.W. I military grp.
8 Second chances for students
9 Its bulbs are milder than garlic
10 Move in an attention-getting way
11 "The Jewel in the Crown" begins it, with "The"
12 One way to think
13 "Check it out for yourself"
18 German mathematician who lent his name to a "bottle"
22 Zealand resident
25 Drum alternative, vehicularly

26 Kind of mud pie
27 Explorer of North America's eastern coast in 1524
31 Player of Det. Eames on "Law & Order: Criminal Intent"
32 Some acts
36 Is an affectionate pooch
37 Indication that there's more: Abbr.
38 Silver: Prefix
39 Some old-fashioned bars
40 Real-life death penalty opponent played by Sarandon in "Dead Man Walking"
41 Folklorist/ musicologist Alan
42 Draw
43 Good profit source
46 Some high-tech images
47 A boring person might have one
51 Being abroad

by Karen M. Tracey

52 Way to turn a ship

53 Cannon shot on a set?

56 ___ corde (music direction)

141

ACROSS

1 Final resting place built in the 17th century
9 Jackson and others
15 Hole that's not filled
16 Demonstrate banking skill
17 Like exiles
18 Distance light travels in 3.3 femtoseconds
19 Sound sometimes followed by an attack
20 "A friend to call my own," per a Michael Jackson hit
21 Reaction to chicken feed
22 "Far From Heaven" director Todd
24 Queens or soldiers
25 Patron saint of hermits
26 Sentences may end with them
28 Car category
29 Creator of a comic strip duo named after a theologian and a philosopher
31 Fine-grained wood
32 Desert rodents
33 Indication of a green light
35 One may be out of control
37 So, in Salerno
38 British Columbia's ___ Mountains
39 "Class Reunion" novelist, 1979
40 Boosted
41 Tank type
42 Pitches
45 Summer turn-on?
46 It might hold gold
47 Black marketeer in "Casablanca"
48 Bygone Buicks
50 Emissary
51 Like some menus
52 Pitched
53 Not at all tight

DOWN

1 Bruiser
2 Rates
3 Big name in slapstick
4 6 letters
5 Building blocks
6 Is repulsed by
7 Rate ___ (be deemed flawless)
8 Skippered
9 "Being an actor is the loneliest thing in the world" speaker
10 They remove letters
11 Repulses
12 Attire around the 1-Across
13 Royal educator
14 Hong Kong's Hang ___ Index
21 Had some
23 Satirist Ward
24 ___ seat
26 Voting booth information
27 1947 western serial film
29 Cowardly
30 Title vampire of film
32 Girl Scouts founder Low
34 Diphthong dividers
36 Mehrabad Airport setting
37 Film holder
39 One of the Sopranos
41 Stately old court dance
42 Get the best of
43 Posthumous Pulitzer winner of 1958
44 Ravi Shankar played it at Woodstock
45 Do a taxing task?
48 Low-grade paper
49 It may pop on a plane

by Martin Ashwood-Smith

142

ACROSS

1 Brand seen near razors
5 They're in seats
15 Cover-up during a shower
16 Philosophy of Montague or Santayana
17 Inquire about a union contract?
19 Roman ___
20 Color faintly
21 One may be prayed to: Abbr.
22 Connect
24 Crash accompanier
26 Alter in a clothing store?
28 Trumpeter with a prominent neck
32 Home to Stratford: Abbr.
35 Quarter master?
39 They benefit personally
41 East Coast sobriquet
42 Crane component

43 One symbol of the 41-Across
44 Filled treats
46 Certain joe
50 Kind of joe
54 Seek change?
57 Father of Eleazar, in the Bible
59 Psychics claim to see them
60 Meteorological shocker?
63 Something often written under
64 Model Melissa Aronson, familiarly
65 Hardly happy
66 Relative of a chestnut

DOWN

1 For what it's worth
2 Play genre
3 Sing the parts of in succession
4 Be published
5 It'll cover you: Abbr.
6 Brand seen near razors, once
7 Losing the fuzz?

8 Heavens: Prefix
9 Word of politesse
10 St. ___ (Caribbean hot spot)
11 "My God!," as cried by King David
12 Actress Long and others
13 U.S.A.F. NCO
14 Hook go-with?
18 Not so rarely
23 Something to practice
25 City near Padua
27 "London Fields" novelist, 1989
29 Superior setting: Abbr.
30 Hairy clue-sniffer
31 It may delve into a derailment: Abbr.
32 Supervising
33 Seaman whose last words were "God and my country!"
34 Some are level: Abbr.

36 Kindergarten "grade"
37 Dishes (out)
38 Biological interstices
40 Even
45 Brennan's successor on the Supreme Court
47 One working on the side?
48 Seize, in a saying
49 Edible pomegranate parts
51 Many an ad
52 Province next to Piacenza
53 Mocha setting
54 River feature
55 Wellsian race
56 Beauties
58 It may be dropped
61 Spring setting in Chi-Town
62 Had the edge

by Victor Fleming

143

ACROSS

1 Rears
6 Jurist who wrote "A Matter of Interpretation," 1997
12 Like theater seating
14 Delivering a tirade
16 Coming from both sides
17 Kind of gland
18 Writer of "Commentarii de Bello Gallico"
19 Makes privy to
20 Watching Letterman or Leno, say
21 Medical inspiration?
22 Not merely thought
23 The Bucharest Buffoon of the court
24 Partition
25 ___ clue
26 Grasping things more slowly
28 Muhammad's favorite wife

33 Boldness to a fault
35 Western wear
37 It's machine-readable
41 Breaker of the 400-meter freestyle world record at the 2000 Olympics
42 "Dig in!"
43 Bandleader with the #1 hit "Blues in the Night"
44 Indications that things have changed?
45 Baseballer Fernando Valenzuela's nickname
46 Like a pleasant aroma
47 Crybaby
48 Precede
49 It turns over before it runs
50 Job woe
51 They branch off

DOWN

1 Get into
2 Potential
3 1960s catchphrase
4 Like a foundling
5 They're often packed away for the summer
6 Prophesy
7 Verbally run down
8 King who infamously demanded half of Rome's Western Empire as a dowry
9 Rain forest flora
10 Cantillate
11 One may act for an actor
13 Theologian Kierkegaard
14 Long, thin strip
15 Before coming out?
25 Inclination
27 Star treks?
29 Levels
30 Supply-and-demand problem

31 Consonant
32 Ostensible
34 "On your feet!"
36 Serape sporters
37 Charlie of swing
38 Embodiment
39 Stay
40 Party get-together
41 Writer's development
42 They're tough to run in

by Joe Krozel

144

ACROSS

1 Like a hunk
5 Perch for a bighorn
9 Puppets
14 Trade name of daminozide
15 Saab model
16 Nirvana attainer
17 Big name in bags
19 Internet forum menace
20 Shakes
21 Major Côte d'Ivoire export
22 Where to get rubbed the right way?
23 Second-largest city in New Hampshire
25 They're often garnished with orchids
29 Act like a bull?
30 Edge
33 They may call the shots
35 Early Saint Laurent employer
36 Winner of four consecutive Emmys for his sitcom role as a prosecutor
38 "Zip" follower
39 Snorkeling spot near Honolulu
40 Weekly msg.
41 Break
42 Get down
43 Refresher between courses
46 Matching pair marking
47 Race beginning?
49 Not too tight?
54 Zulu relative
55 Like some questions
56 Get smart
57 Pteridologist's specimen
58 Waiting aid
59 Cashiers
60 Org. created by Carter in 1979
61 Gear to help you hear

DOWN

1 Transcaucasian capital
2 Half an Asian capital?
3 Some nutrients
4 Peach variety
5 To whom Stubb and Flask answered, in literature
6 Unlike fairies
7 Shakespeare's mother's maiden name
8 Takes a continental tour, e.g.
9 Inconsistent
10 He recorded all 32 Beethoven piano sonatas in the 1960s
11 Response to a ding-dong?
12 Simba's mate
13 The Vire River flows through it
18 Minnesota twin?
24 Three Mile Island is in it
25 Goya subjects
26 Cell part
27 Jennifer Weiner best seller made into a 2005 film
28 Removes, as paint
31 Crumbs
32 Is rapacious
34 Rapacious flier
35 Words followed by a wish list
37 Home ruler?
41 Sounds like an old floorboard
44 Nascence
45 Fox home
47 Fair
48 Street sign word
50 It can make waves
51 Apt. part
52 Act precipitately
53 One of its flavors is Dulce de Leche

by Karen M. Tracey

145

ACROSS
1 Landlocked European
5 1946's "Giant Brain"
10 "Séance on ___ Afternoon" (1964 suspense thriller)
14 Greek goddess Athena ___
15 Planet ruled by Ming the Merciless in "Flash Gordon"
16 Second start?
17 Landscaper's project
19 1920s leading lady ___ Naldi
20 Fastest ocean liner ever in a transatlantic crossing (3 days, 12 hours, 12 minutes)
22 Free
23 Catawampus
24 Showbiz bookings
25 Big man in Oman
27 Inexperienced with
29 Old White House monogram
30 Baseball's Dark and Downing
32 Asian flatbread
33 Copy cats?
34 Private reading?
39 Greek war god, to Greeks
40 Season opener?
41 French seasoning
42 Word with part or port
43 Bank structures?
45 Branches
49 Bellyache
51 Non-coffee order at Starbucks
53 Busts in a museum, e.g.
54 Patriotic display
57 Trans ___ (Kyrgyz/Tajik border range)
58 Oscar-winning portrayer of Police Chief Bill Gillespie, 1967
59 Block division
60 Send
61 Spoonful, say
62 Henry James biographer Leon
63 ___ a fox
64 Prefix with -zoic

DOWN
1 He wrote "Life has no meaning the moment you lose the illusion of being eternal"
2 Old Testament God
3 Peter out
4 Azerbaijan's capital
5 Send, in a way
6 1973 Ali jaw-breaker
7 Highest-grossing film of 1996
8 Like some ports
9 π and others
10 Record for the record books
11 Didn't retire, maybe
12 Double ___
13 Maid of honor and best man, e.g.
18 Twists
21 Parlor pic
26 Hearing things
28 Performed the role of
31 Star of India and others
33 It may be down
34 It may make people jump to a conclusion
35 Broke a court rule
36 Dog originally bred to hunt otters
37 PAC for those who pack?
38 Live
43 Prep, e.g.: Abbr.
44 California county

by Peter A. Collins and Joe Krozel

46 Bath beads maker
47 Like best friends
48 Disc holder
50 Gabardine, e.g.

52 They're placed in the center of a table
55 Single stroke
56 Remain

146

ACROSS

1 Rock samples
10 Rub together
15 Any
16 "Proceed slowly"
17 Salad ingredient
18 Keen
19 Author of "Time's Arrow," 1991, a novel written in reverse chronological order
20 They're observed in the evening
22 Actress Scala
23 Henchmen
27 "Pushing Daisies" star ___ Pace
28 Lights
30 Punk
31 Uncomfortable, in a way
33 Québec's Festival d'___
34 Post ___ (after-the-fact)
35 Start of a confession
42 Auto finish?
43 Influential 1996 video game

45 Drink whose name suggests its vitamin content
46 Yellow squares, often
47 Sch. founded by a president
48 Receiver of some contributions
50 Year that Acre fell in the First Crusade
51 Freeze
52 Uncomfortable
57 Oil source
58 Contents of a certain household box
59 Relates to
60 Cocktails lacking hard liquor

DOWN

1 Rappers' wrappers
2 They're opposed
3 Talk to two 2-Down, say
4 Mumble after a fumble
5 Hero of "Boyz N the Hood"
6 Excite, with "up"

7 ___ psychology
8 Outmoded preposition
9 Waitstaff
10 Actress co-starring in TV's "Burn Notice"
11 Spring's opposite
12 "Just Give Me a Cool Drink of Water 'Fore I Diiie" poet
13 They're often playing at home
14 Cut up, with "around"
21 It begins with an E (in two ways)
23 Throws up
24 Genealogical discovery
25 Budgetary bigwig, for short
26 They have connections
29 Some pellets
30 ___ Minh
32 Is in Athens?
35 French bread
36 Milky
37 Multipart art

38 Defibrillator user, for short
39 RICO Act enforcer
40 School
41 Agent of change
42 Word that first appears in Matthew 1:1
44 Movie critics, sometimes
46 Water bearers
49 Bottom of the sea?
50 Birthplace of poet Paul Verlaine
53 You could stand to lose it
54 Delta, for one: Abbr.
55 BBC's Sports Personality of the Century
56 Black-throated ___ (Asian bird)

by Trip Payne

147

ACROSS

1 Reduced fare?
10 Not much
14 Writer on pictures
16 Bagels, essentially
17 Going bonkers for the British?
18 Eczema treater
19 "___ Blues" (track on the Beatles' "White Album")
20 Response to being elbowed, maybe
22 "Dilbert" character who was reincarnated as his own clone
24 Driver's helper
25 Kind of question
26 Indicator of high-level staff?
28 Companion for Pan
30 Suffix with 49-Across

31 Prehistoric stone tool
33 Show great anticipation
35 Home for a 28-Across
37 Kachina doll makers
38 Bruiser's display
42 Maximally balanced
46 Professional grp. with its own insurance agency
47 Visibly elated
49 Part of a number
50 Tyke
52 Set-___
54 1924 co-defendant
55 Clown
58 General in the Taiping Rebellion
59 Dramatic honor
60 Beige attribute
62 It's folded before dinner
63 Staged
64 Blackmailer in an 1850 novel
65 Restive

DOWN

1 Certain hauling fee
2 "The Bald Soprano" playwright, 1950
3 It's stuffed in a restaurant
4 Letterhead abbr.
5 Ship part
6 Paul who won a Golden Globe for "American Graffiti"
7 Brought down
8 Surname of three generations of Flemish old masters
9 Solar system discovery of 2003
10 Maker of the Lynx and Jaguar systems
11 Where Quechua is spoken
12 Writer whose words are twisted?

13 Outcome disallowed by the N.H.L. in 2005
15 Victim of terrible teasing
21 Second, e.g.
23 Country star Urban
27 Kansas mil. reservation with the U.S. Cavalry Museum
29 Old Fenway nickname
32 Waffling
34 Part of some audiophiles' collections
36 One making a journey with a gurney
38 Bigger than big
39 Shape shifters?
40 Fancy
41 Best in a one-on-one
43 Body art?
44 Followers of some meals
45 "Drop City" novelist, 2003

by Brad Wilber

48 Way in

51 Before making the cut?

53 Option at Sleepy's

56 Orange, peach or strawberry product

57 Imperfection

61 Interrogator's red-flag raiser

148

ACROSS

1 Louisiana State won the first one in 1968
10 Kneecaps, e.g.
15 Neighbor of Kaliningrad
16 Recipient of much praise
17 Source of charcoal wood
18 Mondavi competitor
19 Fashionable meeting place?
20 Sack
21 Facial or racial preceder
22 Abyssinian language?
23 Like the Angkor ruins
25 A little over three grains
26 2001 Nobel Peace Prize recipient
28 Indy Jones and others
30 Dungeons & Dragons player option
31 "I reckon so"
33 Wilt Chamberneezy, more familiarly
34 Olympic sprinter ___ Boldon
35 Line on which a dip needle is horizontal
40 Where private messages are sent?: Abbr.
41 Word before and after "and"
42 Needing buoying
43 36th of 50: Abbr.
44 Ones with stalking feet?
46 Macho stereotype
50 Fan setting
52 Splinter, to Woody Woodpecker
54 Go off
55 Tonsorial accessory
56 "The ___ of Physics" (1975 best seller)
57 City name part that's Dutch for "hedge"
58 Crowing cue
59 1950 Tony winner for Best Actor in a Musical
61 Loomed
62 Slump
63 More desertlike
64 Opposite of torpor

DOWN

1 High-definition video display
2 Astronaut Collins
3 When 58-Across occurs
4 Bond analysts' field?: Abbr.
5 Family name in a Lew Wallace novel
6 Baker's dozen, say
7 Traveler's connection
8 Dish akin to cotoletta alla milanese
9 Papuan port in W.W. II fighting
10 Recreational mathematics construct
11 "Law & Order" actress ___ de la Garza
12 "This one's on me"
13 Countertenor
14 A contraction of
23 Good one
24 Architect Ludwig Mies van der ___
27 First name in objectivism
29 Newbies are often directed to them
32 Spittoon sound
35 Civil War battlefield
36 Crack
37 Person in a mansion
38 Recycle bin, for one
39 Org. concerned with decay
45 Nautical hazard

by Barry C. Silk

47 Stinker
48 River to the Gulf of Mexico
49 Much-needed donations
51 "It's fruitless"
53 Pigeon or dove
57 Dogpatch possessive
59 Bush ___
60 It's periodically observed in Hollywood: Abbr.

149

ACROSS

1 Creator of Stupefyin' Jones
7 Firm
15 This and Sputnik 1 were launched on the same day
17 Soft ground ball that finds its way between infielders
18 ". . . but things could change"
19 High ways?
20 Chinese menu word
21 Sticker by a hospital bed?
23 Year the emperor Decius was born
25 Many a letter to the editor
27 Mopped the floor with
32 Killer ___ (green-skinned "Batman" villain)
33 Engraving tools
35 Coverage provider, for short
36 Acid
38 Classroom groan elicitor
40 Rice-Eccles Stadium athlete
41 Subatomic particle in a collider
43 Hard to watch
44 Cornwall resort port
46 Kimberly of "John Q"
48 Stiff
49 Swim cap material
51 On
54 "In your face!"
55 Prepares to shoot, as an arrow
59 Nitty-gritty
63 Determined one in a kid's song
64 Film editing technique
65 Ice cream shop supply

DOWN

1 Therewithal
2 Satyric expression
3 Columnist who wrote "Baghdad by the Bay"
4 High-tech navigation systems
5 Kept inside
6 Source of blood for blood pudding
7 Nematodes' piercing mouthparts
8 Drives obliquely
9 Some are sculpted
10 Strung souvenir
11 Wish to join
12 N.Y.S.E. nos.
13 It may accompany a promotion, briefly
14 Lithium's número atómico
16 Some plumbing joints
22 Hanging (on)
23 Peer's topper
24 Astrological gray area
25 Rankle
26 Edward IV's birthplace
28 Certain seizure
29 Downs without a break
30 Rousseau novel subtitled "On Education"
31 On the way out?
32 Bikini spec
34 Kind of converter
37 Resident near the Isthmus of Kra
39 Not at all practical
42 Turn for the worse
45 Poles work for them
47 The Delaware Prophet's tribe
50 Main call
51 Within
52 Space-scanning proj.

by Doug Peterson

53 Info source for 58-Down
54 Cutting-edge set
56 End notes?
57 Itching (to)
58 Red grp.
60 Typing letters?
61 Next to ___
62 Shortening in recipes

150

ACROSS

1 Response to "Is anyone else here?"
7 Travel mag listing
12 Just over a minority
14 Sports star who wrote the 2008 best seller "A Champion's Mind"
16 "Water that moves you" sloganeer
17 Spanish pork sausage
18 Nighttime noisemaker
19 Shimon's predecessor
21 Sucker, quickly
22 "Mother Goose in Prose" author, 1897
24 Cause of some food recalls
25 Busiest
26 Spirit
28 Sob syllable
29 All ___ (card game)
30 Complete, as a task
32 Is hardly extravagant
34 Summon a servant, maybe
36 Polynesian libation
37 Round
40 Gate-breaching bomb
44 Sour fruit
45 Planet visited by Spaceman Spiff in "Calvin and Hobbes"
47 It's often unfounded
48 Chain of treeless rolling hills
49 County in Missouri or county seat in Arkansas
51 "___ Said" (1961 hit)
52 Floor
53 April Fools' Day activity
55 Turn sharply
56 Drink with lemon juice
58 Appropriation
60 Brat Pack member
61 Ancient Roman writer of comedies
62 Initiated unpleasantly
63 Hemmed and hawed

DOWN

1 Southwestern shrubs yielding a cosmetic oil
2 Not with it
3 Screen
4 Day "Cheers" was on: Abbr.
5 Tangled and interwoven
6 Cartoonist Segar
7 Believer advocating universal brotherhood
8 Uncontrollably
9 D.C.-based news org.
10 Convenient kind of window
11 Some charity events
13 Clyde ___, "Beau Brummell" playwright, 1890
14 Junk
15 Belts
20 Sites of some exhibits
23 Sponged
25 Fragrant hair dressing
27 Is way cool
29 Fin
31 Cap'n, say
33 Criticize
35 Flair
37 Larghetto
38 Staple of northern Italy
39 Urge
41 Not just great
42 Court
43 Never seemed to end
44 Metalworking tool
46 Mill fill
49 Fell through the cracks?
50 Hit below the belt
53 Queen's quarters
54 Big name in cycling helmets
57 Casablanca wear
59 Lack of organisation?

by Matt Ginsberg

151

ACROSS

1 Squidward's neighbor on Nickelodeon
10 Do before I do's
14 Academic goal, for some
15 Did really well
16 Sal Tessio's portrayer in "The Godfather"
17 Is concupiscent
18 Parmesan alternative
19 Chills
21 Skeletal opening?
22 Thing you don't want to twist
24 Pronunciation guide std.
25 Home of Riding Mountain National Park
29 Go ___ some length
30 Furnish with battlements, as a castle
32 Language spoken in Assam, India
33 Approach the shore on board?
34 Corroded
36 Recurring metrical beat
37 Dinosaur with large thumb spikes
39 Trey trio
40 Drain
41 See 8-Down
42 Indian employed as a British soldier
43 It may be fair
46 Wife of Pylades
48 Antarctic dweller
51 It's often kept under lock and key
52 What you might do after failing
55 Give out
56 Setting in Pago Pago
57 Its motto in Eng. is "It grows as it goes"
58 Things that turn people off?

DOWN

1 Market purchase
2 Numbered rental
3 Old company telephone line
4 Cured and smoked salmon
5 Use one's zygomatic muscles
6 It follows that
7 Starting word
8 With 41-Across, one you go way back with
9 Classic novel with a chapter titled "My Breaking In"
10 Holy Ark's location
11 1961 #1 hit for Bobby Lewis
12 First Italian course?
13 An elephant has a long one
15 Astringent fruit
20 Rio "hello"
22 Stuck
23 Kidder's cry
26 MacGyver's first name on "MacGyver"
27 Safety equipment
28 Terre dans l'eau
29 Athens sch.
30 Helped out
31 Bunker mentality?
32 Game played with a sack called a goose
35 Scotland's longest river
38 Ltr. center
40 Ending with what, in verse
42 Problem with a sebaceous gland
44 Words written on some test papers
45 "The Cat's Meow" actor, 2001
47 Core
48 Like Luther: Abbr.
49 Name-dropper's abbr.?

by Dave Tuller

50 Pre-takeoff cry?

53 Good thing to be sheltered from

54 End of many riddles

152

ACROSS

1 Exuberant gesture with splayed fingers
10 Snake in the grass
15 Captain's command
16 Coat cut
17 Safe
18 Something gays and straights have in common?
19 Phrase
20 Sideshow Bob's last name on "The Simpsons"
22 "Vous ___ ici" (French map indication)
24 Studio props
25 Onetime Nascar outlet
26 Like some gems and old movies
28 Corriere della ___, Italy's top-selling newspaper
29 Vexed look
30 Registers, with "in"

32 Longfellow or Millay, by birth
34 Tree with heart-shaped leaves
37 Tack item
38 Mrs. Wingfield in "The Glass Menagerie"
39 Maker of the first electric compact calculator
40 Rtes. with plazas
41 More than brown
43 In accordance with
47 One going steady?
48 They may be fingered
50 ___-tyme
51 Work stoppage?
54 Island in the Thames
55 Red-haired Disney princess
56 "Deliverance" actor
58 Central point

59 Something pulled out in church
60 Handle
61 "I sympathize"

DOWN

1 Traditional March birthstone
2 Sharp
3 Antiallergy brand
4 Common field trip destination
5 Kind of club
6 "You shouldn't have"
7 Location of the 44-Down
8 Suffers through a boring meeting, maybe
9 Closer to 10?
10 Shrouds
11 "My God," in Aramaic
12 Bars for a cell?
13 Wide-eyed ones
14 Picker-uppers?

21 Foals : horses :: crias : ___
23 Preakness flowers, familiarly
27 All ___
29 Baseball player known as Mr. White Sox
31 Extra in "Broken Arrow," 1950
33 "Votre toast," for one
34 Radiodensity indicators
35 Early containers
36 Rest
37 Like a style of painting with sharply delineated forms
39 "Wayne's World" actress
42 Chat
44 River facetiously described as "a mile wide at the mouth, but only six inches deep"

by Tyler Hinman and Byron Walden

45 White, in fiction, or Brown, in real life
46 Enter again
48 Item with a pegbox

49 Nick of college football who was twice A.P. Coach of the Year

52 "Dogs"
53 Frequent phone booth user
57 Powdery evidence

153

ACROSS

1 No backbreaker
9 Was a catalyst for
15 Add to marginally?
16 Stealthy sort
17 One running through town
18 Exclamation near a runway
19 City in Veneto
20 Cubist who painted "Violin and Glass"
22 Bird notable for walking rather than hopping
23 Triple Crown winner between Whirlaway and Assault
25 Master
28 Not tall
29 Preach
31 Perfume named for Baryshnikov
32 It's just over a foot
33 Plot segment
34 Indian currency
37 Take the wrong way?
38 Ring site
39 Tony award nominee for "Anna Christie," 1993
40 It's sometimes heaping: Abbr.
41 Fishtail, e.g.
42 "The Mary Tyler Moore Show" weatherman
43 Place where kids may feed kids
46 New Mexico's El ___ National Monument
47 Emulate Cyrano
48 Nov. 11 honoree
52 Mardi Gras song that was a 1965 hit for the Dixie Cups
54 Pulitzer-winning William Kennedy novel
56 Good place to look when you're sole-searching?
57 It doesn't add up
58 Waiting list?
59 Kind of mattress pad

DOWN

1 Amounted
2 Last pharaoh of Egypt's Fifth Dynasty
3 Ruffled state
4 It'll give you an edge
5 Financial report abbr.
6 It's hard for laymen to understand
7 Port on the Sea of Japan
8 Song standard from Broadway's "Jubilee," 1935
9 Hub northwest of LAX
10 Nation
11 "Show Boat" girl who sings "Life Upon the Wicked Stage"
12 Like tiny tots
13 Like much pulp
14 Everglades deposit
21 Stretch marks, e.g.
23 Peak projection
24 Financial adviser's suggestion
25 Bluffing bar game
26 Emergency racetrack turnoff
27 Wicked king of Israel
30 Tennis star Zvonareva
31 U.S.M.C. E-8
32 Faint, to Shakespeare
33 Jay or Ray
35 "___ Have" (Jennifer Lopez #1 hit)
36 Classic novel whose title means "rover"
41 Steamship employee
42 Get ready for a bomb
44 Reservation holder
45 Free-falling phenomenon
46 Paste in Asian cookery
48 One whose mouth and lip may be painted
49 TV opponent of Ares
50 Exploit
51 Starting point for un inventeur
53 Has one's fill and more, briefly
55 Foreign policy grp.

by Brad Wilber

154

ACROSS

1 Grunt site
4 Pageant attire
10 Pen name
13 Vegetable sometimes grown as a flower
14 Walrus-skin boats
15 Spain's Victoria Eugenia, familiarly
16 Seafood restaurant locale
17 Mafia runners
18 I.C.U. figure
19 Bad bill collector?
20 Perfectly, after "to"
21 1847 novel involving a mutiny
22 Tape speed abbr.
23 It comprises the 10-Down, 34-Across and a third part found elsewhere in the grid
26 Kind of pork
28 Best Actress winner for "The Great Ziegfeld," 1936

29 Musical with the song "It's the Hard-Knock Life"
30 Proceed effortlessly
33 Sample
34 Part of the 23-Across
37 Bit of autumn decoration
40 QB who was the Super Bowl XXXIII M.V.P.
41 Itchy
45 Revolt
47 Ball of fire
48 One that bets are on
52 AWOL catchers
53 Roger of stage and screen
54 Sugar
55 Genealogical listings: Abbr.
56 Certain council member: Abbr.
57 Black mark
59 Kind of reed
60 Standoff
61 Birthplace of St. Clare
62 Chest contents
63 Tarsus : foot :: incus : ___
64 Admits
65 ___ admin

DOWN

1 Not provide fully
2 Subject of Article III Section 3 of the Constitution
3 Ball material
4 One of two cars besides a Cadillac named in Springsteen's "Pink Cadillac"
5 The Brothers ___ (violinmakers)
6 Popular fraternity, familiarly
7 Actress Veronica of "Hill Street Blues"
8 Barely make, with "out"
9 Job application info: Abbr.
10 Part of the 23-Across
11 Ruling
12 Church office
13 Perfect conditions
21 "Withhold no atom's atom ___ die": Keats
23 The Little Flower of Jesus

24 Manx relative
25 Certain shooter
27 Sample, in a way
30 Quote the raven?
31 River to the Volga
32 "___ questions?"
35 Map abbr.
36 ___ Juan
37 Marked down
38 "O, what a noble mind is here o'erthrown!" speaker, in Shakespeare
39 One with a stake in 48-Across, say
42 Nintendo product
43 Has working
44 Family in Upton Sinclair's "Oil!"
46 Conditions
47 Public transportation to New York's Yankee Stadium
49 Wordsworth, e.g.
50 Denver's ___ University
51 Response to a disbeliever

by Peter A. Collins

55 Spoils
57 ___ the Stockbroker on "The Howard Stern Show"
58 Literary inits.

155

ACROSS

1 Runs through a petcock, e.g.
10 They have big bells
15 Best Director of 2001
16 Setting of Queen Beatrix Airport
17 One might create a spread
18 Garson ___, writer and director of Broadway's "Born Yesterday"
19 Apportionment word
20 City founded during the Cherokee Strip land run
21 United
22 "___ of you . . ."
24 Fond of
26 Itinerary abbr.
27 Food giant based in Springdale, Ark.
29 Trade, informally
30 It has a play of colors
31 Desirable trunk feature
35 He crushed Hannibal at Zama
37 Bright
38 1980 Truffaut film that won 10 César awards
40 Not give way
41 Herd locale
42 Introducer of the math symbol "e"
46 European conductor ___ Klas
47 Unagi restaurant suppliers
50 Be enough for
51 Like avocado skins
53 Quotable types
55 Stars play in it: Abbr.
56 Shorthand inventor Pitman
57 Act of Supremacy institutor
59 Rwandan people
60 Relative of alliteration
61 Track asset
62 Health club offering for aerobic workouts

DOWN

1 Discussion ender
2 Passed, as in a parade
3 1993 N.L. batting champ Galarraga
4 Christian trigram
5 City east of Saint Lawrence Island
6 Tony
7 "The Great Dictator" Oscar nominee
8 "New York, New York" lyricist
9 Most famous resident of Warm Spr., Ga.
10 Like some seats
11 Orenburg is on it
12 Thing with a sweet ring to it?
13 "Hair" song with birthday wishes to a president
14 Wear for Peppermint Patty
21 "The Impresario" composer
23 Lose it
25 Queen for whom an element is named
28 Vacation spot for some oenophiles
30 Repellent
32 Alfred ___, "Footbridge at Argenteuil" artist
33 Shuttle destination
34 Of particular interest to a completist
35 Bolsters
36 Like many clerics
38 Something dreadful
39 Who said "I'll try anything once, twice if I like it, three times to make sure"

by Brad Wilber

43 Cause of a dry spell in the Midwest
44 Business school course-
45 Hinges
47 Battle of Cabra victor, 1079
48 Shampoo shelfmate
49 It's often seen next to a chair
52 Private residence?
54 Coordination, briefly
57 Boasts
58 ___-de-Marne, France

156

ACROSS

1 They lack private parts
10 Part of a capital's name meaning "flower"
15 Unable to get out of a bad situation
16 Is far from a homebody
17 Marmots and prairie dogs
19 "Uncle Tom's Cabin" girl
20 Gets acquainted with something good
21 Fashion
22 Wranglers, e.g.
23 Spot announce-ment?
24 Coloratura Christiane ___-Pierre
25 A Scot has one
26 ___ level
29 The 1965 William Shatner film "Incubus" is in it
32 Generates returns
33 From the heart
35 They may be thrown over the shoulder
38 Squared
42 Quickly
44 Fraternity letters
45 Terre Haute sch.
46 With 6-Down, "Curious . . ."
47 Early advocate of bloodletting
49 "The Far Shore of Time" author Frederik
50 Mechanical trade
53 Source of Caravane cheese
54 Cardinal relatives
56 Red ___
57 Its symbol is a globe composed of jigsaw puzzle pieces
58 World War I period
59 Like some families

DOWN

1 Jesus cursed one in Matthew 21
2 Headway
3 Improvised
4 Fraternity, e.g.
5 Thinner than thin
6 See 46-Across
7 Where M.S.T. and P.S.T. can be found
8 Home of la Sorbonne
9 Jilt
10 LAX info: Abbr.
11 New York's Five ___ Bike Tour
12 Ant-Man, Iron Man, Wasp or Thor, in Marvel Comics
13 1999 A.L. Rookie of the Year Carlos
14 Divides by type
18 Tech., for one
22 San ___
25 French naval base in heavy W.W. II fighting
27 Oregon and Idaho's ___ Canyon
28 Country singer Collin ___
30 Protection: Var.
31 Corrupt, in a way
34 "A Yank at ___" (1942 Mickey Rooney film)
35 Shows contempt for
36 57-Across offering
37 Show, as past events
39 Little ___, island in the Bering Strait
40 Herald
41 Tries to loosen
43 Brute
48 When four bells ring on the middle watch
49 It may give you a buzz
51 Memorable 1996 hurricane along the Eastern Seaboard
52 Corrida sounds
53 Corrida cloak
55 Snatch

1	2	3	4	5	6	7	8	9		10	11	12	13	14
15										16				
17								18						
19						20								
21					22							23		
24				25					26	27	28			
29			30				31		32					
			33					34						
35	36	37				38						39	40	41
42				43		44						45		
46				47	48						49			
50		51	52							53				
54								55						
56					57									
58					59									

by Byron Walden

157

ACROSS

1 Be against
5 Equal measures?: Abbr.
9 Undercroft
14 Her face began to circulate in 2000
16 Grizzled
17 Feature of the 1925 opera "Wozzeck"
18 Warmly welcome
19 "Lucrezia Borgia" composer
20 1920s–'60s Tennessee congressman B. Carroll ___
21 "Holiday in Havana" star, 1949
22 A Buddhist might be found in one
24 Spring
26 "The Merry Adventures of Robin Hood" author Howard
28 Clip
32 Enters gradually
34 Bear fruit
35 California city near Bakersfield
36 Historical decorum disdainer
38 Outdated communications
39 Dramatic exhalation
40 Danish beer brand
42 Old bolt shooter
44 "Something to Talk About" Grammy winner, 1991
49 Bum
50 Go downhill fast
52 Gut flora
53 Gut reaction?
54 Screen ___
55 Least comfortable
56 Big shock wave producer, briefly
57 Gershwin title character
58 Musical score abbr.

DOWN

1 Carne ___ (roasted beef dish)
2 Mongolian for "hero"
3 Big East b-ball powerhouse
4 "Lost" actress Raymonde
5 Related thing
6 Child actor Carl who played Alfalfa
7 Dog owner, often
8 Saws
9 Plot
10 Fragrant fruit used for jellies and confections
11 Musical accompaniment to many a comedic chase scene
12 Alternative to Travelocity or Orbitz
13 River near Hadrian's Wall
15 Adds spice to
23 Farming machine
25 Some a cappella music
27 Biblical 905-year-old
28 Nos. on some lotion bottles
29 Litter member that's almost always female
30 On one's game
31 He wrote "Time eases all things"
33 Plant with long ribbonlike leaves
37 Drumbeat
38 Tugboat fees
41 Jersey, e.g.
43 Jersey, e.g.
45 Bit of harlequinade
46 Relatively remote
47 Word that might accompany finger-pointing
48 Non-permanent residences
49 Pueblo site
51 Bucolic backdrops

	1	2	3	4		5	6	7	8		9	10	11	12	13
14					15						16				
17											18				
19											20				
21							22			23					
				24	25							26			27
28	29	30	31						32		33				
34										35					
36						37		38							
39					40		41								
	42			43							44	45	46	47	48
49						50			51						
52						53									
54						55									
56						57				58					

by Karen M. Tracey

158

ACROSS

1 Attendant
5 No mild pepper
10 Yearly loan figs.
14 Chooses badly
15 Lead role in a classic Arthur Miller play
16 Upstate New York county
17 Eventful stretches
18 Friendly side in a debate
20 Officer's request, at times
22 Rival of Roach in early film comedy
23 Asymmetry, as in a relationship
25 Wile E. Coyote, often
26 Overhead supporter
27 Ruminate (over)
29 Determine the innocence or guilt of
30 Orléans pronoun

31 Feodor III's successor as czar
33 Explanatory information about this puzzle is revealed by reading these in the clues
37 Its streets are immortalized in a classic cowboy ballad
38 Govt. agency creation
40 Head
43 "The Thinker," for one
44 On-call accessory
47 Rakes' shedmates
49 Make more important
51 Opening of a toast
53 Reinforced
54 Energize
56 Leucite source
57 Edit menu command
58 Titled
59 Two fives for ___

60 ESPN anchor Wingo
61 Result of polishing
62 Split

DOWN

1 Implement in a kitchen
2 Station information
3 Tripping over one's feet
4 Hardly necessary
5 Expert dealmaker
6 Optimists keep them alive
7 Parent's challenge
8 Part of French Indochina
9 Overtly
10 State Farm competitor
11 Incense burner, at times
12 Tears may be brought to one's eyes
13 Ever-vigilant sort
19 One possible answer to "Where are you?"

21 Frankfurt-to-Copenhagen dir.
24 Ticket taker?
28 "How to Make an American Quilt" author Whitney ___
31 Entreated
32 Well-proportioned
34 Of soundest mind
35 Remaining leery of
36 Draw together
39 Take vengeance
40 Option for dressing down
41 Barkeep's gizmo
42 Event for a marshal
44 Extorts
45 Nafta's overseas counterpart
46 Tiny biter
48 Entrap
50 Rob of "Melrose Place"
52 Eyecup's shape
55 Domitian's "I love"

by Matt Ginsberg

159

ACROSS

1 Big catch of 2003
8 Applauded with shouts
15 Estate taxes, e.g.
17 Grosbeak relatives
18 Common sight in Venezia
19 Temp. reducers
20 It's north of the Dodecanese Islands
21 Line pair
22 Joseph ___ Ratzinger, birth name of Pope Benedict XVI
24 Casual rejection
25 Nigerian native or language
26 "Fess up!"
28 La ___ Caspienne
29 Parts of some studios
31 11-Down's request
33 Reactionaries
34 "Valley of the Dolls" novelist
35 ___ Building, company headquarters erected in 1908 in New York City, at the time the tallest building in the world
36 Crunchy cafe treats
38 Want ad abbr.
39 Herbal brew
41 Sentence part: Abbr.
42 Looped vase handle
44 Disables
45 Title apiarist of a 1997 film
46 Like shoes and socks
48 French shooting match
49 Cager who starred in "Kazaam"
50 Tons of work to do
53 Carnival offerings
54 Digestion and circulation
55 Intrepid palace employees

DOWN

1 Like many Net connections
2 Without reservations
3 Try to get a better view, say
4 Some Spanish murals
5 "Phineas Finn" character Barrington ___
6 Serpent's tail?
7 Wood and others
8 Five-time winner of the Copa do Mundo
9 TV canine
10 Prizes for video production
11 One on a strict diet
12 Operator's line
13 It included the Eastern and Western fronts
14 There's sometimes no room for it
16 Maj. superiors
22 Having no aisles, in architecture
23 Allergies often affect them
26 Major messes
27 Object of Cavaradossi's affection
30 Dyne-centimeter
32 Red giant?
34 Be no slouch in class?
35 Oceanographers' references
36 Words from the heart?
37 Having no spleen
40 Southern snappers, briefly
43 Old tombstone abbr. meaning "at the age of"

by Joe Krozel

45 Dark
47 Recom-
      mended
      intake
49 Work ID

51 O.T. book
52 Title of
      respect
      in 8-Down:
      Abbr.

160

ACROSS

1 Washington is just above it
10 About
15 Believe
16 What things might be written in
17 "Whatever"
18 Some bucks and does
19 Garage stock
20 The Brady boys or girls
21 One opinionated to a fault
22 Ear piece
25 The Minotaur was fed seven of these annually
27 High-maintenance
28 Firm
30 Relatively recent arrival?
31 They appreciate 59-Down
33 She gave Odysseus a magic veil
34 Feldman's co-star on "The Two Coreys"
37 Impression-able
38 Minimal progress
39 Maximum: Abbr.
40 Glider-towing plane
42 "A Footnote to History" author's inits.
43 State in Elysium
44 Ingredient in chocolat
48 Quarterback Cunningham
50 Home of Weber State University
51 Some lilies
52 Red man?
56 Hipster
57 Two-time "Dancing With the Stars" co-winner Julianne
58 Fully posted?
61 Succeed
62 Adjunct to some pens
63 Believes
64 North Pacific carnivores

DOWN

1 William Howard Taft, by birth
2 Chuck Berry title girl who's repeatedly asked "Is that you?"
3 Come about
4 Plotters' place
5 "So ___ have I invoked thee . . .": Shak.
6 Opening for milk?
7 One who's not straight
8 Bell town in a Longfellow poem
9 Blood flow measurers
10 Garbage collectors
11 Settled
12 "Don't even bother!"
13 Kind of defense
14 It's found between exits
23 Latin word in a quotation book
24 City in Arthur C. Clarke's "The City and the Stars"
26 Squaring-off site
28 Kids' entertainer who won 12 Emmys
29 College expenses
32 Herringbone, e.g.
34 Cheered
35 Forsaken
36 "Don't even bother!"
38 Far from baggy
40 Turns red, maybe
41 Prefix with lateral
45 Record keeper
46 Parent
47 Inscribes, e.g.
49 Free of sticky stuff
53 François-___ de Chateaubriand
54 Chase in films
55 Last ruler of the Ptolemaic dynasty, informally

by Robert H. Wolfe

59 It's appreciated by 31-Across

60 Buddhist monastery

161

ACROSS

1 Park near Philly's City Hall, site of the LOVE statue
9 One might help you on your return
15 Drawer
16 "Ciao!"
17 Fazing
18 Not easily understood
19 John Wayne's L.A. alma mater
20 Sticky paint resins
22 Sierra Club founder
23 Alewife's relative
25 Prefix with facsimile
26 A root crop
27 Picked styles?
29 Prepares with hot seasoning
31 Fine threads
33 Put out
34 Grey Cup sports org.
37 Bedtime stories?
39 River surrounding Navy Island

41 Head word
42 Reliever's triumph
44 1925 trial name
45 Confirmation to a busboy
47 "Das Glasperlen-spiel" novelist
48 Some pens
51 With no apparent purpose
53 Arnsberg is on it
54 One of two that make one
55 Gas pump option
57 Had no catching up to do
58 Secret area of anatomy?
60 Sari-clad royal
62 Do a pit job
63 Cuts off
64 N.C.A.A. rival of George Mason
65 1966 hit for the Capitols

DOWN

1 It was captured by British forces in 1917
2 Result of a combustion explosion
3 Eponym of a national forest in New Mexico
4 Election figure: Abbr.
5 With 59-Down, Rudolph Valentino's "Blood and Sand" co-star
6 Pitching a bit
7 Totally beat
8 Pair of diamonds?
9 Reunión attendees
10 Performance piece?
11 Skate-boarders compete in them
12 Alternative to a pillbox
13 Anorak wearer
14 They're on the same level

21 Dartmoor setting
24 One isn't sharp
26 It'll help you lighten up
28 They're the fault of faults
30 One of Tennessee's state symbols
32 Lot
34 Enclosed in a case, as seeds
35 Toning skin lotion
36 Passé video store offering
38 To have, in Tours
40 It may follow convention
43 Not foreign
45 Opposite of exodus
46 Texas's westernmost county
48 Dig find
49 Polish person?
50 Part of some biography titles
52 Bumpkin

by Barry C. Silk

55 Dark cover
56 Dixieland group?
59 See 5-Down
61 Period in Indian history

162

ACROSS

1 Drug combination?
15 Many a vigilante
16 Call for dishes
17 Going for
18 Unspoken language
19 Not in the dark
20 Scent
22 River that meets the Thames at London
23 Very hot star
25 Insinuating
26 No walk in the park
27 Players that replaced Minis
29 Base pay recipient?: Abbr.
30 Title holder
31 Pitcher Orlando Hernández's nickname
33 Undercover Playboy Bunny of 1963
35 Continuous series

36 "Lost" Emmy nominee Henry ___ Cusick
37 Sans strife
41 Break, as a habit
44 Started
45 ___ Morris College, in Jacksonville, Tex.
47 Electric guitar model, familiarly
48 Mind
49 Praise for Nero?
51 Bygone boomers
52 Gate info: Abbr.
53 Bebe who co-starred in "The Maltese Falcon," 1931
55 Act on a primal urge
56 "Krapp's Last Tape" playwright
58 Chew out
60 Be postponed
61 Dweller along Lake Volta
62 Doesn't get wrapped up well?

DOWN

1 Not taken to the cleaners?
2 Not perfectly round
3 Come back
4 Major downer?
5 Money-changer's profit
6 Splits
7 W.W. I battle locale near the Belgian border
8 Hoedown moves
9 It may be received after sweeping
10 Sedative target, with "the"
11 Beltway fig.
12 Longtime columnist for The Nation
13 Phone system starting point
14 One set for a future wedding?
21 Pro wrestler Flair
24 "Walk on the Wild Side" singer

26 Upright relatives
28 Platoon part
30 They make lasting impressions
32 Family moniker
34 Roofing material
38 Legalese adverb
39 Like some navels
40 Hyundai model
41 Bear
42 First name in late-night talk, once
43 Automatic sound
46 Réponse affirmative
49 Round midnight?
50 Root of law
53 Band that famously remade "Satisfaction" on its first album
54 Work to help one get 57-Down
57 See 54-Down
59 Night spot

by Joe Krozel

163

ACROSS
1 Hindenburg's predecessor as German president
6 Cousin of an alewife
10 Longtime name in news-gathering
14 Drive participant
15 Heads of Italy
16 Gifford's talk-show replacement
17 Place for a tie
19 Magnito-gorsk's river
20 Summer cooler
21 Biblical trial word
22 Manages to get through
23 Roger of "Cheers"
24 Multiplied
25 One doing fitting work
27 Hue similar to cyan
33 Miss at a rodeo
36 Off for a stretch
37 Brand of octane booster
38 Oscar winner for "The Bridge on the River Kwai"
41 Water-skiing variety
42 She, to Schiaparelli
46 Credit report tarnisher, briefly
47 First holder of the title Supreme Governor of the Church of England
53 Calls for passage
54 Governing group
55 Origination point
56 Epithet coined for the 2002 State of the Union address
57 Toe trouble
58 Recommend highly
59 Toy with tassels
60 Dr. Foreman's portrayer on "House"
61 Title aunt in a 1979 best seller
62 Plant ___

DOWN
1 The rough vis-à-vis a green
2 Summer headgear
3 Bring to the boiling point
4 2001 Emmy nominee for "The West Wing"
5 Quality
6 Elaborate solo vocal composition
7 It might be kicked after being picked up
8 With celerity
9 Like some tracts
10 Sternum attachment
11 Alveoli, e.g.
12 Enter la-la land
13 Spiel preparer
18 Cheerful, in Châlons
26 Sports winners
28 Stationery topper
29 Count
30 Second-century year
31 Phil Rizzuto, on the Yankees
32 Headed up
33 Burner locale
34 Court crowd-pleaser
35 Executed part of a 34-Down
39 Shuts up
40 Group with the 1967 #2 hit "Georgy Girl," with "the"
43 English poet Smith
44 Butcherbird or woodchat
45 Like super-markets
48 Locale of Theban ruins
49 Part of the body next to the sacrum
50 Ritz rival
51 Catullus's "Odi et ___"
52 U.K. equivalent to an Oscar

by Frank Longo

164

ACROSS

1 Item with clear face value?
6 One who may have connections
14 Certain blues
16 Cry of relief at an accident scene
17 "Haw"
18 Provoked
19 Roadside stand offering
20 NATO member since 2004
22 Grp. with the debut single "10538 Overture"
23 Rectangular array that's identical when its rows and columns are transposed, as this puzzle's grid
27 Stud alternative
28 Fruity
29 Fruit salad waste
30 Where pizza originated
31 Some collectible Dutch prints
34 Round-bottomed vessels
35 Split and boned entree
36 A choli is worn under it
37 Kind of paper
40 Pondering, informally
43 Many a goddaughter
45 "Collage With Squares Arranged According to the Laws of Chance" artist
46 Revealed the end to?
48 One involved in future deals?
49 Who wrote "I dwelt alone / In a world of moan, / And my soul was a stagnant tide"
50 Some early "astronauts"
51 Lecture, in a way
53 Magazine sales
55 Courtside seats?
56 Honey
57 Cockamamie
58 Automaker Maserati
59 Tots

DOWN

1 Hindu musician's source material for improvisation
2 Methyl orange or Congo red
3 Woman's name meaning "peace"
4 Elementary stuff
5 They may be seen on a lake's surface
6 1963 Elizabeth Taylor/Richard Burton drama
7 Dinosaur, so to speak
8 Turkey setting
9 A little cleaner?
10 "Hostel" director Roth
11 Completely straight-forward
12 Title woman of a story from James Joyce's "Dubliners"
13 Electron-transferring reactions, briefly
15 Country music's ___ Brothers
21 Prunes
24 1990s HBO sketch comedy series
25 Obi-Wan's apprentice
26 Some are heaping: Abbr.
31 Dido
32 German chancellor, 1998–2005
33 Specialty cookware item
34 Drop off
36 End of many business names
37 Trough
38 Polish stripper
39 Some dupes
41 Brand of insecticide strips
42 Doesn't skip
44 Self-response to "Must we put up with this?"
47 Believer in al-Hakim as the embodiment of God
52 Home of Presque Isle Downs racetrack
54 Be a different way?
55 Wrench part

by Mike Nothnagel and Byron Walden

165

ACROSS

1 Unpleasant face covering
4 "O Fortuna" composer
8 Notice in a restaurant
13 Battery, e.g.
15 Fifth-century pope called "the Great"
16 1973 musical for which George S. Irving won a Tony for Best Actor
17 Stat for a state
18 "Can-Can" song
20 Unexpected info source
21 Edgy?
22 Member of a NATO land since 2004
23 Manual component
25 It's all relatives
26 Old Mideast org.
27 A long one is 12% "longer" than a short one
28 Emulate a woman, in "I Am Woman"
32 Aggressive guarding option
37 Bad thing to drive into
38 What some dogs and flaming daredevils do
39 Winter Olympics maneuver
40 Get into
41 From left to right: Abbr.
42 Plasma alternatives, briefly
43 As required
45 It's taken in court
49 Was compelled
51 Added power, in slang
53 "Tell me more . . ."
55 Coin with 12 stars on both the front and back
56 It's often filtered
57 Fee-faw-fum

58 Company V.I.P.'s: Abbr.
59 Do nothing worthwhile
60 Minuscule part of a 34-Down: Abbr.
61 Surprise winner of 1948: Abbr.

DOWN

1 Citation abbreviation
2 Tusks, e.g.
3 Lionel to Drew Barrymore
4 Number between scenes
5 1941 Disney film based on a Kenneth Grahame story, with "The"
6 They're sold in oversize rolls
7 Bygone emporium
8 Autumn arrival
9 Like some confessions
10 Simple
11 Tizzy

12 Adventure
14 Result in serious damage
19 It follows directions
24 Many an ad
28 Shakes off new distractions
29 Away, in a way
30 Clarifying link
31 Invoice abbr.
32 Third baseman Melvin
33 "He eateth grass as ___": Job 40:15
34 See 60-Across: Abbr.
35 Tiny fraction of a foot-pound
36 F on a physics exam
42 1969 Omar Sharif title role
44 Nomadic dwellings
45 Piece of punditry
46 Book of Mormon's longest book

by Joe Krozel

The New York Times

SMART PUZZLES
PRESENTED WITH STYLE

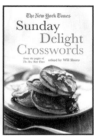

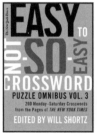

Available at your local bookstore or online at www.nytimes.com/nytstore

St. Martin's Griffin

1

S	C	R	E	W		A	L	S	O		S	P	E	W
O	H	A	R	A		N	O	O	N		L	A	V	A
F	O	U	R	M	I	N	U	T	E	M	I	L	E	R
A	O	L		P	L	O	D		O	V	I	N	E	
		D	U	L	Y		C	L	I	E	N	T	S	
H	A	R	E	M	S		W	H	I	R	R			
E	V	A	C		S	H	I	N	E		B	A	G	
F	O	R	O	L	D	T	I	M	E	S	S	A	K	E
T	W	A		A	R	O	S	E		P	R	I	M	
	S	M	A	R	T		P	L	A	I	N	S		
D	E	S	P	I	T	E		R	E	A	M			
A	L	I	E	N		P	E	A	S		P	S	I	
F	O	R	E	A	N	D	A	F	T	S	A	I	L	S
O	P	E	D		A	I	R	E		O	R	L	O	N
E	E	N	S		P	E	E	R		S	K	E	E	T

2

C	H	E	F	S		W	I	P	E		I	D	O	L
U	B	O	A	T		A	P	E	X		D	E	M	I
D	O	N	Q	U	I	X	O	T	E		E	N	I	D
			B	R	E	D		C	H	A	N	T	S	
S	I	D	E	B	A	R		G	R	A	T	I	S	
U	S	O	P	E	N		L	O	A	V	E	S		
R	A	C	E	D		M	O	N	T	E		Q	B	S
G	A	T	E		F	O	R	G	E		E	U	R	O
E	C	O		E	L	V	E	S		B	R	A	I	N
		R	E	T	A	I	N		G	A	M	I	N	G
	S	Q	U	A	R	E		P	A	R	A	D	E	S
C	O	U	R	S	E		Z	E	R	O				
E	L	L	I	E		D	A	I	R	Y	Q	U	E	E	N
D	I	N	K		U	N	T	O		U	R	G	E	S
E	D	N	A		P	A	I	N		E	N	O	L	A

3

C	A	R	A	F	E		A	B	C	S		A	H	S
C	L	E	V	E	R		M	E	A	L		L	E	I
C	E	S	A	R	R	O	M	E	R	O		T	Y	R
	T	I	M		G	O	T	O		S	I	D	E	
C	H	A	L	I	C	E			B	A	T	M	A	N
E	A	R		L	E	A	H		X	R	A	Y	S	
O	D	E	S	S	A		R	E	N	E	E			
	J	A	C	K	N	I	C	H	O	L	S	O	N	
		A	I	S	L	E		I	S	S	U	E	D	
F	L	A	R	E		O	D	E	S		T	W	O	
J	O	K	E	R	S		T	E	A	R	O	S	E	
O	T	I	S		C	H	I	C		R	E	F		
R	I	N		H	E	A	T	H	L	E	D	G	E	R
D	O	T		O	N	Z	E		E	N	D	A	S	H
S	N	O		T	E	E	M		S	A	Y	S	S	O

4

S	M	E	L	L		S	C	U	L	L		H	O	G
I	G	L	O	O		H	O	S	E	A		A	C	E
T	R	Y	T	R	Y	A	G	A	I	N		N	E	E
			T	E	M	P	S			D	E	G	A	S
C	A	D	E	N	C	E		S	A	L	T	I	N	E
O	N	O	R		A	R	M	E	N	I	A	N		
V	I	N	Y	L			E	L	A	N		T	S	P
E	S	T		I	M	I	T	A	T	E		H	O	E
Y	E	S		G	A	V	E			S	P	E	W	S
		T	I	A	M	A	R	I	A		O	R	E	O
B	O	O	K	M	A	N		N	I	P	P	E	R	S
R	U	P	E	E		P	U	R	E	E				
I	N	N		N	E	V	E	R	S	A	Y	D	I	E
E	C	O		T	O	I	L	E		L	E	A	R	N
F	E	W		S	N	I	T	S		E	S	S	E	S

5

```
C H A T ■ S O L E ■ R A P I D
H A L O ■ A V O N ■ A M E B A
A M E N ■ F E E D ■ G O D O T
S L U G G E R W I L L I E ■ ■
M E T A L ■ K E N Y A ■ S D S
S T S ■ U Z I ■ G E N E T I C
■ ■ P E E L E ■ ■ L A N A ■
P A L E Y E L L O W C O L O R
U R A L ■ ■ S P O O N ■ ■ ■
P U L L T A B ■ O E R ■ P A T
A T A ■ A R E A S ■ G E O D E
■ L A B R A T S M I L I E U
S N A R L ■ T R U E ■ I N S T
E R N I E ■ L I M A ■ O T T O
C A D E T ■ E A S T ■ T E E N
```

6

```
M I R E D ■ H A F T S ■ C R O
A C E L A ■ A W A I T ■ H I C
P U B L I S H O R P E R I S H
■ ■ E Q U A L ■ P R A N K S
F U N R U N ■ S C E N T ■ N I
O N O ■ I D I ■ A R S E N I C
R T E ■ R A M P S ■ D O N O
M A X F I E L D P A R R I S H
E M I R ■ O S A G E ■ S O O
R E T I R E S ■ R E N ■ E L S
■ ■ T E N T H ■ G E T S E T
G L A Z E R ■ U S A G E ■
L O U I S I A N A P A R I S H
I N N ■ E C L A T ■ D R E A R
B E T ■ S H I N E ■ E A R L S
```

7

```
T O M S ■ W A R T S ■ D E J A
I N I T ■ E L I O T ■ E X A M
E T N A ■ B L A I R ■ S P R Y
R O O T O F A L L E V I L ■ ■
■ P R U N E ■ ■ S T A ■ O R C
■ ■ S E E Y A ■ C L O S E R
R A T ■ S T E M T H E T I D E
A T R A ■ A N O ■ T V A D
L E A F T H R O U G H ■ E S O
P A N C H O ■ T R Y O N ■ ■
H M S ■ E R S ■ M Y E Y E
■ P L A N T M A N A G E R S
S H O E ■ E R I C A ■ A S I A
E A S E ■ T E R M S ■ T E E D
T R E K ■ S W E E T ■ E S S O
```

8

```
A D L E R ■ G A R T H ■ D A T
C R U D E ■ A L O H A ■ R O O
M A N U A L L A B O R ■ A R K
E G G ■ M I A M I ■ D A N T E
■ ■ P E R S O N A L L O A N
A R M A D A ■ ■ W I G ■ ■
P O U R ■ S P O O F ■ E B B
S P I R I T U A L L E A D E R
E E R ■ G E E S E ■ N I T A
■ ■ E N E ■ ■ Z A N T A C
D I A G O N A L L I N E ■
R O T O R ■ L E O N A ■ A P O
A W E ■ A L L T U C K E D I N
M A S ■ N A O M I ■ I R E N E
A N T ■ T O T E S ■ N E S T S
```

9

```
M E L O N   W A L T   E M M A
E X U D E   A R I A   F O E S
L I B E R A L B E N E F I T S
S T E R O I D     P U R E E
      D O I   W I S E S T
S E T T E E   N I E C E
I C I E R   E D N A   S P F
M O D E R A T E D R I N K E R
P L Y     G O N O   G U I L E
  P L A N T   M O T T L E
M O H A I R   S R I
A V E R T     E M E R A L D
C O N S E R V A T I V E T I E
R I C E   A I D A   A B O V E
O D E S   S N A G   N A M E D
```

10

```
L I M O   P A A R   I N C U R
E C O L   O N C E   S O U S E
G O O D N I G H T S S L E E P
O N T H E S L Y   T U T
      A G E E   P R E E M I E
N O T B A D   K R I S   O C T
O R B I T   S N I P   S U E Y
B E T T E R M O U S E T R A P
U I E S   O I L S   R A N G E
T D S   L O L L   H O R S E S
S A T H O M E   M O T T
    D W I   G E N I U S E S
B E S T K E P T S E C R E T S
O L I V E   D O A S   N E U T
T I P S Y   A S S T   S K I S
```

11

```
A P E   H I T C H   A D E P T
E R S   A C U R A   R E V U E
S I S I S E N O R   A B A T E
O M E N   J A P E   M I N T S
P A N A M A   F I T
    C M A J O R S C A L E
S L O P S   T U N E   A X O N
H O B O   F A L S E   R E N O
E V I L   E L I E   I D L E S
S E E Y O U L A T E R
    E N D     N E T T L E
P A S S E   O R C A   A R A B
E L I T E   S E A B R E E Z E
W I L E Y   H E L L O   E E R
S T O R E   A L L E N   D D T
```

12

```
S N A R E   J E A N   A F A R
A E S O P   U C L A   S I M I
P H I L I P R O T H   S N I P
S I T E   E O N     B E I G E
    P A T R O B E R T S O N
S P I L L S     A B A S H
M E T A L   E U R O S   L A M
E A S Y   P R M E N   D I K E
E T A   W A R P S   L E N I N
  S T E N O     D E P E N D
P I E R R E R E N O I R
E M C E E     L I E   I V E S
D A R N   P A U L R E V E R E
A G E D   R I D E   G E N I E
L E T S   O D E S   O S I E R
```

13

T	E	S	T		C	O	P	E	S		L	A	Z	Y
A	X	L	E		A	W	A	R	E		A	R	O	O
S	P	O	T		D	E	L	L	A		B	I	O	S
T	O	W		D	E	N	S	E	F	O	R	E	S	T
E	S	C	O	R	T	S		A	P	E				
		O	N	U	S		T	O	R	E	A	D	O	R
A	B	O	M	B		J	E	W	E	L		U	P	A
J	A	K	E		H	O	M	E	R		A	M	I	N
O	R	E		S	O	A	P	S		E	B	B	E	D
B	A	R	I	T	O	N	E		S	L	E	W		
		N	A	S		O	I	L	L	A	M	P		
O	B	T	U	S	E	A	N	G	L	E		I	I	I
L	O	R	I		G	L	A	R	E		E	T	N	A
E	X	I	T		O	A	T	E	N		L	E	O	N
G	Y	M	S		W	R	E	S	T		O	R	S	O

14

S	T	E	V	E		J	A	C	K		I	B	M
E	R	R	O	R	S		A	L	E	E		N	E	A
C	O	N	A	N	O	B	R	I	E	N		J	A	Y
T	D	S		I	N	A	G	E	S		L	E	N	O
	L	E	S	S	O	N		A	E	S	I	R
M	I	M	I		I	N	T	I	M	A	T	E	S
A	T	P	E	A	C	E		O	N	E		
J	O	H	N	N	Y		C	A	R	S	O	N
		T	A	M		D	E	N	E	U	V	E
A	B	O	M	I	N	A	T	E		S	N	A	G
S	O	L	O	S		G	I	B	E	A	T	
H	O	S	T		R	E	D	U	C	E		P	R	O
T	H	E		T	O	N	I	G	H	T	S	H	O	W
O	O	N		A	N	T	E		O	N	T	I	M	E
N	O	S		P	A	A	R		A	L	L	E	N

15

Z	E	R	O		B	O	W	S		S	L	A	B
A	X	E	S		O	L	E	O		C	O	R	E
P	I	N	T		O	L	I	N		A	V	I	D
S	T	E	E	L	(E)	M	A	G	N	O	L	I	A	S
		R	O	B		H	E	M	A	N
J	I	B		T	O	A	S	T	S		G	T	O
A	D	A	P	T	O	R		S	C	A	T
B	I	G	M	O	M	M	A	(S)	(H)	O	U	S	E
B	O	G	S		S	T	O	P	P	E	R
A	M	Y		G	R	O	P	E	S		S	R	I
	J	A	N	E	T		R	E	S	
P	R	E	L	U	D	E	T	O	(A)	(K)	I	S	S
R	E	A	L		A	L	A	I		I	N	L	A
A	N	N	O		C	L	O	D		R	O	O	F
M	O	S	T		T	O	S	S		T	R	E	E

16

C	A	S	H		D	E	B	R	A		F	E	S	T
A	C	L	U		E	N	T	E	R		A	M	I	E
C	R	U	M	B	C	R	U	S	T		J	A	G	S
T	E	M	P	E	R	A	S		D	W	I	G	H	T
I	S	P		R	I	G		B	E	A	T			
		C	R	E	E	P	Y	C	R	A	W	L	Y
E	N	J	O	Y	S		A	T	O	M		H	U	E
P	E	A	T		I	C	E		D	A	T	A
I	A	N		L	A	N	E		S	A	U	T	E	S
C	R	E	D	I	T	C	R	U	N	C	H		
		R	O	T	H		S	O	T		R	P	I
B	A	N	A	N	A		R	A	W	O	N	I	O	N
A	G	O	G		C	R	A	B	C	R	E	O	L	E
R	E	D	O		K	U	K	L	A		A	T	O	P
E	D	E	N		S	T	E	E	P		P	S	S	T

17

L	A	K	E		H	E	M	P		G	A	M	M	A
I	D	E	S		O	B	I	E		A	V	I	A	N
S	H	E	S	A	L	A	D	Y		Z	E	S	T	Y
T	O	N	E	R		N	I	O	B	E				
S	C	E	N	T	S			T	A	B	A	S	C	O
			Y	O	U	R	E	S	O	V	A	I	N	
C	A	P	S		P	R	E			S	A	L	T	S
A	N	I	N		S	N	E	R	D		I	S	E	E
V	I	S	O	R			V	E	E		L	A	S	T
I	M	A	B	E	L	I	E	V	E	R				
L	E	N	S	M	E	N			R	E	C	T	O	R
			N	A	C	H	O			A	L	I	V	E
J	A	B	B	A		H	E	S	A	R	E	B	E	L
A	L	I	E	N		E	L	L	Y		A	I	R	E
B	E	N	E	T		S	L	O	E		T	A	T	E

18

L	A	L	A		J	E	T	S		O	R	B	I	T
E	T	A	S		A	R	O	N		D	E	L	C	O
G	E	T	T	I	N	G	C	O	L	D	F	E	E	T
I	M	H	I	P		S	K	O	A	L		S	S	T
O	P	E	N	E	D			T	W	O		S	H	E
N	O	R		C	U	E	S		S	T	A	Y	E	R
		H	A	N	D	I	N			T	O	E	S	
	C	H	I	C	K	E	N	I	N	G	O	U	T	
F	O	A	L			N	A	T	I	O	N			
E	R	R	O	R	S		I	S	B	N		E	M	I
R	N	A		A	O	K			S	E	A	M	A	N
U	P	S		I	N	R	E	D		I	T	E	R	S
L	O	S	I	N	G	O	N	E	S	N	E	R	V	E
E	N	E	R	O		N	O	A	H		A	G	E	R
S	E	D	A	N		A	L	L	Y		M	E	L	T

19

M	A	S	K		H	U	M	U	S		E	F	O	R
U	N	T	O		U	N	A	P	T		T	R	I	O
S	C	A	R		S	A	Y	N	O		H	E	L	D
T	H	R	E	S	H		B	E	M	I	N	E		
D	O	R	A	T	H	E	E	X	P	L	O	R	E	R
O	R	Y		P	U	P		T	S	E		I	W	O
		K	A	S	E	M				A	D	E	N	
	J	O	E	T	H	E	P	L	U	M	B	E	R	
H	U	N	G			H	E	N	C	E				
A	D	E		S	A	C		E	T	D		A	L	A
R	O	S	I	E	T	H	E	R	I	V	E	T	E	R
	L	O	C	K	I	N		T	I	N	H	A	T	
I	S	I	N		I	N	T	E	L		D	O	P	E
D	E	C	I		N	U	R	S	E		E	M	I	R
E	X	E	C		S	P	E	E	D		D	E	N	Y

20

J	O	U	S	T		J	O	E	Y		J	O	S	H
O	P	R	A	H		E	N	N	E		A	R	E	A
J	E	S	S	E	J	A	M	E	S		N	E	A	T
O	L	A		M	A	N	Y			I	D	I	O	T	S
		J	A	Y	S		T	K	O	S				
	A	B	A	S	E		M	E	N	O	H	U	N	G	J	U	R	Y
S	L	A	C	K		M	E	N	O		O	N	E	A
E	L	M	O		J	C	R	E	W		P	I	N	K
R	O	B	B		E	G	O	S		P	L	O	T	S
F	R	I	J	O	L	E	S		G	A	I	N	S	
		A	B	L	E		M	A	N	N				
H	A	R	V	E	Y		F	A	L	A		A	L	I
A	L	A	I		J	O	E	J	A	C	K	S	O	N
H	U	R	T		A	L	T	O		H	I	T	O	N
A	M	E	S		R	E	A	R		E	X	A	M	S

21

M	Y	S	T	■	■	C	A	S	T	■	S	P	A	M
R	O	T	O	R	■	O	B	E	Y	■	E	R	G	O
B	U	R	M	A	■	R	A	C	K	E	T	E	E	R
U	R	I	■	I	M	P	■	■	E	X	T	E	N	T
R	E	C	K	L	E	S	S	■	■	C	O	N	D	O
N	I	T	E	■	T	E	C	H	I	E	■	S	A	N
S	T	E	V	E	■	■	H	A	L	L	S	■	■	■
■	■	R	I	C	K	R	O	L	L	I	N	G	■	■
■	■	■	N	O	O	I	L	■	■	N	O	E	L	S
H	A	M	■	C	O	B	A	L	T	■	B	R	E	T
A	R	U	B	A	■	■	R	O	C	K	S	T	A	R
R	O	S	A	R	Y	■	■	O	U	I	■	R	K	O
R	U	C	K	S	A	C	K	S	■	S	Q	U	A	B
I	S	L	E	■	W	H	E	E	■	S	E	D	G	E
S	E	E	R	■	■	S	I	G	N	■	■	D	E	E	S

22

S	L	E	D	■	A	L	M	S	■	D	A	Z	E	D
P	E	P	E	■	L	E	A	H	■	O	B	A	M	A
E	G	O	S	■	I	A	G	O	■	M	A	G	U	S
W	A	X	I	N	G	P	O	E	T	I	C	■	■	■
S	L	Y	■	U	N	T	O	■	E	N	I	G	M	A
■	■	■	A	L	E	■	■	S	A	G	■	L	E	X
■	F	U	L	L	D	I	S	C	L	O	S	U	R	E
E	L	L	A	■	■	B	O	O	■	■	L	E	I	S
W	A	N	I	N	G	I	N	T	E	R	E	S	T	■
E	R	A	■	I	R	S	■	■	R	A	W	■	■	■
S	E	R	E	N	E	■	S	O	U	P	■	M	A	R
■	■	N	E	W	H	A	M	P	S	H	I	R	E	■
A	B	C	T	V	■	A	B	E	T	■	E	N	T	S
T	U	T	E	E	■	U	R	G	E	■	L	E	O	I
M	Y	R	R	H	■	L	E	A	D	■	M	O	O	N

23

J	A	M	B	■	E	M	I	L	■	A	R	M	E	D
E	S	A	I	■	R	E	N	O	■	L	E	O	N	A
S	I	N	G	L	E	O	C	C	U	P	A	N	C	Y
T	A	E	B	O	■	W	H	I	R	■	S	O	S	■
■	■	■	A	L	S	■	■	G	O	O	■	■	■	■
D	O	U	B	L	E	I	N	D	E	M	N	I	T	Y
I	T	T	Y	■	E	D	I	E	■	A	S	T	R	A
G	T	E	■	S	P	E	N	C	E	R	■	I	A	L
A	E	R	I	E	■	A	J	A	X	■	A	N	N	I
T	R	I	P	L	E	L	A	Y	E	R	C	A	K	E
■	■	L	A	T	■	■	■	S	A	C	■	■	■	■
■	S	H	E	■	T	A	C	K	■	C	E	L	I	A
Q	U	A	D	R	U	P	L	E	B	Y	P	A	S	S
V	E	R	G	E	■	E	U	R	O	■	T	O	N	I
C	R	E	E	D	■	X	E	N	A	■	S	S	T	S

24

B	L	A	M	E	■	P	E	R	T	■	C	E	L	L
R	O	L	E	S	■	I	C	E	R	■	A	Q	U	A
A	G	E	N	T	■	C	O	P	A	■	S	U	M	O
T	O	S	S	A	S	A	L	A	D	■	T	I	P	S
■	■	■	A	T	T	Y	■	■	S	E	G	A	■	■
A	C	T	■	E	R	U	P	T	■	A	V	A	S	T
B	R	E	T	■	I	N	A	■	L	O	O	K	M	A
B	A	T	H	■	P	E	T	C	O	■	T	I	E	S
A	Z	O	R	E	S	■	C	R	O	■	E	T	A	T
S	Y	N	O	D	■	C	H	E	F	S	■	A	R	E
■	■	■	W	A	S	H	■	S	A	P	S	■	■	■
B	A	J	A	■	P	I	T	C	H	A	T	E	N	T
O	L	A	F	■	I	S	E	E	■	C	A	M	E	O
R	A	V	I	■	T	O	R	N	■	E	V	I	A	N
G	N	A	T	■	E	X	I	T	■	K	E	R	R	Y

25

M	A	O		A	R	T	S		J	O	I	N	T	S
A	R	R	I	V	E	A	T		A	G	R	E	E	D
S	I	G	M	A	C	H	I		M	A	I	T	A	I
T	E	A	S		O	O	P	S		U	S	S	R	
S	S	N		K	N	E	E	H	I	G	H			
		M	O	I		N	U	D	E		M	D	S	
A	L	U	M	N	A		D	S	T		C	O	A	T
W	I	S	E	G	U	Y		H	A	I	R	D	Y	E
E	R	I	N		R	A	W		G	L	U	E	O	N
S	A	C		P	A	P	A		L	D	L			
	C	L	E	A	R	S	K	Y		P	R	E		
	L	I	S	A		T	H	E	O		A	L	O	T
M	U	D	P	I	E		E	V	A	N	B	A	Y	H
I	N	L	A	N	D		R	E	L	I	A	N	C	E
A	G	E	N	T	S		O	R	A	L		E	E	L

26

A	B	A	C	I		T	A	C	T		O	M	A	N
M	A	C	O	N		O	S	H	A		P	O	L	O
P	A	L	M	S		M	E	I	R		A	B	I	T
	S	U	B	U	R	B	A	N	M	A	L	I	B	U
		A	L	A		O	A	F		L	I	P		
M	U	S	T	A	N	G	E	S	C	A	P	E		
A	P	U		R	A	I	L		R	O	H	A	N	
H	I	N	T		T	A	C	O	S		P	O	K	E
I	N	D	I	A		I	D	O	S		M	I	X	
	A	C	C	O	R	D	E	L	E	M	E	N	T	
S	K	Y		T	O	E		T	A	U				
H	Y	B	R	I	D	V	E	H	I	C	L	E	S	
A	R	E	A		L	I	R	A		O	L	L	I	E
R	I	S	K		E	V	I	L		W	A	L	L	Y
P	E	T	E		S	E	C	T		S	H	A	K	E

27

A	B	R	U	P	T		L	A	I	R		T	S	O
P	R	O	M	O	S		A	I	D	E		A	B	E	T
B	A	N	A	N	A	S	P	L	I	T		G	O	A	T
	I	R	I	S		I	C	A	N	S	O			
E	L	I	T	E		L	E	M	O	N	C	R	E	A	M
L	O	S	E	S	I	T		A	A	A	S		S	L	A
I	C	A	R	U	S		A	C	H		A	T	T	N
	A	P	P	L	E	C	R	U	M	B	L	E		
T	I	C	S		D	U	O		A	R	C	A	D	E
I	N	N		O	M	A	R		S	P	O	O	K	E	D
C	H	E	R	R	Y	M	A	S	H		W	A	S	P	S
K	O	W	T	O	W		E	A	R	N				
L	U	T	E		O	R	A	N	G	E	C	R	U	S	H
E	S	O	S		R	O	B	O		B	O	U	R	N	E
D	E	N		D	E	E	R		S	W	E	L	L	S

28

D	I	S	M	A	Y		M	A	S	K		T	R	Y
E	L	A	I	N	E		O	M	N	I		H	I	E
F	O	U	N	T	A	I	N	P	E	N		A	S	A
O	N	C	U	E		D	E	L	E		R	T	E	S
G	A	Y	E		M	I	T	E	R	J	O	I	N	T
		T	R	A				S	O	D	S			
A	S	H		E	M	A	I	L		C	E	A	S	E
C	H	A	M	P	A	G	N	E	C	O	O	L	E	R
H	A	L	A	L		E	N	N	I	S		L	E	G
	F	R	A	U				T	E	L				
H	O	K	E	Y	P	O	K	E	Y		I	R	A	N
O	W	N	S		T	U	N	A		A	N	I	M	E
L	E	O		W	A	T	E	R	I	N	G	C	A	N
E	N	T		O	K	R	A		T	O	U	C	H	E
S	S	S		N	E	E	D		S	N	A	I	L	S

29

```
A C T E D █ W A I L █ R S V P
L A H T I █ E M M A █ O H I O
D R E A M A B O U T █ B O A T
E G G █ E T C █ S E G U E █ █
N O A H █ L A B █ R E S H O T
█ █ P A J A M A B O T T O M S
█ █ L A S █ R U N S █ R I P █
E P S O M █ S T Y █ M I N T S
█ D O H █ P A P A █ K A T █ █
A L A B A M A B O R D E R █ █
M E D I C I █ S L O █ M A S S
█ █ O S K A R █ D N A █ M C I
N E W T █ B E A M A B O A R D
O V E R █ L A V A █ O R D I E
R E D O █ E D E N █ O B A M A
```

30

```
M U M █ A S A P █ █ G A M E S
O N O █ F O N D A █ A G O G O
W I T H O U T Q U E S T I O N
G S H A R P █ █ R A P █ █ █ █
L O R I █ █ T S A R █ A R M █
I N A L L L I K E L I H O O D
█ █ █ █ I A M I █ █ D A L A I
M A Y B E Y E S M A Y B E N O
S W E E T █ █ U T I L █ █ █ █
N O T L O O K I N G S O H O T
█ L I T █ S E T S █ █ N I G H
█ █ █ █ U S N █ █ C O U P L E
A I N T G O N N A H A P P E N
I D E A L █ Y O Y O S █ I R E
M O O D Y █ █ W E P T █ E S T
```

31

```
I R I S H █ T O M S █ E A R P
M A R L O █ A R A T █ X B O X
A R O A R █ L E G A L P A D S
M E N W A L K O N M O O N █ █
S R O █ T U B █ U P A █ D O A
█ N E I L A R M S T R O N G █
█ █ █ D O L C E █ █ H E N I E
K I R I █ S K I D S █ L S T S
I C O N S █ █ G O T T I █ █ █
█ W E C A M E I N P E A C E █
I R K █ A L G █ A L I █ M A O
█ █ F O R A L L M A N K I N D
A F O R T I O R I █ T I L D E
B E R G █ N O O N █ E L I O T
E D D Y █ E S N E █ D O O R S
```

32

```
C R I M E █ G A R P █ C H A F F
H A R E M █ O R A L █ H A L L E
A T A L E O F T W O C I T I E S
R E Q █ R A R E █ █ A R E T E S
█ █ █ S I T E █ D O R A █ █ █ █
█ L E T T H E M E A T C A K E █
W A L R U S █ E L K S █ L I R E
A B I E S █ E S P Y █ S I L A S
R E Z A █ W A S H █ A T C O S T
█ L A M A R S E I L L A I S E █
█ █ █ █ P A T S █ A G R A █ █ █
P T B O A T █ █ E G A D █ F R O
F R E N C H R E V O L U T I O N
C O A C H █ O R E O █ S A L V E
S P R E E █ T E N N █ T R E E S
```

33

R	E	A	M	■	■	F	E	L	L	S	■	B	R	A
A	N	V	I	L	■	L	A	S	S	O	■	R	A	M
J	O	E	S	A	T	U	R	D	A	Y	■	Y	I	P
A	C	R	O	B	A	T	■	■	T	B	I	L	L	S
S	H	Y	■	O	M	E	G	A	■	E	S	C	■	■
■	■	F	R	E	D	R	I	C	A	P	R	I	L	■
N	O	T	E	S	■	■	E	D	E	N	■	E	D	U
E	L	A	N	■	A	N	N	A	N	■	E	E	L	S
R	E	X	■	P	L	O	D	■	■	U	N	M	E	T
D	O	R	I	S	E	V	E	N	I	N	G	■	■	■
■	E	R	A	■	A	L	L	O	T	■	B	A	N	■
T	A	L	E	N	T	■	■	E	T	R	U	R	I	A
E	L	I	■	D	O	N	N	A	A	U	T	U	M	N
A	G	E	■	Q	U	I	P	S	■	E	A	T	E	N
R	A	F	■	S	T	A	R	T	■	H	E	D	Y	■

34

A	I	D	E	■	F	I	J	I	■	B	A	N	K	S
G	R	O	G	■	O	R	A	N	■	I	Q	U	I	T
H	O	W	G	O	E	S	I	T	■	R	U	N	N	Y
A	N	N	E	X	■	■	L	E	N	D	I	N	G	■
■	■	■	D	E	C	K	■	R	O	B	■	■	■	■
A	H	A	■	N	O	W	A	N	D	A	G	A	I	N
C	A	M	S	■	L	A	M	■	T	A	W	N	Y	■
E	L	O	C	U	T	I	O	N	P	H	R	A	S	E
R	E	C	O	N	■	■	N	O	R	■	B	R	E	T
B	R	O	W	N	B	A	G	G	E	R	■	E	T	S
■	■	■	E	B	B	■	O	P	A	L	■	■	■	■
■	J	E	E	R	S	A	T	■	J	I	B	E	D	■
W	E	B	T	V	■	C	O	W	P	A	L	A	C	E
I	R	A	T	E	■	U	N	I	T	■	A	C	H	E
Z	I	N	E	S	■	S	E	G	A	■	C	H	O	P

35

A	L	T	A	R	■	T	A	P	S	■	H	G	T	S
D	I	O	D	E	■	A	L	O	T	■	A	R	A	L
Z	Z	T	O	P	■	L	O	L	A	■	D	O	R	A
■	■	■	P	U	N	C	H	A	N	D	J	U	D	Y
L	E	F	T	B	E	■	A	R	L	O	■	C	Y	S
I	M	A	■	L	E	E	■	E	T	C	H	■	■	■
S	O	C	K	I	T	T	O	M	E	■	F	O	C	I
A	T	T	I	C	■	U	A	E	■	R	O	M	A	N
S	E	C	T	■	H	I	T	T	H	E	S	A	C	K
■	H	E	L	I	■	■	S	E	A	■	R	T	E	■
A	W	E	■	E	G	G	S	■	E	L	I	X	I	R
D	E	C	K	T	H	E	H	A	L	L	S	■	■	■
M	A	K	E	■	I	N	O	N	■	I	A	M	B	S
E	V	E	N	■	Q	U	O	I	■	F	I	E	R	Y
N	E	R	O	■	S	S	T	S	■	E	D	G	A	R

36

R	U	N	O	F	F	■	S	A	W	S	■	C	A	B
S	T	A	P	L	E	■	C	R	O	P	■	O	L	E
T	A	M	P	E	R	P	R	O	O	F	■	M	C	I
■	■	E	S	E	■	E	A	S	E	■	S	M	O	G
S	O	T	■	C	O	P	P	E	R	P	L	A	T	E
I	N	A	H	E	A	P	■	■	I	E	S	T	■	■
R	E	P	O	■	T	E	R	R	A	C	E	■	■	■
■	S	E	M	P	E	R	P	A	R	A	T	U	S	■
■	■	■	B	U	S	S	I	N	G	■	E	N	T	S
■	P	A	R	R	■	■	C	U	D	D	L	E	S	■
P	A	P	E	R	P	U	S	H	E	R	■	■	I	M	S
E	R	A	S	■	A	N	T	E	■	Y	A	K	■
R	I	C	■	S	U	P	E	R	P	O	W	E	R	S
P	A	H	■	A	S	I	A	■	S	U	N	L	I	T
S	H	E	■	P	E	N	D	■	I	T	S	Y	O	U

37

A	C	E	S	■	A	F	B	S	■	S	T	U	D	S
D	O	L	T	■	M	O	A	T	■	T	U	T	E	E
H	A	I	R	S	P	R	A	Y	■	O	B	E	S	E
O	C	T	A	L	■	T	E	R	M	P	A	P	E	R
C	H	E	W	E	D	■	D	O	N	G	S	■	■	■
■	■	P	E	O	N	■	N	O	A	■	D	S	L	■
I	N	M	O	T	I	O	N	■	■	P	H	O	T	O
V	I	A	L	■	S	H	O	R	T	■	A	M	Y	S
A	N	G	L	O	■	G	O	E	S	N	E	X	T	■
N	O	S	■	U	M	P	■	W	A	N	D	■	■	■
■	■	S	T	I	E	S	■	R	E	S	A	L	E	■
C	A	K	E	W	A	L	K	S	■	A	T	B	A	Y
A	M	A	T	I	■	L	I	N	E	D	A	N	C	E
P	I	L	O	T	■	E	N	I	D	■	N	E	E	R
E	D	E	N	S	■	T	K	T	S	■	D	R	Y	S

38

M	I	C	■	T	O	N	I	■	I	M	P	A	L	E
I	N	A	■	I	D	I	D	■	N	A	R	N	I	A
S	K	I	L	O	D	G	E	■	G	L	I	D	E	S
S	E	R	E	■	S	H	O	R	E	L	E	A	V	E
M	Y	O	P	I	A	■	O	M	A	R	■	■	■	■
■	■	E	A	R	P	■	M	A	R	■	A	R	F	■
S	N	O	W	L	E	O	P	A	R	D	■	J	O	E
T	A	B	■	■	M	A	N	■	■	A	P	R	■	■
A	T	E	■	S	O	P	H	I	A	L	O	R	E	N
B	O	Y	■	H	U	E	■	A	T	O	P	■	■	■
■	Y	E	T	I	■	■	A	G	E	N	T	S	■	■
S	P	E	E	D	L	I	M	I	T	■	R	O	A	N
C	A	N	A	D	A	■	S	R	I	L	A	N	K	A
A	N	D	R	E	W	■	G	A	L	E	■	O	E	R
M	E	S	S	R	S	■	S	E	T	S	■	S	N	L

39

S	W	A	P	■	P	A	R	T	B	■	D	A	M
R	O	W	E	D	■	I	T	I	S	I	■	O	R	E
T	R	A	D	E	S	C	H	O	O	L	■	T	E	A
A	S	K	■	C	U	S	S	■	L	O	M	A	N	■
S	T	E	E	L	E	■	D	A	N	Z	A	■	■	■
■	■	B	A	R	T	E	R	S	Y	S	T	E	M	■
I	K	N	O	W	■	W	R	O	T	E	■	R	D	A
S	P	A	N	■	D	I	A	N	A	■	V	I	D	I
L	A	N	■	M	A	N	S	E	■	S	I	X	A	M
E	X	C	H	A	N	G	E	R	A	T	E	■	■	■
■	Y	O	R	K	E	■	■	N	E	W	A	G	E	■
D	I	D	O	K	■	S	A	K	E	■	N	O	G	■
D	O	R	■	S	W	I	T	C	H	P	L	A	T	E
A	W	E	■	U	B	O	A	T	■	S	A	M	M	S
Y	A	W	■	P	A	N	G	S	■	M	E	E	T	■

40

C	Z	A	R	■	M	A	T	H	■	F	E	S	T
R	E	L	O	■	R	A	D	I	O	■	O	N	C	E
O	R	E	O	■	E	X	U	L	T	■	O	L	A	N
C	O	C	K	T	A	I	L	■	T	A	T	A	R	S
■	■	S	O	D	■	T	A	I	L	P	I	P	E	■
U	T	E	■	L	E	S	■	R	E	A	R	■	■	■
P	I	P	E	D	R	E	A	M	■	S	I	T	O	N
S	N	I	P	■	S	L	Y	L	Y	■	N	O	P	E
Y	A	C	H	T	■	D	R	E	A	M	T	E	A	M
■	■	E	U	R	O	■	T	R	A	■	■	■	■	■
T	E	A	M	G	A	M	E	■	D	D	E	■	■	■
I	M	M	E	S	H	■	G	A	M	E	C	O	C	K
N	A	I	R	■	R	E	A	V	E	■	A	M	A	N
G	I	G	A	■	A	R	D	E	N	■	R	O	B	E
E	L	A	L	■	H	E	S	S	■	D	O	S	E	■

41

T	A	N			E	R	U	P	T			B	A	B	A	R
A	S	A			R	A	T	I	O			A	R	U	B	A
D	I	S	A	R	M	A	N	D	H	A	M	M	E	R		
A	F	A	R			S	H	A	D	E			A	P	S	E
		A	T	E					R	O	N					
D	I	S	M	I	S	S	A	M	E	R	I	C	A		
A	N	T	I	C			M	O	O	S	E			A	V	E
T	K	O	S			B	E	R	R	Y			S	P	A	T
E	E	L			N	E	A	T	O			M	A	R	I	A
	D	I	S	B	A	R	A	N	D	G	R	I	L	L		
		A	C	T					A	R	T					
I	M	A	M			O	A	T	E	R			R	I	L	E
D	I	S	B	A	N	D	O	N	T	H	E	R	U	N		
O	C	E	A	N			I	N	N	E	R			A	M	Y
L	E	A	S	T			N	E	E	D	S			S	P	A

42

B	I	D	E	N			C	L	I	O			O	N	A	N
A	D	A	N	O			A	E	R	O			R	E	L	Y
D	O	N	T	M	O	V	E	A	M	U	Z	Z	L	E		
F	I	G			S	C	I			P	R	O	P	S		
I	D	E	D			T	A	R	S	A	L			E	T	A
T	O	R	I	C			R	I	C	H			W	R	A	P
		T	U	B			N	A	P			E	C	R	U	
	B	U	Z	Z	I	N	G	T	A	B	L	E	S			
K	A	T	E			T	E	L			H	A	L			
I	S	I	S			O	M	E	N			R	E	C	U	R
D	S	L			P	H	O	T	O	N			S	A	S	E
	T	I	E	T	O			L	E	S			M	E	D	
F	U	Z	Z	A	N	D	F	E	A	T	H	E	R	S		
U	B	E	R			E	Y	E	S			E	E	R	I	E
N	A	D	A			Y	E	W	S			P	R	A	D	A

43

I	C	E	R	S			T	O	M	B			D	E	A	F
S	A	M	O	A			I	N	G	A			U	C	A	L
P	R	I	M	P			G	I	R	D			L	O	R	I
S	T	R	A	I	G	H	T			G	A	L	L	O	N	
		N	E	A	T			C	U	N	N	I	N	G		
S	T	R	O	N	G			C	L	Y	D	E				
A	H	A			S	E	A	L	E			A	S	H	E	S
W	I	S	E			S	P	E	A	K			S	I	C	K
S	N	A	C	K			S	A	N	E	R			G	H	I
		L	O	S	E	R			N	A	C	H	O	S		
S	I	M	I	L	E	S			B	A	N	A				
O	N	A	P	A	R			S	L	I	P	P	E	R	Y	
L	U	G	S			A	S	T	I			A	T	R	I	A
I	S	M	E			P	E	E	N			S	O	B	E	R
D	E	A	D			H	A	R	D			T	R	E	N	D

44

T	A	C	O			S	M	A	R	T			A	B	R	A
A	L	A	N			P	U	S	H	Y			B	E	E	P
T	I	N	K	E	R	S	H	O	R	T	S	T	O	P		
A	T	A	P	R	I	C	E			R	O	A	S	T		
		A	T	L			L	I	A	R						
E	V	E	R	S	S	E	C	O	N	D	B	A	S	E		
N	E	R	V	E			H	O	N	E			S	P	A	
I	T	I	S			T	R	I	M	S			S	P	I	T
A	C	C			O	R	E	L			S	I	C	E	M	
C	H	A	N	C	E	F	I	R	S	T	B	A	S	E		
		U	T	E	S			E	T	O						
O	B	A	M	A			B	R	A	I	N	I	A	C		
D	O	U	B	L	E	P	L	A	Y	C	O	M	B	O		
D	A	R	E			G	O	T	T	I			M	A	L	T
S	T	A	R			O	L	S	E	N			E	X	E	S

45

```
S P E E D   L I L T   Z E A L
A L I K E   I N O R   A L T A
J A G G E D E D G E   I L E S
A C H   P O N Y E X P R E S S
K E T T L E S     L E N T O
    B O Y S   B A L E
B R A T     D O G P A D D L E
L O L A   M E N U S   R I O T
T O L L P L A Z A   I S T O
      E B R O   I K E S
A S T A R     A T E D I R T
M A R C U S W E L B Y   D E O
O X E N   H I D D E N G E M S
R O V E   A N N E   E R N I E
E N I D   G E A R   S E T T E
```

46

```
F R I S K   Z A C K   A S E A
W I C C A   U P O N   C U L T
D O E R R   L E V I   C A V E
  T R E A S U R E T R O V E S
    W O N       W I S E S T
T R I C K O R T R E A T
N O V A E   H A H A S   M M E
U T E P   T I M O R   J O E L
T O S   W A N E D   A E O N S
      T R I E D A N D T R U E
S O L E I L     E M B
T R A C T O R T R A I L E R
R A S H   R O M A   R A R E R
A T T N   E W A N   E C L A T
P E S O   D A N G   S K E D S
```

47

```
H T T P   S O L E   S C U F F
E I R E   A V O W   T O R R E
R A I N   R A R E   A R N A Z
B R O C C O L I R A B E
S A S H A Y S   P L A T E S
    A L A   O D I E   A L P
R U N N I N G B E A R   T I E
A T I T   E O E   R U H R
K I X   B A R E M I N I M U M
E C O   O H M S   M E G
S A N D R A     O P I A T E S
    R E B A M C E N T I R E
L I V E D   M O E T   O B I E
A M I G O   F R A U   N E C K
S P A S M   M E N S   I R A S
```

48

```
L A U D E D   L A I   S M E E
E L N I N O   I N K   T A T A
A D D S T O   S T E W A R D S
P E A C H F U Z Z   A N G S T
T R Y   R U S T   M R T
    H O S S   D A S H I N G
A L I E N   T O U R   E S A U
P U P A E   E T S   K M A R T
S L O T   J E T T   A A N D E
O L D S O U L   M A N N
    T N T   R O E G
C A I R O   C O P S A P L E A
A L S O R A N S   O R I G I N
P E A K   A B E   P O L I C E
P E K E   A C S   S O L D E R
```

49

```
G R A S P   B A S E   A Q U A
L A S E R   U R L S   C U P S
A G I L E   S E A T   T O S S
D U F F Y S T A V E R N
      O I L     O O H E D
  F I N N E G A N S W A K E
  D E L     O B O E   Z I A
G I L L I G A N S I S L A N D
U S O   A S I N     E R G
M C N A M A R A S B A N D
P O S T S     O A R
    H O G A N S H E R O E S
A S E A   I T O O   T E R R A
L A W N   G O T O   H A S I D
A X E D   S P A N   A L O N E
```

50

```
A A R P   G L I B   A R S O N
R I A L   O O N A   Q U E U E
U S D A   S C A N   U S E R S
B L A C K H A W K   A S I
A E R I E   L E A H   O N E S
      D I G S   B A G   G L O
G I G O L O   E L I A   R I B
U R L   L A W Y E R S   E T E
T O A   O T H E   D O D D E R
E N S   R E I   J O V E
N Y S E   E Z R A   E L A T E
    W S J   B U C K N A K E D
R I A T A   A L O U   Y I P E
A R L E N   N E B R   E R I N
F A L S E   G R I T   D A D S
```

51

```
S M A R T S   P A R   S I M S
A C T I  I I   I O U   O N I T
C H O P S T I C K S   N E N E
R A M     S R O   H E A D E R
E L I S E   A T T E N T I O N
D E C I D E     R E T A B L E
    T I R A D E       L A R
  T H E E N V E L O P E
A P O     O R S I N O
P O L E C A T     Z A P A T A
O N E M O M E N T   N E T W T
S C R E W S   U S A     T O T
T H A R   T A K E M Y W I F E
L O N G   E N E   E A G L E S
E S T E   L E D   N O N A R T
```

52

```
A L A W   S T O A T   O W E S
S E G A   T O M C A T   H O M O
T I O S   E R E N O W   D R I P
A F G H A N P R E S I D E N T
      S N O O T   N R A
G R E A T G R A N D P A R E N T
R I A L S     E X A M   T O O
I A T E   T R A G I C   S H O W
E T E   S H E D     I N A N E
G A R A G E D O O R O P E N E R
    L T D   N O R S E
  T H E S E C R E T G A R D E N
H O A X   A R I S T A   S E X Y
S U Z I   D A M I E N   A M E N
T R E S   B E E N S   T I D Y
```

53

	S	A	G		F	I	G	H	T		M	O	B	Y
A	C	N	E		A	C	R	I	D		O	R	L	E
M	O	A	N		T	E	E	N	S		I	B	I	S
P	U	L	L	A	H	E	A	D		F	R	A	T	S
E	T	Y		L	O	S	T		C	R	E	C	H	E
R	E	T	R	I	M		W	H	O	O	S	H	E	D
E	D	I	E		E	H	U	D	S					
	C	A	P	T	A	I	N	A	H	A	B			
		R	E	S	T	S			M	I	R	A		
A	N	I	S	E	T	T	E		H	A	T	R	E	D
M	A	R	T	Y	R		W	H	O	M		D	V	D
A	P	E	R	S		S	H	O	W	C	A	S	E	S
Z	O	N	E		S	L	A	N	T		B	E	A	T
E	L	I	A		R	O	L	E	O		R	E	L	O
D	I	C	K		O	B	E	Y	S		A	D	S	

54

S	P	O	K	E		S	K	E	E		A	B	B	A
L	E	C	A	R		P	O	U	R		K	A	E	L
I	N	T	R	O		C	O	R	A		I	S	N	O
G	R	E	A	T	L	A	K	E	S		N	I	N	E
H	O	T	T	I	E			K	E	Y		L	I	V
T	D	S		C	A	E	S	A	R	S	W	I	F	E
		S	A	R	A	H		S	L	I	C	E	R	
M	A	G	I			T	O	N		P	A	R	A	
A	D	O	N	I	S		J	U	D	G	E			
G	H	O	S	T	W	R	I	T	E	R		S	T	U
N	E	D		O	A	K		N	O	S	P	I	N	
A	S	I	S		P	E	R	R	Y	W	H	I	T	E
T	I	D	Y		P	L	I	E		S	E	R	T	A
E	V	E	N		E	L	L	A		U	R	A	L	S
S	E	A	S		D	Y	E	D		P	A	L	E	Y

55

J	A	I	L	S		A	F	A	R		S	O	S	A
I	N	L	E	T		R	O	T	E		I	R	O	N
M	A	K	E	A	S	T	R	O	N	G	C	A	S	E
		R	I	O		T	I	E	A	K	N	O	T	
S	A	C		N	A	B			G	R	O	G		
C	R	O	P	S	P	R	A	Y	E	R		E	N	O
H	E	M	I		Y	O	R	E		E	N	R	O	N
U	T	E	N	N		N	B	A		T	A	I	L	S
L	O	T	T	E		C	O	S	T		A	N	T	I
Z	O	O		S	H	O	R	T	W	I	N	D	E	D
	T	A	S	E			Y	I	N		S	S	E	
O	N	E	S	I	D	E	D		S	C	I			
N	O	R	W	E	G	I	A	N	T	H	R	O	N	E
I	R	M	A		E	R	N	E		E	A	S	E	S
T	A	S	S		D	E	K	E		S	Q	U	A	T

56

A	M	M	O		T	R	O	T	S		A	C	I	D
L	O	A	F		R	O	X	I	E		E	D	N	A
E	O	J	F	R	A	Z	I	E	R		S	P	U	R
P	R	O	T	E	M		D	R	E	W		L	I	T
H	E	R	O	D		J	E	O	N	A	M	A	T	H
		D	I	E		D	E	C	A	Y				
O	J	E	B	I	D	E	N		O	T	E	R	I	
L	A	V	A		S	P	E	N	D		T	R	O	D
E	R	A	S	E		O	E	J	P	E	S	C	I	
	P	I	T	A	S		A	S	H					
E	J	O	C	O	C	K	E	R		O	F	U	S	E
N	O	R		N	E	I	N		A	N	U	B	I	S
A	L	A	S		S	L	O	P	P	Y	J	O	E	S
C	I	T	E		I	L	L	E	R		I	A	N	A
T	E	E	N		T	S	A	R	S		S	T	A	Y

57

```
B A N J O   L O C A L   M U M
O C E A N   O C H R E   E N O
F R U S T R A T I O N   N P R
F E T C H E D   A G A T E S
    H E X   M O R T G A G E
A C T A S   S U R   H A L
M O E   L E T S G O   I N K S
I T M A Y B E T A K E N O U T
E S P N   B L A N D A   T H E
    T I X   M R S   S T E N T
F A S T F O O D   S T R
U N F A I R   M E L I N D A
N I A   L I B R A R Y B O O K
G O T   E B O N Y   M A I Z E
O N E   S I N A I   E L R E Y
```

58

```
R O B   B I N G E   S C R A M
O P E   I D E A L   C R U D E
B E E   N E W T O   H A D I T
I R R I G A T E   E M M E T S
N A G S       P N O M
  H A S A H E A R T   E W E S
S O R   M E M B E R   D E V A
C U D   C A B O V E R   S A L
U S E S   R E V U E S   T N T
D E N T   T R E E S T U M P
    A A H S       R O I S
C H A S M S   R U M P U N C H
H A S H E   T U B E R   R O E
A S H E N   O M E G A   O N E
S H E D S   S P R A Y   E E N
```

Each shaded box contains a word square.

59

```
E L M I R A   S C A M   S H E
L I O N E L   T H R I L L E R
S N O C A P   S I N C E R E R
    N A C H O   O H M
N O W   H A D J   A U G H T
E V A D E   D A N G E R O U S
D E L I S H   C O O L   N N E
I R K S   A S K M E   J E T T
C L I   F L O S   S P A T E S
K I N G O F P O P   A M O R E
S E G A R   N U L L   O S S
    P E P   N O M A S
A L O E V E R A   A T C O S T
F A L S E T T O   M O T O W N
B Y E   R E E K   S P I N E T
```

60

```
S T A H L       T A B   A O K
A I R I E R   O H N O   N R A
D R U G D I C T I O N   J A R
R O T H   P A T E   E B O L A
    S H O W O F A D O U B T
L O V E I S       P R Y
R I O A C T I V I T Y   T P K
O S I S   L A Z   P R I E
N E D   R O L L E R B L I N G
    C O W   H O A X E S
M A I L I N G D R E S S
A C R E S   E Y E S   M O D I
B A A   T A K E O U T A N A D
E S Q   E L K S   S H T E T L
L E I   R A O   U V R A Y
```

61

A	C	T	A	S		A	L	P		S	I	E	G	E
S	H	A	L	T		B	I	C		C	L	A	R	A
T	I	K	K	I		C	M	L		I	O	T	A	S
O	N	E	A	R	M		B	A	M		I	S	N	T
		C	L	I	M	B		B	A	L	L	A	D	E
T	R	A	I	N	S	E	T		R	I	O	T	E	R
D	A	R	N			G	R	A	M	S				
S	T	E	E	R		T	U	B		P	I	P	E	S
				U	C	O	N	N		T	R	E	E	
W	I	E	S	E	L		K	E	R	O	S	E	N	E
E	N	D	U	S	E	R		R	E	N	A	L		
T	H	E	N		O	A	R		O	L	D	A	G	E
T	A	N	G	O		N	O	R		O	A	T	E	N
E	L	I	T	E		B	O	O		A	T	E	S	T
D	E	C	O	R		Y	T	D		N	E	S	T	S

62

S	T	U	F	F		E	T	O	N		M	C	C	I
L	I	N	E	A		R	A	F	T		A	H	A	B
I	N	D	E	X		R	U	T	H	E	N	I	U	M
G	E	O			P	O	R	E		L	I	N	T	
H	A	N	K	A	A	R	O	N		S	L	A	I	N
T	R	E	A	T	S			R	E	A	S	O	N	
			R	O	S	E	A	T	E		E	N	E	
		B	A	R	A	C	K	O	B	A	M	A		
B	O	A		G	U	A	N	A	C	O				
E	N	C	O	D	E			T	E	A	B	A	G	
T	E	T	R	A		S	U	P	E	R	B	O	W	L
M	E	A	L		E	V	E	S		R	N	A		
F	O	R	T	Y	F	O	U	R		H	U	M	I	D
E	R	I	E		R	U	L	E		I	N	A	N	E
D	E	A	D		A	L	A	S		T	O	N	G	S

63

M	A	L	A	R	I	A	L		G	A	N	D	H	I
O	N	E	H	O	R	S	E		I	B	E	R	I	A
N	O	N	S	T	O	P	S		A	S	W	A	R	M
Y	D	S			B	E	S	T		E	T	T	E	S
			S	H	O	R		J	O	N	S			
	E	P	C	O	T		S	M	U	T		H	E	M
U	L	E	E	S		A	L	A	R		M	I	M	I
T	W	E	N	T	Y	S	I	X	S	T	A	T	E	S
I	A	T	E		A	M	E	X		O	L	M	E	C
L	Y	E		G	N	A	R		A	F	T	E	R	
			J	A	G	R		A	G	U	A			
V	I	S	O	R		A	C	M	E		A	R	C	
A	N	T	I	C	S		H	O	T	C	O	C	O	A
I	R	A	N	I	S		I	C	E	C	R	E	A	M
N	E	C	T	A	R		C	O	N	C	O	R	D	E

64

J	A	B		C	O	R	G	I		A	M	T	O	C
A	L	E		O	D	E	O	N		B	I	E	R	S
C	I	R		B	O	A	R	D		O	X	E	Y	E
K	E	E	P	O	N	L	O	R	R	Y	I	N		
U	N	T	I	L			U	A	E		T	I	C	S
P	S	S	T		C	O	N	G	A	Q	U	E	U	E
			A	L	O	U	D			U	P	S	E	T
H	A	M		O	P	T		A	M	I		T	D	S
E	L	U	T	E		E	X	U	D	E				
W	I	S	E	B	L	O	K	E	S		L	I	M	P
N	E	I	N		A	C	E		V	I	D	E	O	
		C	A	T	C	H	S	O	M	E	Z	E	D	S
H	U	B	B	A		R	O	T	O	R		A	L	I
A	R	O	L	L		E	U	R	O	S		L	E	T
P	I	X	E	L		S	T	O	N	E		S	Y	S

65

A	R	M	A	N	D			E	M	B	A	R			P	F	C
B	E	A	V	E	R			V	E	R	S	E			A	O	L
A	P	T	I	T	U	D	E	T	E	S	T				L	U	X
F	R	E	S	H	M	A	N	S	E	N	A	T	O	R		
T	O	Y				U	S	S				M	A	M	I	E
	S	O	P	H	O	M	O	R	E	J	I	N	X		
S	N	O	W				U	R	N				N	O	T
C	O	L	L	E	G	E	S	T	A	T	I	O	N	
D	O	O			R	A	P				E	S	S	E
J	U	N	I	O	R	P	A	R	T	N	E	R		
S	T	E	N	T			B	A	I				S	A	P
	S	E	N	I	O	R	D	I	S	C	O	U	N	T	S
A	I	L			T	H	E	I	M	M	O	R	T	A	L	S
M	G	S			I	N	A	N	E			L	E	E	R	A	T
I	N	E			S	O	R	E	N			A	S	S	E	S	S

66

C	U	B	S			D	I	V	A			F	U	Z	Z	Y
U	S	O	C			E	M	I	T			O	K	I	E	S
R	E	F	I			A	N	E	W			R	E	P	E	L
B	U	F	F	A	L	O	W	I	N	G	S		
S	P	O	I	L	S			L	E	I			I	D	O
	L	I	L	Y	L	I	V	E	R	E	D
E	D	N	A			N	A	E			N	E	G	A	T	E
T	R	U	R	O			G	M	S			N	O	N	E	T
A	L	B	I	N	O			E	U	R			S	I	R	S
T	A	B	L	E	T	E	N	N	I	S		
S	O	Y			C	O	X				D	A	Y	S	P	A
	J	U	S	T	A	D	D	W	A	T	E	R
N	A	B	O	B			O	P	A	L			C	A	S	T
O	M	A	N	I			L	O	D	E			H	I	T	S
D	I	G	I	T			S	P	A	R			T	R	O	Y

67

C	P	A	S			S	L	O	P			C	U	F	F	S
H	E	M	P			T	O	N	E			U	T	I	L	E
A	R	E	A	C	O	D	E	S			P	E	R	O	N
R	U	N	N	I	N	G	A	T	A	B			E	S	T
		K	N	E	E	L			M	O	S	E	S
M	R	D	E	E	D	S			I	B	A	R	S	
G	O	O	D			O	V	E	R	A	C	T	S	
M	A	N			K	E	Y	W	O	R	D			A	H	H
T	R	O	P	I	C	A	L			B	P	O	E
		T	E	N	O	R			D	E	B	E	E	R	S
D	E	I	G	N			D	O	P	E	S		
T	I	N			L	O	S	E	C	O	N	T	R	O	L
S	A	T	I	E			U	P	I	N	S	M	O	K	E
A	N	E	R	A			M	O	L	Y			A	X	I	S
R	A	R	E	R			S	T	E	M			N	Y	E	T

68

N	I	N	E			O	L	A	N			P	A	S	S	E
O	N	O	R			T	I	N	E			E	M	P	T	Y
L	A	M	A			T	O	N	E			S	M	I	T	E
E	T	A	S			O	N	U	S			T	O	R	E	
S	I	N	E	W				L	O	G				I	R	A
S	E	S	S	I	L	E			N	A	P	S	T	E	R
			S	O	R	E			L	A	T	E	S	T
S	T	A	N	D	A	R	D	W	O	R	K	D	A	Y
P	E	R	I	O	D			S	O	R	T		
I	S	T	H	M	U	S			P	E	E	V	I	S	H
N	T	H			P	C	B				D	O	L	C	E
	F	O	R	T			O	R	B	S			I	L	E	X
C	L	U	E	R			F	O	R	E			D	I	N	O
O	E	S	T	E			F	I	R	E			O	N	E	S
S	W	E	D	E			S	L	R	S			F	I	V	E

69

D	I	T	S		E	V	E	R		C	O	B	R	A
E	V	R	Y		M	A	X	I		A	D	O	U	T
M	A	I	N		B	L	A	C	K	P	E	A	R	L
O	N	A		D	E	S	C	E	N	T			
T	O	G	A	E	D		T	R	I		K	E	E	L
E	V	E	N	T		M	A	S	T		I	M	N	O
			N	A	P	A	S		T	A	K	I	N	G
A	S	T	A	I	R	E		R	E	W	I	R	E	S
D	I	A	B	L	O		N	O	R	A	D			
A	T	I	E		B	O	O	M		R	E	M	I	T
N	U	L	L		L	O	G		I	D	E	A	T	E
			P	E	L	T	E	R	S		S	R	S	
S	A	N	T	A	M	A	R	I	A		S	A	I	L
O	D	E	O	N		L	I	N	T		P	L	E	A
Y	E	G	G	S		A	L	E	E		P	A	D	S

70

M	G	S		P	A	N	D	A	S		P	F	F	T
E	L	O		O	B	O	I	S	T		E	R	I	E
G	O	U	N	D	E	R	T	H	E	K	N	I	F	E
	B	L	A	S	T		T	E	R	I		S	T	N
C	A	M	P			B	O	R	N	W	I	T	H	A
B	L	U	E	I	C	E			A	I	R			
S	I	S		N	I	E	C	E			A	S	S	
	S	I	L	V	E	R	S	P	O	O	N	I	N	
M	C	I			S	T	O	N	E		D	A	S	
			P	A	C		C	O	N	C	E	P	T	
O	N	E	S	M	O	U	T	H			H	O	P	E
F	A	N		B	A	B	E		M	O	O	R	E	
F	O	R	K	I	T	O	V	E	R	B	U	D	D	Y
A	M	O	I		E	L	Y	S	E	E		E	T	A
L	I	N	T		S	T	E	A	D	Y		R	O	Y

71

C	A	B	O	T		D	A	B	S		C	A	S	H
A	L	E	R	O		E	L	L	E		A	L	A	S
L	O	R	I	S		E	D	O	M		N	E	X	T
L	U	N	G	C	A	P	A	C	I	T	Y			
			A	A	R	P			H	O	U	S	E	
S	K	I	M		C	U	R	T	A	I	N	R	O	D
M	A	G	I	C		R	A	R	E	R		A	L	I
I	B	N		E	M	P	R	E	S	S		N	A	T
T	O	O		T	A	L	I	A		T	R	U	C	E
H	O	R	S	E	S	E	N	S	E		U	S	E	D
S	M	E	A	R			O	N	C	D				
			M	A	I	D	E	N	V	O	Y	A	G	E
U	M	P	S		T	O	R	O		N	A	S	A	L
Z	E	R	O		E	S	A	U		G	R	I	N	S
I	R	O	N		M	E	S	S		A	D	A	G	E

72

B	I	O	L		B	O	S	C	H		M	A	C	E
R	A	R	E		O	R	T	H	O		A	L	A	S
E	M	A	G		B	R	E	E	D	S	H	I	L	L
A	N	N	U	L	S		W	A	S	H	O			
D	O	G	M	A		S	A	P		A	G	A	T	E
S	T	E	E	R		T	R	O	U		A	L	M	A
			E	D	I	T			T	E	N	D	E	R
E	C	U	A	D	O	R		M	A	R	Y	A	N	N
G	A	S	L	O	G		A	S	H	E				
A	R	I	L		S	E	V	E		S	H	E	E	P
L	E	A	S	T		M	O	C		T	I	L	D	E
			I	O	N	I	C		R	U	D	E	S	T
N	E	W	Z	E	A	L	A	N	D		E	V	E	S
F	R	E	E		S	I	D	E	A		H	E	L	I
L	A	B	S		H	O	O	T	S		I	N	S	T

73

B	O	L	E		R	C	A	S		J	E	S	S	E
O	P	E	N	W	E	A	V	E		E	T	A	T	S
C	A	T	C	H	E	S	G	L	I	T	C	H	E	S
A	L	S		A	L	B		A	N	S	E	L	M	O
	B	R	E	A		S	U	E	T					
S	C	R	A	T	C	H	E	S	I	T	C	H	E	S
T	O	O	H	O	T		S	I	T		A	L	A	
U	C	O	N	N		I	T	E		A	D	R	A	G
M	O	S		R	N	A		A	R	I	S	T	A	
P	A	T	C	H	E	S	B	R	I	T	C	H	E	S
	H	I	V	E		O	M	I	T					
A	N	T	I	G	U	A		U	H	S		S	R	A
M	A	T	C	H	E	S	S	T	I	T	C	H	E	S
A	T	O	L	L		O	N	E	N	E	G	A	T	I	V	E
D	O	P	E	Y		N	O	S	H		N	A	S	A

74

A	P	E	R	S			S	I	R	E		R	E	P
R	O	D	E	O		I	N	N	E	R		A	G	E
R	I	D	D	L	E	C	A	K	E	S		I	R	A
			T	I	M	O	R		K	E	R	N	E	L
M	I	R	A		I	N	L	A	W		C	A	T	S
O	N	A	P	A	R		L	E	G	A	L			
N	A	V	E	L		M	O	T	E	L		C	A	M
E	N	E		P	R	O	V	O	K	E		O	R	E
T	E	N		H	U	L	A	S		A	S	H	E	N
		I	P	A	N	A		S	N	O	O	T	S	
A	L	M	A		T	R	A	L	A		P	L	E	A
M	E	A	D	O	W		L	I	N	E	R			
B	A	G		R	O	W	I	N	G	P	A	I	N	S
E	V	E		C	R	A	C	K		I	N	D	I	E
R	E	S		S	K	Y	E		C	O	O	P	T	

75

X	E	N	I	A		M	O	R	K		B	Y	R	D
A	L	O	N	G		O	N	E	I		L	E	A	N
N	I	E	C	E		R	E	A	D		U	L	N	A
D	O	N	A	L	D	R	U	M	S	F	E	L	D	
Y	T	D		I	R	O	N		M	G	M			
		A	M	Y	W	I	N	E	H	O	U	S	E
A	L	I	B	I		T	E	A		N	I	T	A
N	O	N	S	T	O	P		O	L	D	D	E	A	R
E	C	T	O		S	O	W		O	A	S	T	S
W	A	L	L	A	C	E	B	E	E	R	Y		
	U	N	U		Y	L	E	M		I	Z	E
N	A	T	A	L	I	E	P	O	R	T	M	A	N
B	E	B	E		A	B	A	A		O	A	S	I	S
A	R	A	L		T	I	T	S		O	T	E	R	O
R	O	S	Y		E	S	S	O		M	A	T	E	R

76

★	C	O	M	E		★	L	A	W		A	S	K	★
L	O	P	E	Z		S	A	R	A		D	A	I	S
E	L	E	N	I		T	W	I	G		A	B	L	E
T	A	L	O	N		E	N	D	O	W	M	E	N	T
			R	E	A	P		N	R	A				
★	C	L	A	S	S		B	A	S	I	N	E	T	S
L	E	A	H		A	B	E	L		S	T	A	R	E
A	L	B		I	N	O	R	O	U	T		T	E	N
S	L	A	Y	S		S	T	E	R		M	E	A	T
T	O	N	E	L	E	S	S		S	T	A	N	D	★
		S	E	N		B	A	A	L					
S	A	N	D	S	T	O	N	E		S	A	L	S	A
I	S	E	E		A	R	E	A		T	B	I	L	L
T	O	R	A		I	M	E	T		E	A	S	E	L
★	F	O	R		L	E	D	★		D	R	A	W	★

★ = IN/OUT

77

P	R	I	M	E	R	■	T	M	I	■	C	E	D	E
L	A	R	E	D	O	■	I	O	C	■	A	T	O	M
A	D	O	R	E	S	■	P	I	E	■	R	U	N	T
T	I	N	■	N	E	W	S	S	T	O	R	I	E	S
O	A	F	■	■	■	O	T	T	E	R	■	■	■	■
S	L	E	D	■	A	M	E	■	A	D	A	P	T	S
■	N	O	F	E	A	R	■	A	M	U	S	E		
L	E	C	T	E	R	N	■	S	P	I	N	N	E	R
S	T	E	E	R	■	P	I	C	N	I	C	■		
T	O	S	S	U	P	■	O	S	S	■	O	H	M	S
■	■	L	A	I	L	A	■	B	O	P				
V	O	L	L	E	Y	B	A	L	L	S	■	O	R	I
E	T	A	S	■	O	E	R	■	A	R	A	W	A	K
T	O	R	A	■	L	A	I	■	S	T	I	L	L	E
S	E	A	T	■	A	M	S	■	S	A	S	S	E	D

78

Z	A	P	S	■	C	A	T	■	S	H	I	F	T
I	D	E	A	■	G	O	R	E	■	M	A	N	I	A
P	L	A	N	■	R	O	T	C	■	E	S	S	E	X
P	A	R	K	C	I	T	Y	U	T	A	H	■	■
O	I	L	■	R	E	I	■	M	E	R	■		
■	R	E	V	E	R	S	E	S	P	L	I	T	
Q	U	O	T	E	■	O	E	D	■	R	A	N	I
L	U	N	G	E	■	B	A	H	■	M	O	C	K	S
A	I	D	E	■	D	O	M	■	P	E	S	K	Y
N	E	U	T	R	A	L	S	H	A	D	E	■	
A	T	E	■	E	L	I	■	A	L	I			
■	D	R	I	V	E	M	E	C	R	A	Z	Y	
A	D	I	E	U	■	I	L	L	S	■	A	G	U	N
L	I	N	E	N	■	A	B	E	T	■	N	E	R	O
G	E	A	R	S	■	N	E	T	■	G	R	E	W

79

B	E	A	D	■	S	L	I	P	■	A	D	I	P
L	P	G	A	■	T	I	T	L	E	■	R	E	N	E
A	H	A	B	■	A	F	O	U	L	■	I	C	E	D
N	O	P	■	A	L	T	■	T	O	E	■	R	A	E
C	R	E	A	T	E	■	O	P	E	N	E	R	S
■	P	R	A	T	T	■	E	R	R	A	N	T	
A	S	T	A	I	R	E	S	■	A	S	E	A	
T	N	T	■	P	R	A	T	T	L	E	■	E	S	L
I	D	E	D	■	C	R	U	E	L	E	S	T
P	R	E	A	M	P	■	A	N	T	I	S
S	O	L	D	E	R	S	■	D	E	S	I	G	N
O	M	G	■	T	O	P	■	A	O	L	■	R	I	O
V	E	R	O	■	S	I	N	E	W	■	H	E	A	D
E	D	E	N	■	Y	E	A	R	N	■	E	N	N	E
R	A	Y	E	■	L	E	O	S	■	P	E	T	S

80

W	E	S	S	O	N	■	L	I	S	■	A	L	A	E
A	N	T	E	C	E	D	E	N	T	■	R	A	S	A
I	D	O	N	T	D	R	I	V	E	■	E	N	T	S
S	E	C	S	■	I	S	H	E	■	A	G	E	2
T	A	K	E	S	5	■	T	R	A	■	E	R	O
S	R	S	■	A	F	I	R	E	■	S	O	L	I	D
■	E	R	O	S	E	■	G	A	O	L	S			
P	A	R	A	L	L	E	L	O	G	R	A	M		
A	M	I	N	D	■	L	E	G	I	T				
I	R	E	N	A	■	A	S	K	O	F	■	O	V	O
N	O	N	■	C	A	P	■	S	T	U	P	O	R
4	D	A	Y	■	B	I	G	3	■	N	I	L	E
T	I	M	E	■	B	E	O	R	I	G	I	N	A	L
H	E	E	P	■	I	C	E	S	K	A	T	E	R	S
S	S	N	S	■	E	E	S	■	E	L	Y	S	E	E

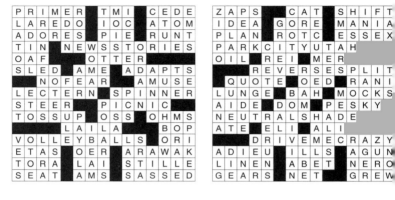

81

S	A	L		R	O	I	L			F	E	S	T	S
U	G	O		E	R	N	E		S	I	X	E	R	S
N	I	C	O	T	I	N	E		Y	A	P	P	E	R
S	T	A	N	D	B	Y		O	N	S	E	T	S	
E	A	T	S		I	C	O	N	O	C	L	A	S	T
T	T	O	P	S		R	E	P	O	S	T	E	D	
S	E	R	E	N	A		I	I	S		E	S	S	
		C	O	I	N	F	L	I	P	S				
D	B	L		R	O	I		S	T	O	L	A	F	
W	A	I	T	A	S	E	C		A	R	O	L	L	
I	N	C	O	M	P	L	E	T	E		T	I	T	O
D	E	N	I	E	S		R	E	M	O	T	E	S	
C	A	N	I	N	E		C	O	N	I	F	E	R	S
M	I	S	T	E	D		E	M	I	L		R	E	E
I	D	E	E	S		O	P	E	D		S	D	S	

82

E	L	A	L		R	A	H	S			L	U	L	L
M	I	L	A		I	C	E	T		C	O	P	A	Y
A	B	E	T		P	E	R	O	G	A	T	I	V	E
I	R	R	E	G	A	R	D	L	E	S	S			
L	A	T	T	E			S	E	A	C	A	L	F	
		E	T	N	A		N	R	A		E	R	R	
E	X	C	E	T	E	R	A			F	R	A	U	
P	R	O	N	O	U	N	C	I	A	T	I	O	N	S
E	A	R	S			A	S	T	E	R	I	C	K	
E	Y	E		C	H	O		T	E	A	S			
	S	Y	R	I	A	N	S			M	T	I	D	A
		C	A	M	E	A	C	R	O	S	S	E	D	
S	U	P	P	O	S	A	B	L	Y		E	S	A	I
K	N	I	T	S		C	R	U	E		E	U	R	O
I	O	N	S			T	E	E	S		D	E	E	S

83

E	E	E	E		M	A	Y			Q	Q	Q	Q
M	E	D	E	A		A	T	V		C	U	T	I	T
F	O	U	R	L	E	T	T	E	R	W	O	R	D	S
			I	I	I	I		T	T	T	T			
S	S	E		G	N	A	T	S		I	M	S	
G	E	T	S	T	H	E	R	E		S	N	E	E	R
O	N	E	T	O	T	E	N		J	I	G	G	L	E
O	O	P		A	H	S		F	A	N		A	L	A
D	R	O	I	D	S		G	A	N	G	S	T	E	R
S	A	U	C	Y		A	N	C	E	S	T	O	R	S
	S	T	E		A	R	C	E	D		O	N	S	
		B	B	B	B		O	O	O	O				
R	E	P	E	A	T	O	F	F	E	N	D	E	R	S
I	N	E	R	T		R	E	F		A	B	D	U	L
G	G	G	G		S	Y	S			Y	Y	Y	Y	

84

H	O	T		M	E	O	W	S		D	E	V	I	L
A	N	A		A	L	P	H	A		O	V	I	N	E
R	E	N		D	E	P	O	T		L	E	X	U	S
M	A	G	L	E	V		L	I	K	E		E	R	S
			V	I	S	C	E	R	A		K	N	E	E
S	I	T	I	N		O	T	I	S		U	S	S	R
T	R	O	I		C	A	T	C	H	E	R			
E	A	R		P	A	T	H		M	O	D	E	L	A
P	E	T	R	O	V		E	R	I	N		T	A	G
		B	R	E	E	D	E	R		R	O	M	E	
S	E	M	I		A	J	O	B		Z	O	N	E	D
A	X	E	S		R	E	G	A	L	E	S			
M	A	N		A	T	M	S		O	P	E	N	U	P
O	C	T	A	L		P	O	A	C	H		O	L	E
A	T	A	L	L		L	U	C	K	Y		S	N	L
S	A	L	T	Y		O	T	T	E	R		E	A	T

85

85

A	T	P	L	A	Y	■	U	N	I	■	P	C	T	S
D	I	R	I	G	I	B	L	E	S	■	R	A	H	S
E	L	E	V	E	N	+	T	W	O	■	O	S	I	S
E	S	S	E	S	■	A	R	T	L	O	V	E	R	■
P	I	T	T	■	O	V	A	■	D	R	I	F	T	S
■	T	O	H	A	V	E	■	N	E	E	D	I	E	R
■	■	M	E	R	L	E	■	E	L	E	A	■		
B	I	C	■	A	N	A	G	R	A	M	■	E	N	S
E	T	U	I	■	■	G	A	V	E	L	■			
L	A	T	T	I	C	E	■	O	R	I	N	G	S	
A	D	R	E	N	O	■	Q	U	O	■	O	R	C	S
■	D	A	M	A	S	C	U	S	■	S	N	O	O	P
A	S	T	I	■	T	W	E	L	V	E	+	O	N	E
S	U	E	Z	■	A	T	E	Y	E	L	E	V	E	L
A	P	S	E	■	S	S	N	■	E	L	D	E	S	T

86

C	A	M	P	S	■	P	A	G	E	T	■	L	A	P	D
A	D	I	O	S	■	A	L	A	M	O	■	O	S	O	S
S	H	R	U	G	■	T	O	R	T	R	E	F	O	R	M
H	E	A	R	T	T	R	A	N	S	P	L	A	N	T	■
E	R	G	S	■	O	O	F	■	O	A	T	E	R	S	
W	E	E	■	B	A	L	■	C	T	R	■	M	A	Y	
■	N	O	S	C	O	R	E	■	O	N	A	I	R		
■	F	I	R	S	T	A	M	E	N	D	M	E	N	T	■
R	I	C	A	N	■	R	E	D	N	O	S	E	■		
E	N	E	■	S	S	N	■	I	N	K	■				
N	I	S	S	A	N	■	F	S	U	■					
■	S	T	A	G	E	A	D	A	P	T	A	T	I	O	N
S	H	O	E	R	E	P	A	I	R	■	P	A	T	H	S
C	E	R	N	■	Z	O	R	R	O	■	I	S	A	A	C
I	S	M	S	■	E	P	E	E	S	■	P	H	I	S	H

87

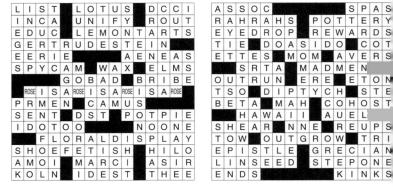

87

L	I	S	T	■	L	O	T	U	S	■	D	C	C	I
I	N	C	A	■	U	N	I	F	Y	■	R	O	U	T
E	D	U	C	■	L	E	M	O	N	T	A	R	T	S
G	E	R	T	R	U	D	E	S	T	E	I	N	■	
E	E	R	I	E	■	■	A	E	N	E	A	S		
S	P	Y	C	A	M	■	W	A	X	■	E	L	M	S
■	G	O	B	A	D	■	B	R	I	B	E			
ROSE	I	S	A	ROSE	I	S	A	ROSE	I	S	A	ROSE		
P	R	M	E	N	■	C	A	M	U	S	■			
S	E	N	T	■	D	S	T	■	P	O	T	P	I	E
I	D	O	T	O	O	■	■	N	O	O	N	E		
■	F	L	O	R	A	L	D	I	S	P	L	A	Y	
S	H	O	E	F	E	T	I	S	H	■	H	I	L	O
A	M	O	I	■	M	A	R	C	I	■	A	S	I	R
K	O	L	N	■	I	D	E	S	T	■	T	H	E	E

88

A	S	S	O	C	■	■	S	P	A	S
R	A	H	R	A	H	S	■	P	O	T	T	E	R	Y
E	Y	E	D	R	O	P	■	R	E	W	A	R	D	S
T	I	E	■	D	O	A	S	I	D	O	■	C	O	T
E	T	T	E	S	■	M	O	M	■	A	V	E	R	S
■	S	R	T	A	■	M	A	D	M	E	N	■		
O	U	T	R	U	N	■	E	R	E	■	E	T	O	N
T	S	O	■	D	I	P	T	Y	C	H	■	S	T	E
B	E	T	A	■	M	A	H	■	C	O	H	O	S	T
■	H	A	W	A	I	I	■	A	U	E	L	■		
S	H	E	A	R	■	N	N	E	■	R	E	U	P	S
T	O	W	■	O	U	T	G	R	O	W	■	T	R	I
E	P	I	S	T	L	E	■	G	R	E	C	I	A	N
L	I	N	S	E	E	D	■	S	T	E	P	O	N	E
E	N	D	S	■	■	K	I	N	K	S

89

90

91

92

93

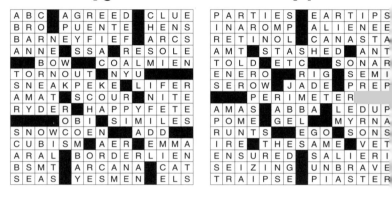

94

95

96

Note: The O's in the corners represent HOOP, RING, CIRCLE and ZERO, each used twice.

97

```
L E A D   . P A T H . . O M A N I
O N C E   . O S H A . . A U T O S
G O D F A T H E R O F S O U L . .
E S C A P E . M D L . . E R S E .
. . C E N T . . U S S . . . . . .
F E D E X C O M P E T I T O R . .
R R R . . Y E A . . N A V A H O .
A R O M A . D Y E . . T E N A M .
N O N A M E . A N O . . . G R E .
C L E V E L A N D P L A Y E R . .
. . S I R . . S P I N . . . . . .
G I G S . Z A P . . O N C A L L .
I V Y L E A G U E S C H O O L . .
B O R E R . O N M E . . O K E D .
B R O W N . N Y P D . . R I B S .
```

98

```
O H O H . B A S S . . A R N E L
K E N O . E T C H . . V O I L A
S H O W E D T H E D O C T O R .
. . S A R A . L E N . . R H O .
N O M O R E . E L L . . L O I S
A N A . S A X . . T R A U M A .
D I R E C T S T R A I T S . . .
A N K L E . E R A . . E T A I L
. M O N I C A S E L E C T S . .
C R Y P T S . C A N . . I S A .
I O W E . S O T . . G O O D A T
N G O . C U Z . . F I R S . . .
E U R O P E A N U N C T I O N .
M E D A L . W A R E . . E N D O
A S S T S . A M Y S . . O N E D
```

99

```
J U D Y . . C L A D . . N O V A
O P I E . . R U B E . . A B E L
A T T S . M I N I M O Z A R T .
D O Z I N G B A T . . R A M B O
. . D U M . . . N O R A S . . .
C A R O M . S E R E N E . . . .
U T E . B O O Z Y W O N D E R .
J O N I . S N I D E . E A V E .
O Z O N E L I N E R S . D I A .
. . S L I C E R . P S A L M . .
. B R O W N . . A R C . . . . .
C R I M E . C O Z Y Y O U N G .
L I O N S D O Z E N . T R O T .
A N T I . O O Z E . . I S S O .
M E S A . S P Y S . . A A H S .
```

100

```
J E W . C H I R P . . W I G G Y
U V A . B A N D O . . S N A R E
G A R Y G Y G A X . J A S O N .
. . O B I E . . . . N O G S . .
C A G Y . N A P S . E E L . . .
O L E O . G R A N D P R I X . .
M E N S A . T I R O . . N Y M .
E K E . G O R E T E X . E L O .
T E R . A N I L . . Y A T E S .
. G A G R E F L E X . B A N E .
. T E N . F A N G . E X E S . .
G A I T . . . D A T A . . . . .
I L O S T . G U M M O M A R X .
V E N T I . A K E E M . P I X .
E X X O N . T E N S E . B O X .
```

101

C	O	R	K	■	G	O	L	E	M	■	E	L	A	L
O	R	A	N	■	A	S	O	N	E	■	N	O	M	E
M	A	N	O	■	L	L	O	Y	D	■	T	W	I	G
A	L	I	T	T	L	E	M	A	D	N	E	S	S	■
■	■	■	T	I	E	R	S	■	L	E	N	■	■	■
A	D	D	S	T	O	■	■	D	E	A	D	S	E	A
N	O	R	■	I	N	T	H	E	S	P	R	I	N	G
T	W	A	S	■	■	H	A	M	■	■	E	X	O	N
I	S	W	H	O	L	E	S	O	M	E	■	E	R	E
C	E	L	A	D	O	N	■	■	A	L	A	R	M	S
■	■	■	K	I	A	■	T	U	C	K	S	■	■	■
■	E	V	E	N	F	O	R	T	H	E	K	I	N	G
A	V	I	S	■	E	M	O	T	E	■	O	D	O	R
M	E	N	U	■	R	I	V	E	T	■	U	L	N	A
P	R	E	P	■	S	T	E	R	E	■	T	E	E	M

102

L	I	M	I	T	■	S	H	I	E	R	■	I	N	T
E	N	O	K	I	■	K	A	T	I	E	■	N	O	R
G	R	E	E	N	W	I	T	H	N	V	■	D	R	E
S	E	N	S	E	I	■	P	A	S	S	B	O	O	K
■	■	■	■	A	S	P	I	C	■	■	R	O	O	S
N	E	P	O	R	T	I	N	A	S	T	O	R	M	■
S	W	A	P	■	E	N	S	■	U	R	N	■	■	■
C	E	L	E	B	R	E	■	A	L	Y	S	S	A	S
■	■	■	R	O	I	■	A	T	E	■	O	H	I	O
■	M	E	A	W	A	R	D	W	I	N	N	E	R	S
S	O	W	N	■	■	A	R	O	M	A	■	■	■	■
W	H	I	T	E	L	I	E	■	A	G	G	I	E	S
I	A	N	■	R	U	N	N	I	N	G	O	N	M	T
P	I	G	■	O	C	E	A	N	■	E	R	N	I	E
E	R	S	■	S	I	D	L	E	■	R	E	S	T	S

103

A	C	N	E	■	C	A	N	C	E	L	■	S	A	P
C	O	A	X	■	O	V	I	E	D	O	■	H	S	T
C	O	U	PED	E	V	I	L	L	E	S	■	A	H	A
U	P	S	I	D	E	S	■	E	N	T	I	R	E	■
S	U	E	T	S	■	■	Q	B	S	■	S	PED	B	Y
E	P	E	E	■	A	S	U	■	■	M	A	G	O	O
■	■	S	A	L	T	I	N	E	S	■	E	R	R	■
S	S	T	■	P	E	D	X	I	N	G	■	D	O	E
U	N	A	■	A	R	S	O	N	I	S	T	■	■	■
B	I	PED	A	L	■	■	T	E	D	■	O	D	I	N
S	T	E	M	■	S	T	E	■	■	G	R	E	C	O
■	C	L	A	M	M	Y	■	T	H	I	N	A	I	R
S	H	A	■	C	A	PED	C	R	U	S	A	D	E	R
K	E	Y	■	C	R	U	S	E	S	■	D	E	S	I
I	D	S	■	I	M	P	I	S	H	■	O	R	T	S

104

C	A	N	A	D	A	■	■	D	E	F	A	M	E
O	N	E	L	A	P	■	R	A	D	A	M	E	S
B	E	W	A	R	E	■	S	A	N	G	R	I	A	S
■	■	S	I	D	E	L	I	N	E	D	■	■
P	A	R	K	A	■	L	E	S	E	■	I	M	A	X
I	D	E	A	■	U	D	D	E	R	■	S	O	R	E
E	M	A	N	A	T	E	D	■	A	T	L	A	S
■	I	D	I	T	A	R	O	D	T	R	A	I	L	■
I	R	E	N	E	■	■	G	O	O	D	N	E	S	S
C	A	R	T	■	S	E	R	G	E	■	T	R	E	Y
E	L	S	E	■	C	R	A	M	■	S	P	E	A	R
■	■	R	O	O	T	C	A	N	A	L	■	■
P	E	D	I	G	R	E	E	■	O	N	A	J	A	G
O	R	I	O	L	E	S	■	R	E	C	E	D	E
P	E	E	R	E	D	■	■	A	R	E	T	O	O

105

```
J O K E · P L I E D · B A J A
E V I L · L O R C A · E X E C
W A R E · A N A R T · A L E E
· L I V I N G Q U A R T E R S
· · E M O · · · S O I · · · ·
B U R N I N G Q U E S T I O N
A T E A T · L U S T Y · L X I
T E A M · B O A T S · S E E K
C R I · E R A S E · S A N Y O
H O M E C O M I N G Q U E E N
· · · L O U · · · A F C · · ·
S T R I N G Q U A R T E T S
T W I X · H U R L S · P R E Z
L O C I · A A L T O · A U R A
O D O R · M Y S O N · N E A P
```

106

```
T M A N · E M I L · O H J O Y
J E R I · Y O D A · B U E N O
M A R M · E B A Y W I N D O W
A G E O F · · H U H S · · · ·
X R A Y O F H O P E · L I V E
X E R · C I A · E V O K E D
· · T U R B A N L E G E N D
C B E R S · L I E · T O A D Y
R A D I O S A M I G O S · ·
U R G E N T · N N E · A M E
Z E E S · A W E S C R A V E N
· · D R A X · S Q U A D
E X T R A E X T R A · U L N A
M Y B A D · E O N S · A S I S
O Z A W A · S L A P · S E T H
```

107

```
A G R A · C R A B · C H O K E
W E A N · N I L E · H O T E L
O R I G I N O F S P E C I E S
L E N I N · · A T O M · S P A
· S N E A K · I N L A · ·
· C H A R L E S R D A R W I N
P L O · T A R T · B E A M E
A I W A · S N A C K · A F E W
S M E L T · · H O E S · F A T
A B R A H A M L I N C O L N
· N E R O · L O R R E · ·
O K S · A A R E · A N I S E
R E P U B L I C A N P A R T Y
B R O N C · T R O Y · T O L E
S I T E S · Z U L U · E N O S
```

108

```
F R E E T · B E T · A C T I V
A I R C A N A D A · B O O L A
T H E G R U D G E · B R A I N
H A L · T I D E · J O S H E D
E N O S · T O O K I T E A S Y
A N N E E · G U N N · T I C K
D A G A M A · T A X I · R U E
· · T I N S · R E D A · ·
S S S · R O T C · D E J A V U
A H A S · D I A Z · S O D A S
F A T A L E R R O R · B E T S
E L I D E S · F O I L · L I C
S A R I N · S I M P A T I C O
E L I S T · E R I E C A N A L
X A C T O · P E N N Y L A N E
```

109

```
A C R O S T I C ■ ■ W A G E S
T H E N E R V E ■ H A U L U P
L I A R L I A R ■ A R T U R O
A L L A L O N E ■ S N O C A T
R E I M S ■ R A S H ■ H O S T
G A S P ■ W E L K ■ B A S I E
E N T ■ R A I S I N B R E A D
■ ■ S O R T ■ P O O P ■ ■
J A C K D E M P S E Y ■ B R O
O G R E S ■ A L A S ■ W E E P
U R A L ■ S N A G ■ W E D G E
R E S E C T ■ T R A I N M A N
N E S T L E ■ T A L L T A L E
A T E O U T ■ E D U C A T E S
L O R N E ■ ■ R E M O T E S T
```

110

```
C R A I G S L I S T ■ S A G S
M A G N A C A R T A ■ C U R T
O R A N G E P E E L ■ O N E A
N E R O ■ N A S ■ M A T T E R
■ ■ C A T T ■ C U T T I N G
A F T E R S ■ R A D I O E R A
D R A N K ■ M E R I T ■ M I Z
A U S T ■ V E D I C ■ W A V E
M I T ■ P C L A B ■ T I M E R
S T E W A R D S ■ M U S E R S
A S S O R T S ■ R O T H ■
P A G O D A ■ P A R ■ L A C E
P L O D ■ P R I Z E F I G H T
L A O S ■ E A T O N E S H A T
E D D Y ■ S H A R O N T A T E
```

111

```
M A Y T A G R E P A I R M A N
O N E M O M E N T P L E A S E
S T R I K E S A B A L A N C E
T O E ■ A N I M A L S ■ G E D
E N V O Y ■ D O R E ■ S I N N
S I A M ■ B E R N ■ A C E T O
T O N I E R ■ S U N B U R S T
■ ■ T R A P ■ M E L S ■ ■
P O E T I C A L ■ A Y E S H A
A N N E E ■ V E S T ■ M E O N
R E C D ■ S I S I ■ D E A N S
I F A ■ P A L O M A R ■ D O W
N O R S E L I T E R A T U R E
G O T I N T O H O T W A T E R
S T A R S I N O N E S E Y E S
```

112

```
I T H A D ■ D I E ■ E T A L
T H E R E S M O R E ■ L O R E
S A L M A H A Y E K ■ A R E A
Y T D ■ D A R E ■ I P A S S
■ W I T H I N E A R S H O T
A L A M O ■ O N E S I E ■ ■
S I T A R S ■ E L I S ■ L G A
S P E C I A L ■ S C H M E A R
N O R ■ G R A B ■ S W A Y Z E
■ ■ C H A I R S ■ H I D E S
F R E E T H R O W L I N E ■
J E L L S ■ N O E S ■ N H L
O P A L ■ B A Z O O K A J O E
R A T E ■ O P E N S E S A M E
D Y E D ■ W E D ■ Y P R E S
```

113

```
  N O S U C H T H I N G
  C O M P L A I N A B O U T
G O V E R N M E N T I S S U E
A M E L I A       D E T R E
R E L E T   P E K E   D A N L
B U T T   L I N E D R I V E S
S P Y   H A S H E D O V E R
    C A N T A B I L E
  B R A N D O N L E E   T A P
S L A M D A N C E S   T A T A
Y E L P   U S E R   B A R M Y
M E L O N         P A X T O N
S P I R A L S T A I R C A S E
  S E E Y O U I N C O U R T
  D E S C E N D A N T S
```

114

```
F A I R S H A K E   P E E N S
A L M A M A T E R   A R I E L
C O R P U L E N T   L A S E R
T E E S   L A T E R I S E R S
      J E S U   O N E N D
  C O M E   E C R U   S H O P
L O U V E R   K E G S   O W E
S L I P P E R Y W H E N W E T
A D J   S P E C   S T E E L E
T H A T   O T O S   B U R L
  A B O A T   L I L Y
B R O W N S T O N E   B O H O
A B A C K   I N E E D A N A P
L O R A L   T E A K E T T L E
D R D R E   O L D S C H O O L
```

115

```
  C F O       M R S
  C R E V E     C O E U R
L A U R E L S   D O L O R E S
A B E R R A T I O N S   G T O
P A L E S T I N E   H E I L
S L A T H E R S   S T A P L E
  S N O O D     R E H I R E
    D U E   P R O N E T O
S H U T   P R E M A R I T A L
P U N   R E L A T E   E N E
I M U S   O V I N E   A C T A
T O S C A   E E C   E S T O P
T R U E C O N F E S S I O N S
E M A N A N T   R O S A R I O
D E L E T E S   S W E N S O N
```

116

```
T I M E W A R P   K E I T H S
O S O L E M I O   O P T O U T
S A I L B O A T   H O O P L A
C A R E S S   I L L S   D A G
A C E R   M O E S   J O S E
    Y A W I N G   B I L K S
S T E   S A L S A   A L L I E
W A X W O R K   L O S T A R T
A X T O N   M E A D E   R T S
Z E R O G   A N G E L O
I V E S   L I T E   B L O C
L A M   A U D I   A T T I L A
A D I E U X   C O Q A U V I N
N E T T L E   E M U L S I O N
D R Y A D S   R E A L E A S Y
```

117

F	L	A	T	■	C	A	P	P	■	D	O	G	E	S
L	I	V	E	D	A	L	I	E	■	E	V	E	N	T
A	A	A	M	E	M	B	E	R	■	R	E	E	V	E
I	N	S	P	A	D	E	S	■	B	A	R	K	I	N
L	A	T	E	F	E	E	■	S	A	I	D	S	O	■
■	■	R	E	N	■	C	O	L	L	O	Q	U	Y	■
A	R	D	E	N	■	G	O	A	D	S	■	U	S	O
L	E	N	D	■	C	A	M	P	Y	■	B	A	L	K
F	D	A	■	S	I	T	B	Y	■	R	E	D	Y	E
A	S	S	U	A	G	E	S	■	B	U	N	■	■	■
■	Q	A	N	T	A	S	■	G	A	N	G	W	A	R
F	U	M	I	E	R	■	F	O	R	S	H	A	M	E
L	A	P	S	E	■	M	A	R	R	I	A	G	E	S
O	R	L	O	N	■	G	R	E	E	N	Z	O	N	E
P	E	E	N	S	■	M	E	N	D	■	I	N	S	T

118

H	A	S	T	A	M	A	N	A	N	A	■	M	P	G
I	S	A	K	D	I	N	E	S	E	N	■	E	R	R
R	A	N	T	A	N	D	R	A	V	E	■	Z	O	O
E	S	T	■	M	E	R	E	■	■	G	L	U	T	S
R	E	E	L	S	■	E	U	L	O	G	I	Z	E	S
■	T	E	Y	■	J	A	S	O	N	■	P	A	G	E
■	■	I	M	U	S	■	S	L	A	S	H	E	S	■
O	P	E	N	I	T	■	■	O	U	T	S	E	T	■
L	I	V	E	D	T	O	■	T	A	X	I	■	■	■
D	R	A	Y	■	E	L	L	E	N	■	C	M	D	■
J	A	M	E	S	D	E	A	N	■	S	K	I	R	T
E	C	A	S	H	■	M	A	R	L	■	N	I	H	■
A	I	R	■	A	L	L	A	B	O	U	T	E	V	E
N	E	I	■	P	E	A	R	L	Y	G	A	T	E	S
S	S	E	■	E	X	P	R	E	S	S	L	A	N	E

119

A	C	E	D	■	F	A	I	L	■	A	S	P	C	A
S	A	L	E	P	R	I	C	E	■	L	O	R	A	X
P	R	E	M	I	E	R	E	S	■	L	U	I	G	I
■	S	C	O	P	E	S	■	S	E	E	P	S	I	N
S	E	T	T	E	R	■	S	I	N	G	S	O	N	G
H	A	R	E	S	■	B	E	S	T	R	O	N	G	■
O	T	I	S	■	H	E	R	M	I	O	N	E	■	■
E	S	C	■	D	E	S	P	O	T	S	■	R	A	D
■	■	A	D	U	L	T	E	R	Y	■	T	O	P	E
■	S	L	I	M	L	I	N	E	■	H	I	F	I	S
M	I	S	S	P	E	N	T	■	B	A	N	Z	A	I
A	N	T	L	E	R	S	■	D	U	F	F	E	R	■
G	E	O	I	D	■	H	A	I	R	T	O	N	I	C
D	A	R	K	O	■	O	P	E	N	S	I	D	E	D
A	D	M	E	N	■	W	E	S	T	■	L	A	S	S

120

M	I	N	S	T	E	R	■	D	E	B	A	T	E	D
O	N	E	L	O	V	E	■	E	Y	E	H	O	L	E
T	H	E	O	R	E	M	■	F	R	A	S	I	E	R
H	E	D	■	C	R	O	N	I	E	S	■	L	V	I
E	R	I	C	H	■	V	O	N	■	T	R	E	A	D
R	I	E	L	■	E	E	R	I	E	■	A	R	T	E
S	T	R	A	W	M	A	T	T	R	E	S	S	E	S
■	■	R	A	I	L	H	E	A	D	S	■	■	■	■
A	S	G	E	N	T	L	E	A	S	A	L	A	M	B
S	A	L	T	■	S	T	A	R	E	■	E	V	I	L
C	R	I	S	S	■	R	S	T	■	A	R	I	S	E
E	D	T	■	O	R	A	T	I	O	N	■	A	T	E
T	I	T	A	N	I	C	■	C	R	E	P	T	U	P
I	N	E	X	I	L	E	■	L	A	N	E	O	N	E
C	E	R	E	A	L	S	■	E	N	T	E	R	E	D

121

```
D I G I T   P A S T T E N S E
E N O T E   A S P A R T A M E
A F L A T   R C A V I C T O R
R E D L E T T E R   T H E G O
O R E O   H O N E S T
L I N   C E N T R E   L A I C
D O G S A G E   S A L E R N O
D R A P E R     H E A T O N
A T T U N E S   W O O F I N G
D O E R   A L D E R S   F E R
    S T A R E S   W I S E
S P O U T   T Y P E F A C E S
H E N R Y V I I I   I V I N S
I N B A L A N C E   L E A S E
A N Y L O N G E R   A R L E S
```

122

```
H A R P E R S   I N F O R M S
E T A I L E D   N O W W H A T
P H I L E A S   S P I N O Z A
C O S T A R   S T E W   D E G
A M I D   D I R T   P E L E
T E N O R S A X   S O A S T O
    W E A L T H   U N I O N
I C A N T S A Y A S I H A V E
N O R M A   I N S I D E
D A M A G E   I T S A L U L U
E L O N   T O N Y   L R O N
T M I   M A D E   A M E B A E
A I R M I L E   O C A N A D A
I N E R T I A   R E L I N E S
L E S S T A R   E Y E C A R E
```

123

```
S I L O   J U B A L   F A C T
I C A N   A S O N E   S N O W
T E M P O R A R Y T A T T O O
P R E O P   G A S M A I N S
A U S T E R E   E R N S T
T N T   R E N T A L S   U K E
  T E A C O Z Y   S K I P
S P A R   D O R A N   K E N S
A L L Y   M D C L X V I
L O L   T E E H E E S   E B B
S T A L E   A S I M M E R
A L T E R E G O   G O P R O
D I S A P P E A R I N G I N K
I N E S   I N F O R   E R I E
P E A T   C A S T E   N E E R
```

124

```
  B O O T C A M P S
  C A P T A I N A H A B
  Q U I E T O N T H E S E T
P U T T   C H E W   A H S
R A Y   K O S H E R   S U E T
E N O   A P T E R   J A F F A
S T U   R I A S   M A X O U T
C U R R A N T   F A B E R G E
I M L A T E   G L I B   T I T
E L O P E   B L A Z E   S T R
N E S T   C O A X E D   C I E
T A S   B R R R   D A V E
  P E R I O D I C T A B L E
  S P A C E N E E D L E
  I S I N G L A S S
```

125

C	A	R	J	A	C	K	■	M	U	S	K	E	T	S
A	R	O	U	S	A	L	■	A	N	T	I	Q	U	E
F	E	S	T	I	V	E	■	P	R	O	C	U	R	E
T	O	T	■	S	E	P	T	■	I	N	K	I	N	D
A	L	E	S	■	S	T	O	D	G	Y	■	P	O	L
N	A	R	C	S	■	O	W	N	■	■	W	A	V	E
■	■	■	O	P	E	C	■	A	L	L	E	G	E	S
B	A	R	R	I	E	R	■	S	E	A	L	E	R	S
E	L	E	C	T	R	A	■	E	X	I	T	■	■	■
S	I	G	H	■	■	C	O	Q	■	C	E	C	U	M
S	E	A	■	L	A	Y	O	U	T	■	R	O	S	E
E	N	T	R	A	P	■	F	E	H	R	■	H	E	S
M	A	T	A	D	O	R	■	N	E	A	T	E	N	S
E	T	A	G	E	R	E	■	C	A	S	H	I	E	R
R	E	S	E	N	T	S	■	E	X	H	O	R	T	S

126

T	A	G	G	E	D	■	Z	I	M	B	A	B	W	E
S	Q	U	A	T	S	■	O	N	E	A	L	A	R	M
Q	U	A	I	N	T	■	O	N	T	H	E	L	A	M
U	I	N	T	A	■	O	L	I	O	S	■	T	I	E
A	L	A	S	■	E	C	O	N	O	■	W	I	T	T
R	I	C	■	G	R	E	G	G	■	Y	A	C	H	T
E	N	O	L	A	G	A	Y	■	W	O	K	■	■	■
S	E	S	S	I	O	N	■	B	I	G	E	A	R	S
■	■	A	L	T	■	S	U	S	A	N	D	E	Y	
J	E	T	T	Y	■	H	T	T	P	S	■	R	P	M
O	R	E	S	■	W	A	R	T	Y	■	L	E	A	P
Y	O	N	■	N	O	V	A	E	■	M	A	N	I	A
F	I	N	D	A	W	A	Y	■	T	E	N	A	N	T
U	C	I	R	V	I	N	E	■	W	E	A	L	T	H
L	A	S	T	Y	E	A	R	■	P	R	I	S	S	Y

127

S	C	U	S	E	■	■	T	E	X	A	S	B	B	Q
E	A	V	E	S	■	I	V	E	G	O	T	Y	O	U
T	H	U	G	S	■	M	I	R	A	N	D	I	Z	E
O	I	L	■	O	N	A	D	I	M	E	■	T	E	S
F	L	A	B	■	A	R	O	L	E	■	B	S	M	T
F	L	E	U	R	D	E	L	Y	S	■	L	E	A	S
■	■	N	U	I	T	S	■	■	K	I	L	N		
■	P	I	E	R	S	■	M	T	W	T	F			
■	D	O	O	R	■	■	A	R	R	O	Z			
S	A	W	N	■	F	O	U	R	O	N	E	O	N	E
A	Y	E	S	■	E	N	D	I	T	■	D	M	A	J
N	P	R	■	I	N	L	I	G	H	T	■	A	M	E
D	E	A	L	S	W	I	T	H	■	E	T	H	I	C
R	E	D	P	L	A	N	E	T	■	M	E	A	N	T
O	P	E	N	E	Y	E	D	■	P	A	N	G	S	

128

C	O	M	I	C	A	L	■	T	W	O	P	A	I	R
A	P	I	S	H	L	Y	■	A	R	T	I	S	T	E
T	E	N	S	I	L	E	■	L	I	O	N	E	L	S
E	N	G	U	L	F	■	L	E	S	S	S	A	L	T
■	■	E	L	E	M	E	N	T	■	■	■			
I	P	O	■	M	I	N	T	■	S	H	I	S	H	
N	O	T	S	T	A	N	D	A	C	H	A	N	C	E
G	E	T	M	I	L	E	A	G	E	O	U	T	O	F
A	T	E	O	N	E	S	H	E	A	R	T	O	U	T
S	E	R	G	E	■	W	A	N	S	■	W	R	Y	
■	■	■	C	E	N	T	E	R	S	■	■			
C	O	M	P	A	R	E	D	■	F	A	T	L	O	T
A	R	E	A	M	A	P	■	L	I	M	E	A	D	E
R	E	G	L	A	Z	E	■	B	R	O	N	Z	E	D
T	O	A	S	T	E	R	■	J	E	S	T	E	R	S

129

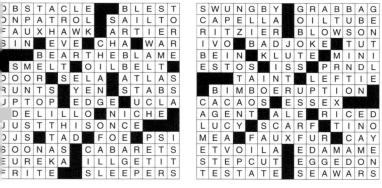

130

131

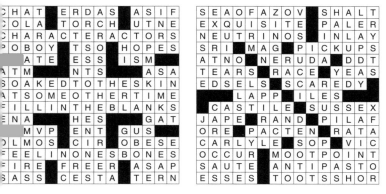

132

133

S	P	A	S	M	S	█	M	A	C	G	Y	V	E	R
T	I	L	T	A	T	█	O	N	L	O	A	N	T	O
A	S	T	A	G	E	█	N	E	E	D	H	E	L	P
S	T	A	R	E	█	V	I	T	A	L	█	C	A	Y
█	A	R	T	E	M	I	S	█	N	I	C	K	█	█
A	C	R	O	█	A	A	M	I	L	N	E	█	█	█
C	H	A	N	G	S	█	S	C	I	E	N	C	E	S
I	I	I	█	E	S	O	█	I	N	S	█	A	N	O
D	O	L	I	T	T	L	E	█	E	S	T	E	E	M
█	█	P	A	R	A	M	U	S	█	I	S	M	E	█
█	H	O	R	A	█	B	A	S	E	P	A	Y	█	█
E	T	E	█	A	N	D	R	E	█	N	O	R	M	A
D	O	A	S	I	S	A	Y	█	S	A	V	E	I	T
N	O	T	A	S	I	D	O	█	I	M	E	A	N	T
A	T	H	L	E	T	E	S	█	B	I	R	N	E	Y

134

T	H	E	S	T	A	R	S	A	N	D	B	A	R	S
H	A	V	E	A	N	O	P	I	N	I	O	N	O	N
U	S	E	T	H	E	T	E	L	E	P	H	O	N	E
M	T	N	█	I	M	A	C	█	█	P	E	T	E	F
P	O	M	█	N	I	L	█	P	R	E	M	E	E	T
█	S	O	N	I	C	█	B	L	A	R	E	█	█	█
A	T	N	O	S	█	C	O	U	P	S	█	W	A	D
M	O	E	T	█	W	A	R	M	S	█	P	E	R	U
S	P	Y	█	T	Y	P	E	B	█	N	O	N	C	E
█	█	G	R	E	E	D	█	R	A	I	T	T	█	█
A	L	L	I	A	S	K	█	L	E	M	█	A	I	N
S	E	I	J	I	█	D	E	B	I	█	S	C	I	█
B	A	N	A	N	A	R	E	P	U	B	L	I	C	S
I	V	E	N	E	V	E	R	T	R	I	E	D	I	T
G	E	N	E	R	A	L	M	A	N	A	G	E	R	S

135

W	E	A	S	E	L	W	O	R	D	S	█	S	C	H
R	I	G	H	T	S	I	D	E	U	P	█	C	I	A
I	N	C	O	H	E	R	E	N	C	E	█	O	R	S
T	E	Y	█	I	V	E	S	█	K	L	A	T	C	H
█	█	I	C	E	D	█	S	C	U	T	T	L	E	█
A	S	A	M	A	N	█	S	H	A	N	T	I	E	S
P	H	I	A	L	█	A	W	A	L	K	█	E	L	O
G	O	R	Y	█	T	C	E	L	L	█	C	D	I	V
A	R	C	█	R	A	R	E	E	█	R	O	O	N	E
R	E	A	R	E	X	I	T	█	S	I	N	G	E	R
S	C	R	I	B	E	D	█	S	H	O	E	█	█	█
C	O	R	T	E	X	█	B	E	A	T	█	P	S	S
O	V	I	█	K	I	S	S	M	Y	G	R	I	T	S
R	E	E	█	A	L	U	M	I	N	U	M	C	A	N
E	R	R	█	H	E	A	T	S	E	N	S	O	R	S

136

S	P	I	N	A	L	T	A	P	█	P	A	E	A	N
H	O	M	E	L	O	A	N	S	█	A	P	P	L	E
A	M	P	L	I	T	U	D	E	█	S	P	I	K	E
L	E	A	S	T	█	R	U	B	E	█	S	A	D	█
O	L	I	O	█	V	O	O	D	O	O	D	O	L	L
M	O	R	N	█	A	R	M	O	R	█	E	D	I	E
█	█	█	I	S	E	E	█	G	L	E	N	S	█	█
Z	I	E	G	F	E	L	D	F	O	L	L	I	E	S
I	D	L	E	S	█	A	L	D	O	█	█	█	█	█
M	E	D	S	█	A	G	G	I	E	█	E	W	O	K
B	O	O	T	S	T	R	A	P	S	█	V	I	B	E
A	G	R	█	T	E	A	L	█	█	D	E	N	T	E
B	R	A	V	O	█	P	A	C	K	I	N	G	U	P
W	A	D	E	R	█	E	X	P	E	R	T	I	S	E
E	M	O	T	E	█	S	Y	L	V	E	S	T	E	R

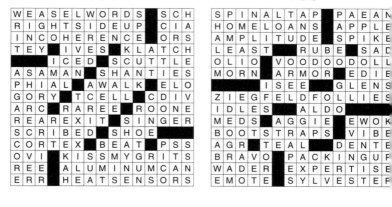

137

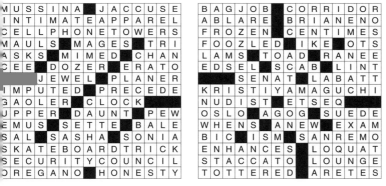

M	U	S	S	I	N	A	■	J	A	C	C	U	S	E
I	N	T	I	M	A	T	E	A	P	P	A	R	E	L
C	E	L	L	P	H	O	N	E	T	O	W	E	R	S
M	A	U	L	S	■	M	A	G	E	S	■	T	R	I
A	S	K	S	■	M	I	M	E	D	■	C	H	A	N
C	E	E	■	D	O	Z	E	R	■	E	R	A	T	O
■	■	J	E	W	E	L	■	P	L	A	N	E	R	■
I	M	P	U	T	E	D	■	P	R	E	C	E	D	E
G	A	O	L	E	R	■	C	L	O	C	K	■	■	■
U	P	P	E	R	■	D	A	U	N	T	■	P	E	W
E	M	U	S	■	S	E	T	T	E	■	B	A	L	E
S	A	L	■	S	A	S	H	A	■	S	O	N	I	A
S	K	A	T	E	B	O	A	R	D	T	R	I	C	K
S	E	C	U	R	I	T	Y	C	O	U	N	C	I	L
O	R	E	G	A	N	O	■	H	O	N	E	S	T	Y

138

B	A	G	J	O	B	■	C	O	R	R	I	D	O	R
A	B	L	A	R	E	■	B	R	I	A	N	E	N	O
F	R	O	Z	E	N	■	C	E	N	T	I	M	E	S
F	O	O	Z	L	E	D	■	I	K	E	■	O	T	S
L	A	M	S	■	T	O	A	D	■	R	A	N	E	E
E	D	S	E	L	■	S	C	A	B	■	L	I	N	T
■	■	■	S	E	N	A	T	■	L	A	B	A	T	T
K	R	I	S	T	I	Y	A	M	A	G	U	C	H	I
N	U	D	I	S	T	■	E	T	S	E	Q	■	■	■
O	S	L	O	■	A	G	O	G	■	S	U	E	D	E
W	H	E	N	S	■	A	N	E	W	■	E	X	A	M
B	I	C	■	I	S	M	■	S	A	N	R	E	M	O
E	N	H	A	N	C	E	S	■	L	O	Q	U	A	T
S	T	A	C	C	A	T	O	■	L	O	U	N	G	E
T	O	T	T	E	R	E	D	■	A	R	E	T	E	S

139

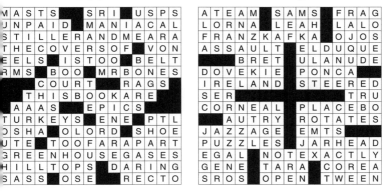

M	A	S	T	S	■	S	R	I	■	U	S	P	S
U	N	P	A	I	D	■	M	A	N	I	A	C	A	L
S	T	I	L	L	E	R	A	N	D	M	E	A	R	A
T	H	E	C	O	V	E	R	S	O	F	■	V	O	N
E	E	L	S	■	I	S	T	O	O	■	B	E	L	T
R	M	S	■	B	O	O	■	M	R	B	O	N	E	S
■	■	■	C	O	U	R	T	■	R	A	G	S	■	■
■	■	T	H	I	S	B	O	O	K	A	R	E	■	■
A	A	A	S	■	E	P	I	C	S	■	■	■	■	■
T	U	R	K	E	Y	S	■	E	N	E	■	P	T	L
O	S	H	A	■	O	L	O	R	D	■	S	H	O	E
U	T	E	■	T	O	O	F	A	R	A	P	A	R	T
G	R	E	E	N	H	O	U	S	E	G	A	S	E	S
H	I	L	L	T	O	P	S	■	D	A	R	I	N	G
S	A	S	S	■	O	S	E	■	R	E	C	T	O	■

140

A	T	E	A	M	■	S	A	M	S	■	F	R	A	G
L	O	R	N	A	■	L	E	A	H	■	L	A	L	O
F	R	A	N	Z	K	A	F	K	A	■	O	J	O	S
A	S	S	A	U	L	T	■	E	L	D	U	Q	U	E
■	■	■	B	R	E	T	■	U	L	A	N	U	D	E
D	O	V	E	K	I	E	■	P	O	N	C	A	■	■
I	R	E	L	A	N	D	■	S	T	E	E	R	E	D
S	E	R	■	■	■	■	■	■	■	■	T	R	U	■
C	O	R	N	E	A	L	■	P	L	A	C	E	B	O
■	■	A	U	T	R	Y	■	R	O	T	A	T	E	S
J	A	Z	Z	A	G	E	■	E	M	T	S	■	■	■
P	U	Z	Z	L	E	S	■	J	A	R	H	E	A	D
E	G	A	L	■	N	O	T	E	X	A	C	T	L	Y
G	E	N	E	■	T	A	R	A	■	C	O	R	E	A
S	R	O	S	■	O	P	E	N	■	T	W	E	E	N

141

T	A	J	M	A	H	A	L	■	J	E	S	S	E	S
O	P	E	N	D	A	T	E	■	A	V	I	A	T	E
U	P	R	O	O	T	E	D	■	M	I	C	R	O	N
G	R	R	■	B	E	N	■	P	E	C	K	I	N	G
H	A	Y	N	E	S	■	C	A	S	T	E	■	■	■
G	I	L	E	S	■	P	A	R	D	O	N	S	■	■
U	S	E	D	■	W	A	T	T	E	R	S	O	N	■
Y	E	W	■	J	E	R	B	O	A	S	■	N	O	D
■	S	I	T	U	A	T	I	O	N	■	C	O	S	I
■	S	E	L	K	I	R	K	■	J	A	F	F	E	■
■	■	H	I	K	E	D	■	P	A	N	Z	E	R	■
C	A	R	E	E	N	S	■	F	A	N	■	O	R	E
U	G	A	R	T	E	■	R	I	V	I	E	R	A	S
L	E	G	A	T	E	■	A	L	A	C	A	R	T	E
L	E	A	N	E	D	■	G	E	N	E	R	O	U	S

142

A	F	T	A	■	I	N	C	U	M	B	E	N	T	S
T	A	R	P	■	N	E	O	R	E	A	L	I	S	M
P	R	O	P	O	S	E	M	A	R	R	I	A	G	E
A	C	L	E	F	■	T	I	N	C	T	■	S	T	E
R	E	L	A	T	E	■	N	O	I	S	E	■	■	■
■	■	R	E	T	A	G	■	■	S	W	A	N	■	■
O	N	T	■	N	U	M	I	S	M	A	T	I	S	T
V	E	S	T	E	D	I	N	T	E	R	E	S	T	S
E	M	P	I	R	E	S	T	A	T	E	■	C	A	E
R	O	S	E	■	■	O	R	E	O	S	■	■	■	■
■	■	■	D	E	C	A	F	■	S	L	O	P	P	Y
B	E	G	■	A	A	R	O	N	■	A	U	R	A	E
E	L	E	C	T	R	I	C	A	L	S	T	O	R	M
N	O	M	D	E	P	L	U	M	E	■	E	M	M	E
D	I	S	T	R	E	S	S	E	D	■	R	O	A	N

143

D	U	F	F	S	■	■	■	S	C	A	L	I	A
I	N	R	O	W	S	■	S	P	O	U	T	I	N	G
S	T	E	R	E	O	■	P	R	O	S	T	A	T	E
C	A	E	S	A	R	■	L	E	T	S	I	N	O	N
U	P	L	A	T	E	■	I	N	H	A	L	A	N	T
S	P	O	K	E	N	■	N	A	S	T	A	S	E
S	E	V	E	R	■	G	E	T	A
■	D	E	N	S	E	R	■	A	Y	E	S	H	A
■	■	■	G	A	L	L	■	C	H	A	P	S
■	B	A	R	C	O	D	E	■	T	H	O	R	P	E
H	A	V	E	A	T	I	T	■	H	E	R	M	A	N
E	R	A	S	U	R	E	S	■	E	L	T	O	R	O
E	N	T	I	C	I	N	G	■	M	O	A	N	E	R
L	E	A	D	U	P	T	O	■	E	N	G	I	N	E
S	T	R	E	S	S	■	■	■	S	E	C	T	S

144

B	U	F	F	■	C	R	A	G	■	P	A	W	N	S
A	L	A	R	■	A	E	R	O	■	A	R	H	A	T
K	A	T	E	S	P	A	D	E	■	T	R	O	L	L
U	N	S	E	T	T	L	E	S	■	C	A	C	A	O
■	■	S	P	A	■	N	A	S	H	U	A	■	■	■
M	A	I	T	A	I	S	■	B	U	Y	■	N	I	P
A	N	N	O	U	N	C	E	R	S	■	D	I	O	R
J	O	H	N	L	A	R	R	O	Q	U	E	T	T	E
A	D	E	E	■	H	A	N	A	U	M	A	B	A	Y
S	E	R	■	G	A	P	■	D	E	P	R	E	S	S
■	■	S	O	R	B	E	T	■	H	I	S	■	■	■
E	T	H	N	O	■	S	E	P	A	R	A	B	L	E
X	H	O	S	A	■	O	P	E	N	E	N	D	E	D
P	R	E	E	N	■	F	E	R	N	■	T	R	A	Y
O	U	S	T	S	■	F	E	M	A	■	A	M	P	S

145

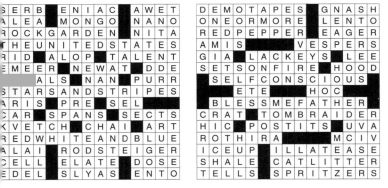

S	E	R	B			E	N	I	A	C		A	W	E	T
A	L	E	A		M	O	N	G	O		N	A	N	O	
R	O	C	K	G	A	R	D	E	N		N	I	T	A	
T	H	E	U	N	I	T	E	D	S	T	A	T	E	S	
R	I	D		A	L	O	P		T	A	L	E	N	T	
E	M	E	E	R		N	E	W	A	T		D	D	E	
	A	L	S		N	A	N		P	U	R	R			
S	T	A	R	S	A	N	D	S	T	R	I	P	E	S	
A	R	I	S		P	R	E		S	E	L				
C	A	R		S	P	A	N	S		S	E	C	T	S	
K	V	E	T	C	H		C	H	A	I		A	R	T	
R	E	D	W	H	I	T	E	A	N	D	B	L	U	E	
A	L	A	I		R	O	D	S	T	E	I	G	E	R	
C	E	L	L		E	L	A	T	E		D	O	S	E	
E	D	E	L		S	L	Y	A	S		E	N	T	O	

146

D	E	M	O	T	A	P	E	S		G	N	A	S	H
O	N	E	O	R	M	O	R	E		L	E	N	T	O
R	E	D	P	E	P	P	E	R		E	A	G	E	R
A	M	I	S				V	E	S	P	E	R	S	
G	I	A		L	A	C	K	E	Y	S		L	E	E
S	E	T	S	O	N	F	I	R	E		H	O	O	D
	S	E	L	F	C	O	N	S	C	I	O	U	S	
		E	T	E			H	O	C					
	B	L	E	S	S	M	E	F	A	T	H	E	R	
C	R	A	T		T	O	M	B	R	A	I	D	E	R
H	I	C		P	O	S	T	I	T	S		U	V	A
R	O	T	H	I	R	A					M	C	I	V
I	C	E	U	P		I	L	L	A	T	E	A	S	E
S	H	A	L	E		C	A	T	L	I	T	T	E	R
T	E	L	L	S		S	P	R	I	T	Z	E	R	S

147

D	I	E	T	P	L	A	T	E			A	B	I	T
R	O	G	E	R	E	B	E	R	T		T	O	R	I
A	N	G	L	O	M	A	N	I	A		A	L	O	E
Y	E	R		W	A	S	I	S	N	O	R	I	N	G
A	S	O	K		T	E	E		T	R	I	V	I	A
G	C	L	E	F		D	R	Y	A	D		I	S	M
E	O	L	I	T	H		S	A	L	I	V	A	T	E
		T	R	E	E		Z	U	N	I				
M	A	C	H	I	S	M	O		S	A	N	E	S	T
A	M	A		L	I	T	U	P		L	Y	R	I	C
M	O	P	P	E	T		T	O	S		L	O	E	B
M	E	R	R	Y	A	N	D	R	E	W		T	S	O
O	B	I	E		N	E	U	T	R	A	L	I	T	Y
T	A	C	O		T	H	E	A	T	R	I	C	A	L
H	E	E	P			I	L	L	A	T	E	A	S	E

148

P	E	A	C	H	B	O	W	L		M	A	I	M	S
L	I	T	H	U	A	N	I	A		A	L	L	A	H
A	L	D	E	R	T	R	E	E		G	A	L	L	O
S	E	A	M		C	A	N			I	N	T	E	R
M	E	W		K	H	M	E	R		C	A	R	A	T
A	N	N	A	N		P	R	O	F	S		E	L	F
			Y	E	P		S	H	A	Q		A	T	O
M	A	G	N	E	T	I	C	E	Q	U	A	T	O	R
A	P	O		S	U	C	H		S	A	D			
N	E	V		L	I	O	N	S		R	A	M	B	O
A	R	E	N	A		N	I	E	C	E		E	R	R
S	T	R	O	P			T	A	O		H	A	A	G
S	U	N	U	P		E	Z	I	O	P	I	N	Z	A
A	R	O	S	E		R	E	C	E	S	S	I	O	N
S	E	R	E	R		A	L	E	R	T	N	E	S	S

149

A	L	C	A	P	P	■	S	T	A	L	W	A	R	T
L	E	A	V	E	I	T	T	O	B	E	A	V	E	R
S	E	E	I	N	G	E	Y	E	S	I	N	G	L	E
O	R	N	O	T	■	E	L	S	■	■	T	S	O	S
■	■	■	N	U	R	S	E	■	C	C	I	■	■	■
■	G	R	I	P	E	■	T	R	O	U	N	C	E	D
C	R	O	C	■	L	A	S	E	R	S	■	H	M	O
C	A	U	S	T	I	C	■	P	O	P	Q	U	I	Z
U	T	E	■	H	A	D	R	O	N	■	U	G	L	Y
P	E	N	Z	A	N	C	E	■	E	L	I	S	E	■
■	■	L	I	T	■	L	A	T	E	X	■	■	■	■
A	S	T	O	■	■	H	A	H	■	N	O	C	K	S
M	E	A	T	A	N	D	P	O	T	A	T	O	E	S
I	T	S	Y	B	I	T	S	Y	S	P	I	D	E	R
D	I	S	S	O	L	V	E	■	P	E	C	A	N	S

150

J	U	S	T	M	E	■	■	B	A	N	D	B
O	N	E	H	A	L	F	■	S	A	M	P	R	A	S
J	A	C	U	Z	Z	I	■	C	H	O	R	I	Z	O
O	W	L	■	Y	I	T	Z	H	A	K	■	V	A	C
B	A	U	M	■	E	C	O	L	I	■	P	E	A	K
A	R	D	O	R	■	H	O	O	■	F	O	U	R	S
S	E	E	O	U	T	■	S	C	R	I	M	P	S	
■	■	C	L	A	P	■	K	A	V	A	■	■		
■	S	P	H	E	R	I	C	■	P	E	T	A	R	D
S	L	O	E	S	■	Z	O	G	■	R	U	M	O	R
W	O	L	D	■	O	Z	A	R	K	■	M	A	M	A
A	W	E	■	H	O	A	X	I	N	G	■	Z	A	C
G	I	N	F	I	Z	Z	■	S	E	I	Z	I	N	G
E	S	T	E	V	E	Z	■	T	E	R	E	N	C	E
■	H	A	Z	E	D	■	■	D	O	D	G	E	D	

151

S	P	O	N	G	E	B	O	B	■	■	S	T	A	G
H	O	N	O	R	R	O	L	L	■	S	H	O	N	E
A	B	E	V	I	G	O	D	A	■	L	U	S	T	S
R	O	M	A	N	O	■	■	C	O	O	L	S	I	T
E	X	O	■	■	A	N	K	L	E	■	I	P	A	
■	■	M	A	N	I	T	O	B	A	■	O	N	A	T
C	R	E	N	E	L	A	T	E	■	K	H	A	S	I
H	A	N	G	T	E	N	■	A	T	E	I	N	T	O
I	C	T	U	S	■	I	G	U	A	N	O	D	O	N
P	I	P	S	■	E	M	P	T	Y	O	U	T	■	
P	A	L	■	S	E	P	O	Y	■	■	U	S	E	
E	L	E	C	T	R	A	■	■	P	E	T	R	E	L
D	I	A	R	Y	■	S	T	A	R	T	A	N	E	W
I	S	S	U	E	■	S	A	M	O	A	T	I	M	E
N	M	E	X	■	E	X	I	T	L	A	N	E	S	

152

J	A	Z	Z	H	A	N	D	S	■	P	E	R	I	L
A	S	Y	O	U	W	E	R	E	■	A	L	I	N	E
S	T	R	O	N	G	B	O	X	■	L	O	N	G	A
P	U	T	■	T	E	R	W	I	L	L	I	G	E	R
E	T	E	S	■	E	A	S	E	L	S	■	T	N	N
R	E	C	U	T	■	S	E	R	A	■	M	O	U	E
■	■	S	O	A	K	S	■	M	A	I	N	E	R	
C	A	T	A	L	P	A	■	H	A	R	N	E	S	S
A	M	A	N	D	A	■	C	A	S	I	O	■	■	
T	P	K	S	■	C	H	A	R	■	A	S	P	E	R
S	H	E	■	C	H	O	R	D	S	■	O	L	D	E
C	O	F	F	E	E	B	R	E	A	K	■	A	I	T
A	R	I	E	L	■	N	E	D	B	E	A	T	T	Y
N	A	V	E	L	■	O	R	G	A	N	S	T	O	P
S	E	E	T	O	■	B	E	E	N	T	H	E	R	E

153

C	U	S	H	Y	J	O	B	■	S	P	E	D	U	P
A	N	N	O	T	A	T	E	■	F	E	L	I	N	E
M	A	I	N	D	R	A	G	■	O	O	L	A	L	A
E	S	T	E	■	G	R	I	S	■	P	I	P	I	T
■	■	C	O	U	N	T	F	L	E	E	T	■	■	■
■	L	E	A	R	N	■	T	R	U	E	■	R	E	V
M	I	S	H	A	■	S	H	I	N	■	A	C	R	E
S	A	C	A	G	A	W	E	A	D	O	L	L	A	R
G	R	A	B	■	L	O	B	E	■	M	E	A	R	A
T	S	P	■	S	L	U	E	■	G	O	R	D	Y	■
■	P	E	T	T	I	N	G	Z	O	O	■	■	■	■
M	O	R	R	O	■	D	U	E	L	■	E	X	G	I
I	K	O	I	K	O	■	I	R	O	N	W	E	E	D
S	E	A	B	E	D	■	N	O	N	S	E	N	S	E
O	R	D	E	R	S	■	E	G	G	C	R	A	T	E

154

■	S	T	Y	■	S	A	S	H	E	S	■	B	I	C
O	K	R	A	■	U	M	I	A	K	S	■	E	N	A
P	I	E	R	■	B	A	G	M	E	N	■	L	P	N
T	M	A	N	■	A	T	E	E	■	■	O	M	O	O
I	P	S	■	T	R	I	P	L	E	C	R	O	W	N
M	O	O	S	H	U	■	■	R	A	I	N	E	R	■
A	N	N	I	E	■	C	O	A	S	T	■	T	R	Y
■	■	P	R	E	A	K	N	E	S	S	■	■	■	■
C	O	B	■	E	L	W	A	Y	■	E	A	G	E	R
U	P	R	I	S	E	■	■	D	Y	N	A	M	O	■
T	H	E	F	A	V	O	R	I	T	E	■	M	P	S
R	E	E	S	■	■	D	E	A	R	■	R	E	L	S
A	L	D	■	S	T	I	G	M	A	■	O	B	O	E
T	I	E	■	A	S	S	I	S	I	■	T	O	Y	S
E	A	R	■	L	E	T	S	O	N	■	S	Y	S	■

155

D	R	A	I	N	S	O	F	F	■	T	U	B	A	S
R	O	N	H	O	W	A	R	D	■	A	R	U	B	A
O	D	D	S	M	A	K	E	R	■	K	A	N	I	N
P	E	R	■	E	N	I	D	■	M	E	L	D	E	D
I	B	E	G	■	K	E	E	N	O	N	■	T	B	A
T	Y	S	O	N	■	■	B	I	Z	■	O	P	A	L
■	W	A	S	H	B	O	A	R	D	A	B	S	■	■
■	S	C	I	P	I	O	■	B	R	A	I	N	Y	■
T	H	E	L	A	S	T	M	E	T	R	O	■	■	■
H	O	L	D	■	L	E	A	■	■	E	U	L	E	R
E	R	I	■	E	E	L	E	R	S	■	S	A	T	E
P	E	B	B	L	Y	■	W	I	T	S	■	N	H	L
I	S	A	A	C	■	H	E	N	R	Y	V	I	I	I
T	U	T	S	I	■	A	S	S	O	N	A	N	C	E
S	P	E	E	D	■	S	T	E	P	C	L	A	S	S

156

F	I	S	H	B	O	W	L	S	■	A	B	A	B	A
I	N	T	O	O	D	E	E	P	■	R	O	V	E	S
G	R	O	U	N	D	S	Q	U	I	R	R	E	L	S
T	O	P	S	Y	■	T	U	R	N	S	O	N	T	O
R	A	G	E	■	J	E	A	N	S	■	■	G	R	R
E	D	A	■	B	U	R	R	■	T	H	R	E	A	T
E	S	P	E	R	A	N	T	O	■	E	A	R	N	S
■	■	G	E	N	U	I	N	E	L	Y	■	■	■	■
S	A	R	I	S	■	S	E	T	T	L	E	D	U	P
P	R	E	S	T	O	■	R	H	O	S	■	I	S	U
I	T	S	■	G	A	L	E	N	■	P	O	H	L	■
T	I	T	F	O	R	T	A	T	■	C	A	M	E	L
S	C	A	R	L	E	T	T	A	N	A	G	E	R	S
A	L	G	A	E	■	W	I	K	I	P	E	D	I	A
T	E	E	N	S	■	O	N	E	P	A	R	E	N	T

157

A	B	U	T	■	T	S	P	S	■	C	R	Y	P	T
S	A	C	A	J	A	W	E	A	■	H	O	A	R	Y
A	T	O	N	A	L	I	T	Y	■	A	S	K	I	N
D	O	N	I	Z	E	T	T	I	■	R	E	E	C	E
A	R	N	A	Z	■	Z	E	N	■	S	T	A	T	E
■	■	E	M	E	R	G	E	■	P	Y	L	E	■	■
S	C	I	S	S	O	R	■	S	E	E	P	S	I	N
P	A	N	O	U	T	■	■	D	E	L	A	N	O	■
F	L	A	P	P	E	R	■	T	E	L	E	X	E	S
S	I	G	H	■	T	U	B	O	R	G	■	■	■	■
■	C	R	O	S	S	B	O	W	■	R	A	I	T	T
M	O	O	C	H	■	A	V	A	L	A	N	C	H	E
E	C	O	L	I	■	D	I	G	E	S	T	I	O	N
S	A	V	E	R	■	U	N	E	A	S	I	E	S	T
A	T	E	S	T	■	B	E	S	S	■	C	R	E	S

158

P	A	G	E	■	C	H	I	L	I	■	A	P	R	S
E	R	R	S	■	L	O	M	A	N	■	E	R	I	E
E	R	A	S	■	O	P	P	O	S	I	T	I	O	N
L	I	C	E	N	S	E	■	S	E	N	N	E	T	T
E	V	E	N	N	E	S	S	■	C	H	A	S	E	R
R	A	F	T	E	R	■	P	O	R	E	■	T	R	Y
■	L	U	I	■	■	P	E	T	E	R	I	■	■	■
■	■	L	A	S	T	L	E	T	T	E	R	S	■	■
■	■	■	L	A	R	E	D	O	■	■	R	E	G	■
T	O	P	■	N	U	D	E	■	B	E	E	P	E	R
S	P	A	D	E	S	■	R	E	L	E	G	A	T	E
H	E	R	E	S	T	O	■	S	E	C	U	R	E	D
I	N	A	C	T	I	V	A	T	E	■	L	A	V	A
R	E	D	O	■	N	A	M	E	D	■	A	T	E	N
T	R	E	Y	■	G	L	O	S	S	■	R	E	N	T

159

H	U	S	S	E	I	N	■	B	R	A	V	O	E	D
I	N	T	E	R	N	A	L	R	E	V	E	N	U	E
S	C	A	R	L	E	T	T	A	N	A	G	E	R	S
P	O	N	T	E	■	A	C	S	■	S	A	M	O	S
E	N	D	S	■	A	L	O	I	S	■	N	O	P	E
E	D	O	■	S	P	I	L	L	I	T	■	M	E	R
D	I	N	E	T	T	E	S	■	N	O	M	E	A	T
■	T	O	R	I	E	S	■	S	U	S	A	N	N	■
S	I	N	G	E	R	■	B	I	S	C	O	T	T	I
E	O	E	■	S	A	G	E	T	E	A	■	P	H	R
A	N	S	A	■	L	A	M	E	S	■	U	L	E	E
M	A	T	E	D	■	T	I	R	■	O	N	E	A	L
A	L	O	T	O	N	O	N	E	S	P	L	A	T	E
P	L	E	A	S	U	R	E	C	R	U	I	S	E	S
S	Y	S	T	E	M	S	■	T	A	S	T	E	R	S

160

O	N	E	D	O	L	L	A	R	■	A	S	F	O	R
H	A	V	E	F	A	I	T	H	■	S	T	O	N	E
I	D	O	N	T	C	A	R	E	■	H	A	R	E	S
O	I	L	■	T	R	I	O	■	B	I	G	O	T	■
A	N	V	I	L	■	■	M	A	I	D	E	N	S	■
N	E	E	D	Y	■	S	T	E	R	N	■	T	O	T
■	■	E	S	T	H	E	T	E	S	■	I	N	C	■
H	A	I	M	■	W	A	X	E	N	■	S	T	E	P
U	L	T	■	A	I	R	T	R	A	I	N	■	■	■
R	L	S	■	B	L	I	S	S	■	S	U	C	R	E
R	A	N	D	A	L	L	■	■	O	G	D	E	N	■
A	L	O	E	S	■	E	R	I	C	■	■	C	A	T
H	O	U	G	H	■	W	E	L	L	A	W	A	R	E
E	N	S	U	E	■	I	N	K	E	R	A	S	E	R
D	E	E	M	S	■	S	E	A	O	T	T	E	R	S

161

J	F	K	P	L	A	Z	A		T	A	X	T	I	P
E	L	I	C	I	T	O	R		I	M	G	O	N	E
R	A	T	T	L	I	N	G		O	P	A	Q	U	E
J	S	C		A	L	K	Y	D	S		M	U	I	R
S	H	A	D		T	E	L	E		B	E	E	T	S
A	F	R	O	S		D	E	V	I	L	S			
L	I	S	L	E	S		S	O	R	E		C	F	L
E	R	O	T	I	C	A		N	I	A	G	A	R	A
M	E	N		S	A	V	E		S	C	O	P	E	S
		I	M	D	O	N	E		H	E	S	S	E	
S	W	A	N	S		I	D	L	Y		R	U	H	R
H	A	L	F		P	R	E	P	A	Y		L	E	D
A	X	I	L	L	A		M	A	H	A	R	A	N	I
R	E	F	U	E	L		I	S	O	L	A	T	E	S
D	R	E	X	E	L		C	O	O	L	J	E	R	K

162

M	O	R	T	A	R	A	N	D	P	E	S	T	L	E
A	V	E	N	G	E	R		O	R	D	E	R	I	N
C	O	S	T	I	N	G		S	I	G	N	I	N	G
H	I	P		O	D	O	R	I	Z	E		L	E	A
I	D	O	L		S	N	I	D	E		S	L	O	G
N	A	N	O	S		N	C	O		S	P	I	N	E
E	L	D	U	Q	U	E		S	T	E	I	N	E	M
W		R	U	N			I	A	N			E		
A	T	P	E	A	C	E		U	N	L	E	A	R	N
S	H	I	E	D		L	O	N		S	T	R	A	T
H	E	E	D		L	A	U	D	E		S	S	T	S
A	R	R		D	A	N	I	E	L	S		E	A	T
B	E	C	K	E	T	T		R	I	P	I	N	T	O
L	I	E	O	V	E	R		G	H	A	N	I	A	N
E	N	D	S	O	N	A	S	O	U	R	N	O	T	E

163

E	B	E	R	T		S	H	A	D		T	A	S	S
D	O	N	O	R		C	A	P	I		R	I	P	A
G	A	R	B	A	G	E	B	A	G		U	R	A	L
I	T	A	L	I	A	N	I	C	E		E	C	C	E
N	E	G	O	T	I	A	T	E	S		R	E	E	S
G	R	E	W					T	A	I	L	O	R	
		E	L	E	C	T	R	I	C	B	L	U	E	
G	A	L		O	N	L	E	A	V	E		S	T	P
A	L	E	C	G	U	I	N	N	E	S	S			
S	L	A	L	O	M				E	S	S	A		
R	E	P	O		E	L	I	Z	A	B	E	T	H	I
A	Y	E	S		R	U	L	E	M	A	K	E	R	S
N	O	D	E		A	X	I	S	O	F	E	V	I	L
G	O	U	T		T	O	U	T		T	R	I	K	E
E	P	P	S		E	R	M	A		A	S	E	E	D

164

R	A	Z	O	R			T	R	A	V	E	L	E	R
A	Z	U	R	E	S		H	E	S	A	L	I	V	E
G	O	L	E	F	T		E	L	I	C	I	T	E	D
A	D	E		L	A	T	V	I	A			E	L	O
S	Y	M	M	E	T	R	I	C	M	A	T	R	I	X
	E	A	R	C	L	I	P		I	N	S	A	N	E
		S	T	E	M	S		N	A	P	L	E	S	
E	S	C	H	E	R	S		W	O	K	S			
S	C	R	O	D		S	A	R	I		F	A	X	
C	H	E	W	I	N	G	O	N		N	I	E	C	E
A	R	P		M	O	O	N	E	D		S	E	E	R
P	O	E		A	P	E	S		R	E	A	D	T	O
A	D	P	A	G	E	S		J	U	R	Y	B	O	X
D	E	A	R	E	S	T		A	S	I	N	I	N	E
E	R	N	E	S	T	O		W	E	E	O	N	E	S

165

E	G	G			O	R	F	F		N	O	M	S	G
T	O	R	T		L	E	O	I		I	R	E	N	E
A	R	E	A		I	L	O	V	E	P	A	R	I	S
L	E	A	K		O	U	T	E	R		L	E	T	T
	S	T	E	P		C	L	A	N					
		U	A	R		T	O	N			R	O	A	R
M	A	N	T	O	M	A	N	D	E	F	E	N	S	E
O	N	C	O	M	I	N	G	T	R	A	F	F	I	C
R	O	L	L	O	N	T	H	E	G	R	O	U	N	D
A	X	E	L		D	O	N		A	C	R			
			C	R	T	S		D	U	L	Y			
O	A	T	H		H	A	D	T	O		S	O	U	P
P	L	E	A	S	E	G	O	O	N		E	U	R	O
E	M	A	I	L		O	G	R	E		S	G	T	S
D	A	L	L	Y		N	S	E	C			H	S	T